SIDNEY LANIER

Sidney Lanier

SIDNEY LANIER

BY

EDWIN MIMS

ILLUSTRATED

BOSTON AND NEW YORK
HOUGHTON, MIFFLIN AND COMPANY
The Riverside Press, Cambridge
1905

Published November, 1905

PREFACE

THE present volume is a biography of Lanier rather than a critical study of his work. So far as possible, I have told the story in his own words, or in the words of those who knew him most intimately. If I have erred in placing undue emphasis on the early part of his career, it was intentional, for that is the part of his life about which least is known. I have intentionally emphasized his relation to the South, in order to avoid a misconception that he was a detached figure. The bibliographies prepared by Mr. Wills for the " Southern History Association " and by Mr. Callaway for his " Select Poems of Lanier " make one unnecessary for this volume.

Of previously published material, I have been greatly indebted to the Memorial by Mr. William Hayes Ward, the fuller sketch by the late Professor W. M. Baskervill, and the volume of letters published by Messrs. Charles Scribner's Sons. For new material, I am indebted, first of all, to Mrs. Sidney Lanier, who has put me

in possession, not of the most intimate correspondence of the poet, but of many letters written by him to his father and friends, as well as
unpublished fragments and essays. She has done
all in her power to make this volume accurate
and trustworthy. Her sons, Mr. Charles Day
Lanier and Mr. Henry W. Lanier, have put
me under special obligations, the latter especially,
by reading the proof of a large part of the volume. Mr. Clifford Lanier, the poet's brother,
put at my disposal a valuable series of letters,
and otherwise aided me. I am indebted to Dr.
Daniel Coit Gilman, Mrs. Edwin C. Cushman,
Judge Logan E. Bleckley, Mr. Dudley Buck,
Mr. Charles Scribner, Mrs. Isabel L. Dobbin,
Mr. George Cary Eggleston, Miss Effie Johnston,
Mr. Sidney Lanier Gibson, and Miss Sophie
Kirk, for placing in my hands unpublished
letters of Lanier. The following have written
reminiscences which have proved especially help-
ful: Dr. James Woodrow, Professor Gilder-
sleeve, Chancellor Walter B. Hill, Professor
Waldo S. Pratt, Mrs. Arthur W. Machen, Mrs.
Sophie Bledsoe Herrick, Mr. F. H. Gottlieb, and
Mr. Charles Heber Clarke. I desire to thank
Messrs. Charles Scribner's Sons and Mrs. Lanier

for permission to quote from the letters and collected writings of Lanier; Messrs. Double-day, Page & Co. for permission to quote from Lanier's " Shakspere and his Forerunners," and the editor of " Lippincott's Magazine," for the quotations from the letters to Mr. Milton H. Northrup. For various reasons I am under obligations to Miss Susan Hayes Ward, Mrs. W. M. Baskervill, Mr. and Mrs. Lawrence Turnbull, Mr. George S. Wills, Mr. J. P. Breedlove of the Trinity College Library, Mr. T. J. Kiernan of the Harvard College Library, Mr. Philip R. Uhler of the Peabody Institute, Mr. J. H. Southgate, Mr. F. A. Ogburn, Mr. Milton H. Northrup, Mr. J. A Bivins, Dr. C. Alphonso Smith, and to my colleagues, Dr. W. P. Few and Dr. W. H. Glasson.

TRINITY COLLEGE, DURHAM, N. C.,
August 12, 1905.

CONTENTS

LIST OF ILLUSTRATIONS

SIDNEY LANIER

INTRODUCTION

THE author of the introduction to the first complete edition of Sidney Lanier's poems — published three years after the poet's death — predicted with confidence that Lanier would "take his final rank with the first princes of American song." Anticipating the appearance of this volume, one of the best of recent lyric poets, who had been Lanier's fellow prisoner during the Civil War, prophesied that "his name to the ends of the earth would go." Indeed, there was a sense of surprise to those who had read only the 1877 edition of Lanier's poems, when his poems were collected in an adequate and worthy edition. Since that time the space devoted to him in histories of American literature has increased from ten or twelve lines to as many pages — an indication at once of popular interest and of an increasing number of scholars and critics who have recognized the value of his work. His growing fame found a notable expression when his picture appeared in the frontispiece of the standard American Anthology, along with those of Poe, Walt Whitman, and the five recognized New England poets.

It cannot be said, however, that Lanier's rank as a poet — even in American, to say nothing of English literature — is yet fixed. He is a very uneven writer, and his defects are glaring. Some of the best American critics — men who have a right to speak with authority — shake their heads in disapproval at what they call the Lanier cult. Abroad he has had no vogue, as have Emerson and Poe and Walt Whitman. The enthusiastic praise of the "Spectator" has been more than balanced by the indifference of some English critics and the sarcasm of others. Mme. Blanc's article in the "Revue des Deux Mondes," setting forth the charm of his personality and the excellence of his poetry, met with little response in France. In view of this divergence of opinion among critics, it may be doubted if the time has yet come for anything approaching a final valuation of Lanier's work. In the later pages of this book an attempt will be made to give a reasonably balanced and critical study of his actual achievement in poetry and criticism.

Certainly those who have at heart the interest of American poetry cannot but wage a feud with death for taking away one who had just begun his career. The words of the great English threnodies over the premature death of men of genius come involuntarily to one who realizes what the death of Lanier meant. It is true that he lived fourteen years longer than Keats and ten years longer than Shelley, and that he was as old as Poe when he died ; but it must be remembered that, so far as his artistic work was concerned, the period from 1861 to 1873 was largely one of arrested development. He is one of the inheritors of unfulfilled renown, not simply because he died young, but because what he had done and what he had planned to do gave promise of a much better and more enduring work. Such men as he and Keats must be judged, to be sure, by their actual achievement ; but there will always attach to their names the glory of the unfulfilled life, a fame out of all proportion to the work accomplished. Poe had completed his work: limited in its range, it is all but perfect. Lanier, with his reverence for science, his appreciation of scholarship, his fine feeling for music, and withal his love of nature and of man, had laid broad the foundation for a great poet's career. The man who, at so early an age and in the face of such great obstacles, wrote the " Marshes of Glynn" and the " Science of English Verse," and who in addition thereto gave evidence of constant growth and of self-criticism, would undoubtedly have achieved much worthier things in the future.

Of one thing there can be no doubt, that his personality is one of the rarest and finest we have yet had in America, and that his life was one of the most heroic recorded in the annals of men. The time has passed for emphasizing unduly the pathos of Lanier's life. He was not a sorrowful man, nor was his life a sad one. His untimely and all but tragic death following a life of suffering and poverty, the appeals made by admirers in behalf of the poet's family, a few letters written to friends explaining his seeming negligence, and a fragment or two found in his papers after death, have been sometimes treated without their proper perspective. A complete reading of his letters — published and unpublished — and of his writings, combined with the reminiscences of his friends in Baltimore, Macon, and elsewhere, will convince any one of the essential vigor and buoyancy of his nature. He would have resented the expression "poor Lanier," with as much emphasis as did Lamb the condescending epithet used by Coleridge. He was ever a fighter, and he won many triumphs. He had the power of meeting all oppositions and managing them, emerging into "a large blue heaven of moral width and delight."

He was a sufferer from disease, but even in

the midst of its grip upon him he maintained his
composure, cheerfulness, and unfailing good humor. He had remarkable powers of recuperation. Writing to his father from San Antonio
in 1872, he said: " I feel to-day as if I had been
a dry leathery carcass of a man into whom some
one had pumped strong currents of fresh blood,
of abounding life, and of vigorous strength. I
cannot remember when I have felt so crisp, so
springy, and so gloriously unconscious of lungs."
During these intervals of good health he was
mentally alert, — a prodigious worker, feeling
" an immortal and unconquerable toughness of
fibre " in the strings of his heart. There was
something more than the cheerfulness that attends
the disease to which he was subject. There was
an ardor, an exuberance that comes only from
" a lordly, large compass of soul." As to his poverty, it must be said that few poets were ever so
girt about with sympathetic relatives and friends,
and few men ever knew how to meet poverty so
bravely. He fretted at times over the irrespon-
siveness of the public to his work, but not so
much as did his friends, to whom he was constantly speaking or writing words of encouragement and hope. Criticism taught him " to lift
his heart absolutely above all expectation save
that which finds its fulfillment in the large consciousness of faithful devotion to the highest

ideals in art." " This enables me," he said, " to
work in tranquillity." He knew that he was
fighting the battle which every artist of his type
had had to fight since time began. In his intellectual life he passed through a period of storm
and stress, when he felt " the twist and cross of
life," but he emerged into a state where belief
overmasters doubt and he knew that he knew.
He was cheerful in the presence of death, which
he held off for eight years by sheer force of will;
at last, when he had wrested from time enough
to show what manner of man he was, he drank
down the stirrup-cup " right smilingly."

Looked at from every possible standpoint, it
may be seen that none of these obstacles could
subdue his hopeful and buoyant spirit. " He
was the most cheerful man I ever knew," said
Richard Malcolm Johnston. Ex-President Gilman expressed the feeling of those who knew the
poet intimately when he said, " I have heard a
lady say that if he took his place in a crowded
horse-car, an exhilarating atmosphere seemed to
be introduced by his breezy ways. . . . He always preserved his sweetness of disposition, his
cheerfulness, his courtesy, his industry, his hope,
his ambition. . . . Like a true knight errant,
never disheartened by difficulty, never despondent
in the face of dangers, always brave, full of resources, confident of ultimate triumph." The stu-

dent at Johns Hopkins University who knew him best said : " No strain of physical wear or suffering, no pressure of worldly fret, no amount of dealing with what are called ' the hard facts of experience,' could stiffen or dampen or deaden the inborn exuberance of his nature, which escaped incessantly into a realm of beauty, of wonder, of joy, and of hope." Certainly the great bulk of his published lectures and his poems bear out this impression. His brother, Mr. Clifford Lanier, says that he would not publish some of his early poems because they were not hale and hearty, " breathing of sanity, hope, betterment, aspiration." " Those are the best poets," said Lanier himself, " who keep down these cloudy sorrow songs and wait until some light comes to gild them with comfort." And this he did.

Lanier, whose career has been here briefly suggested, makes his appeal to various types of men and women. Enjoying the use of the Peabody Library and living in the atmosphere of a newly created university, he gave evidence of the modern scholar's zest for original research ; and in addition thereto displayed a spiritual attitude to literature that is rare. The professional musician sees in him one of the advance guard of native-born Americans who have achieved success in some one field of musical endeavor, while a constantly increasing public,

intent upon musical culture, finds in his letters
and essays an expression of the deeper meaning
of music and penetrative interpretations of the
modern orchestra. Lanier influenced to some
extent the minor poets of his era: who knows
but that in some era of creative art — which let
us hope is not far off — his subtle investigations
and experiments in the domain where music and
verse converge may prove the starting point of
some greater poet's work ? To the South, with
which he was identified by birth and temperament, and in whose tremendous upheaval he bore
a heroic part, the cosmopolitanism and modernness of his mind should be a constant protest
against those things that have hindered her in
the past and an incentive in that brilliant future to which she now so steadfastly and surely
moves. To all men everywhere who care for
whatsoever things are excellent and lovely and
of good report his life is a priceless heritage.

CHAPTER I

ANCESTRY AND BOYHOOD

SIDNEY LANIER was born in Macon, Ga., February 3, 1842. His parents, Robert Sampson Lanier and Mary J. Anderson, were at that time living in a small cottage on High street, the father a struggling young lawyer, and the mother a woman of much thrift and piety. There were on both sides traditions of gentility which went back to the older States of Virginia and North Carolina, and in the case of the Laniers to southern France and England. Lanier became very much interested in the study of his genealogy. He was convinced by evidence gathered from the many widely scattered branches of the family that a single family of Laniers originally lived in France, and that the fact of the name alone might with perfect security be taken as a proof of kinship. On account of their nomadic habits, due to their continual movement from place to place during two hundred years, he found it difficult to make out a complete family history. He was not, nor have his relatives and later investigators been, able to find material for the study of the Laniers in their original home. At one time he expressed a wish that President Hayes would appoint him consul to southern France. Certainly he was at home there in imagination and spirit from the time when as a boy he felt the fascination of Froissart's " Chronicles."

One of the keenest pleasures he had in later life was to discover in the Peabody Library at Baltimore a full record of the Lanier family in England. In investigating the state of art in Elizabeth's time he came across in Walpole's " Anecdotes of Painting " references to Jerome and Nicholas Lanier, whose careers he followed with his accustomed zeal and industry through the first-hand sources which the library afforded. There is no more characteristic letter of Lanier's than that written in 1879 to Mr. J. F. D. Lanier, giving the result of this investigation. He there tells the story of ten Laniers who enjoyed the personal favor of four consecutive English monarchs. Jerome Lanier, he believed, had on account of religious persecution fled from France to England during the last quarter of the sixteenth century and " availed himself of his accomplishments in music to secure a place in Queen Elizabeth's household." His son Nicholas Lanier—" musician, painter, engraver " — was patronized successively by James I,

Charles I, and Charles II, wrote music for the masks of Ben Jonson and Campion and for the lyrics of Herrick, and was the first marshal of a society of musicians organized by Charles I in 1626. He also wrote a cantata called " Hero and Leander." He was the friend of Van Dyck, who painted a portrait of Lanier which attracted the attention of Charles I and eventually led to that painter's accession to the court. He was sent by King Charles to Italy to make purchases for the royal gallery. He and other members of his family lived at Greenwich and were known as amateur artists as well as musicians. After the Restoration five Laniers — Nicholas, Jerome, Clement, Andrewe, and John — were charter members of an organization of musicians established by the king " to exert their authority for the improvement of the science and the interest of its professors." It was a great pleasure to Sidney Lanier to find in the diary of Pepys many passages telling of his associations with these music-loving Laniers. " Here the best company for musique I ever was in my life," says the quaint old annalist, " and I wish I could live and die in it. . . . I spent the night in an exstasy almost; and having invited them to my house a day or two hence, we broke up."

The study of these distant relatives enjoying

the favor of successive English kings must have
suggested the contrast of his own life; but he
was pleased with the fancy that their musical
genius had come to him through heredity, for it
confirmed his opinion that " if a man made himself an expert in any particular branch of human
activity there would result the strong tendency
that a peculiar aptitude towards the same branch
would be found among some of his descendants."

Another Lanier in whom he was interested
was Sir John Lanier, the story of whose bravery
at the battle of the Boyne, in 1690, he first read
in Macaulay's " History of England." Lanier's
hope and belief that the family would some
day be able to fill the intervals satisfactorily
connecting Sir John Lanier with the musicians
of the court have not been realized, nor has
any satisfactory study been made of the coming
of the Laniers to America. The best evidence
of the connection between the two families is
found in a deed recorded in Prince County, Va.,
May 14, 1728, from Nicholas Lanier to Holmes
Boisseau — the name Nicholas being significant.
It is certain that Thomas Lanier, along with
a large number of other Huguenots, settled in
Virginia in the early years of the eighteenth century at Manakin-town, some twenty miles from
Richmond. Some of these Huguenots, notably
the Moncures, the Maurys, the Latanés, and the

Flournoys, became connected with historic families of Virginia. There was a tradition in the Lanier family as well as in the Washington family, that Thomas Lanier married an aunt of George Washington, but this has been proved to be untrue.[1] The Laniers were related by marriage to the Washingtons of Surry County. They established themselves in the middle of the eighteenth century in Brunswick and Lunenburg counties of Virginia, as prosperous planters; they did not, however, rank either in dignity or in wealth with the older gentry of Virginia. In a letter written in 1877 Lanier gives in full the various branches of the Lanier family as they separated from this point and went into all parts of the United States. One branch joined the pioneers who went up through Tennessee into Kentucky and thence to Indiana. The most famous of these was Mr. J. F. D. Lanier, who played a prominent part in the development of the railroad system of the West, and at the time of the Civil War had become one of the leading bankers in New York city. He was a financial adviser of President Lincoln, and represented the government abroad in some important transactions. He was of genuine help to Sidney Lanier

[1] *William and Mary Quarterly*, iii, 71–74, 1895 (article by Horace Edwin Hayden); iii, 137–139, October, 1894 (by Moncure D. Conway, with editorial comment); iv, 35–36, July, 1895 (by the editor, Lyon G. Tyler).

at critical times in the latter's life. His son,
Mr. Charles Lanier, now a banker of New York,
was a close friend of the poet, and after his
death presented busts of him to Johns Hopkins
University and the public library of Macon.

The branch of the Lanier family with which
Sidney was connected, moved from Virginia
into Rockingham County, N. C. Sampson Lanier was a well-to-do farmer — a country gentleman, " fond of good horses and fox hounds."
Several of his sons went to the newer States of
Georgia and Alabama. Of these was Sterling
Lanier, the grandfather of the poet, who lived
for a while in Athens, Ga., and was afterwards
a hotel-keeper in Macon and Montgomery. By
the time of the Civil War he had amassed a considerable fortune. In a letter written in 1844
from Macon we learn that he was an ardent
Methodist. His daughters were being educated
in the Wesleyan Female College in that city, his
son Sidney had sailed recently from Charleston
to France, and expected to travel through Sicily,
Italy, and other parts of Europe on account of
his health. He was giving his younger sons the
best education then attainable in Georgia.

His son Robert Sampson Lanier had four
years before returned from Randolph-Macon
College, Virginia, and was at the time the letter
was written beginning the practice of law. He

never became a lawyer of the first rank, but he was universally esteemed for his " fine presence," his " social gentleness," and his " persistent habit of methodical industry." " During all of his long and active professional life," says the late Washington Dessau, " he never allowed anything to interfere with his devotion to his calling as a lawyer. No desire for office attracted him; no other business of profit or honor ever diminished for a moment his devotion for his professional duties. In the year 1850 he was admitted to the bar by the Supreme Court of Georgia, and from that period down to the time of his death the name of his firm appears in nearly every volume of the reports, indicating the wide extent of his business. . . . As a lawyer, while not aspiring to be a brilliant advocate, he was a most profound and able reasoner, thoroughly versed and grounded in the knowledge of the common law, well prepared with a knowledge of current decisions and in the learning that grows out of them. . . . In his social intercourse he was a gentleman of the purest and most refined type. . . . At his own home, at the homes of others, in casual meetings, in travel, everywhere, he always exhibited toward those who met him an unbroken front of courtesy, gentleness, and refinement." [1]

[1] *Report of the 11th Annual Meeting of the Georgia Bar Association*, Atlanta, 1894.

He was just such a lawyer as Lanier would
have become had he remained in that profession; indeed, son and father were very much
alike. The father was a man of "considerable
literary acquirements and exquisite taste." He
was fond of Shakspere, Addison, and Sir Walter Scott, having the literary taste of the gentlemen of the old South. The letters written
to his son show decided cultivation. They show
also that he was in thorough sympathy with his
son's intellectual life. The letter written by
Lanier to his father from Baltimore in 1873
may lead one to think otherwise. Mr. Lanier
was opposed, as were most of the men of his
section, to a young man's entering upon a musical or poetic career, but more than two hundred letters written by son to father and many
from father to son prove that their relations
during the entire career of the poet were unusu-
ally close and sympathetic. In the earlier years,
Lanier sent his poems to his father, and valued
highly his criticism, and in later years he received from him financial aid and counsel.

While Robert Sampson Lanier was at college
in Virginia he met Mary Jane Anderson, the
daughter of Hezekiah Anderson, a Virginia
planter who attained success in the political life
of that State. They were married in 1840, and
Sidney was their first-born. The poet thus in-

herited on his mother's side Scotch-Irish blood,
an element in Southern life which has been often
underestimated. She proved to be a hard-work-
ing woman, caring little for social life, but thoroughly interested in the religious training of her
children. Her husband, although nominally a
Methodist, was not actively identified with the
church, but willingly acquiesced in the somewhat
rigid Presbyterian discipline that prevailed in
the home. The children — Sidney, Clifford, and
Gertrude — were taught the strictest tenets
of the Calvinistic creed. When Lanier afterwards, in Baltimore, lived a somewhat more
liberal life — both as to creed and conduct —
he wrote: "If the constituents and guardians
of my childhood — those good Presbyterians
who believed me a model for the Sunday-school
children of all times — could have witnessed my
acts and doings this day, I know not what groans
of sorrowful regret would arise in my behalf."

The seriousness of this life was broken, however, on week days. Southern Puritanism dif-
fered from the early New England Puritanism in
a certain affectionateness and sociability. The
mother could play well on the piano, and frequently sang with the children hymns and popular melodies. Between the two brothers there
was from the first the most beautiful relation, as
throughout the rest of their lives: comrades in

boyhood, comrades during the War, comrades in
their first literary work, and to the end. On
Saturdays they went to " the boys' hunting fields
— happy hunting grounds, redolent of hickory
nuts, scaly barks, and rose-blushing, luscious,
haw apples. . . . Into these woods, across yon
marsh, we plunged every permissible Saturday
for a day among doves, blackbirds, robins, plov-
ers, snipes, or rabbits." [1] Sometimes they enjoyed fishing in the near-by brook or the larger
river. The two brothers were devoted to their
sister Gertrude, to whom Sidney referred in later
years as his " vestal sister, who had, more perfectly than all the men or women of the earth,
nay, more perfectly than any star or any dream,"
represented to him " the simple majesty and the
serene purity of the Winged Folk up Yonder."

The beauty of this simple home life cannot well
be overestimated in its influence on Lanier's
later life. He had nothing of the Bohemian in
his nature. He was throughout his life fully alive
to all human ties, fulfilling every relationship,
whether of son, brother, father, husband, or friend.
His other relatives — uncles, aunts, and cousins,
— filled a large place in his early life, especially
his mother's brother, Judge Clifford Anderson,
who was the law partner of Lanier's father and
afterwards Attorney-General of Georgia ; and

[1] Clifford Lanier, *The Chautauquan*, July, 1895.

his father's sister, Mrs. Watt, who from much travel and by association with leading men and women of the South brought into Lanier's life the atmosphere of a larger social world than that in which he was born.

Nor did Lanier live apart from the life in Macon. Although in later years he felt strongly the contrast between himself and his environment, he always spoke of his native place with the greatest affection, and it was among Macon people that he found some of his best friends in his adopted city. Its natural beauty appealed to him from the beginning — the river Ocmulgee, the large forests of oak-trees stretching in every direction, the hills above the city, for which he often yearned, from the plains of Texas, or the flats of Florida, or the crowded streets of Baltimore. The climate was agreeable. Describing this section, Lanier said: " Surely, along that ample stretch of generous soil, where the Appalachian ruggednesses calm themselves into pleasant hills before dying quite away in the seaboard levels, a man can find such temperances of heaven and earth — enough of struggle with nature to draw out manhood, with enough of bounty to sanction the struggle — that a more exquisite co-adaptation of all blessed circumstances for man's life need not be sought." [1]

[1] *Music and Poetry*, p. 134.

Macon was the capital of Middle Georgia, the centre of trade for sixty miles around. There was among the citizens an aggressive public spirit, which made it the rival in commercial life of the older cities, Savannah and Augusta; before the War it was a more important city than Atlanta. It was one of the first towns to push the building of railroads; it became "the keystone of the roads grappling with the ocean at the east and with the waters beyond the mountains at the west." The richer planters and merchants lived on the hills above the city — in their costly mansions with luxuriant flower gardens — while the professional men and the middle classes lived in the lower part of the city. Social lines were not, however, so sharply drawn here as in cities like Richmond or Charleston. Middle Georgia was perhaps the most democratic section of the South. It was a democracy, it is true, working within the limitations of slavery,[1] and greatly tempered with the feudal ideas of the older States, but it was a life which gave room for the development of well-marked individual types. There were many Georgia "Crackers" in the surrounding country; they were even recognized more than in

[1] In Macon a great many citizens had no slaves at all, and even those who had them had only a few. In 1850 the white population was 3323, while there were only 2352 slaves. In 1859, when the population had grown to 8000, the proportion was maintained.

other States as part of the social structure. While
still a young boy Lanier was delivery clerk in the
Macon post-office, and entertained the family at
nights by " mimicry of their funny speech." In
later life he wrote dialect poems, setting forth the
humor of these people, and drew upon their speech
for illustrations of philological changes in language.

In Macon hospitality was regarded as an indispensable, even sacred duty. Cordiality and
kindness in all the ordinary relations of men and
women made up for whatever deficiencies there
were in art and literature. Professor Le Conte,
who lived in Macon during the boyhood of Lanier, speaking of some weeks he spent there during a college vacation, says, " Oh, the boundless
hospitality of those times — a continual round
of entertainments, musicales, and evening parties, . . . horseback rides and boat rides during
the day and piano-playing, singing, fluting, and
impromptu cotillions and Virginia reels in the
evening ! " [1] The Lanier House, a hotel owned
by Sterling Lanier from 1844 to 1854, was the
centre of this social life. Here many distinguished
men were entertained and many receptions were
held. The proprietor was a typical " mine host,"
endeavoring to throw around his guests some
of the atmosphere of the finer Southern homes.

[1] *The Autobiography of Joseph Le Conte.*

In 1851 President Fillmore and his Secretary of
the Navy, John P. Kennedy, visited Macon and
were entertained at this hotel. Macon was not without its cultivated people. Young ladies studied
music in New York and brought into the private
life of the city an atmosphere of musical culture. Now and then students were sent to the
universities of the East. A group of professional
and business men — E. A. Nisbet, Washington
Poe, Charles Day, Colonel Whittle, L. Q. C.
Lamar (in his earlier days) — had the refinement and cordiality characteristic of the old
régime.

The religious spirit ran high in Macon. While
the Presbyterian church had a better educated
clergy and proportionately a greater number of
educated personages among the laity, the Methodist and Baptist churches dominated the life of
the community. Revivals that recall the Great
Awakening in New England in the time of Jonathan Edwards were frequent. The most popular
preacher in Macon — George F. Pierce, afterwards bishop in the Southern Methodist church
— is said to have preached the terrors of the
law so plainly that the editor of a long extinct
Universalist paper said he could smell fire and
brimstone half a mile from the church. The
type of religion that prevailed was emotional,
but in an earlier stage of society it was a great

barrier against immorality. The clergy did not raise the question of the ethics of slavery, — on the other hand they defended it on biblical grounds, — but they did enjoin upon masters the duty of kindness to slaves. Many of them were not cultivated men, but they laid the foundation for a better civilization in a stern and righteous social life which flowered in the next generation. "The only burning issues were sprinkling versus immersion, freewill versus predestination," and over these questions the churches fought with energy. Divided though they were on many points, they agreed in resisting the forces of modern thought that were making for a more liberal theology.

Although the people of Macon were thoroughly alive to the commercial, social, and religious welfare of the community, they provided no adequate school system. Lanier was schooled " in small private one - roomed establishments, taught by a Mrs. Anderson, a Mr. Hancock, or by that dear old eccentric dominie, ' Jake ' Danforth. One of these schools stood in a grove of oak and hickory-nut trees and was called the 'Cademy. Sidney was bright in studies, but while parsing, reading, writing, and figuring, he was also chucking nuts from the tops of the tall trees, sympathizing with the dainty half-angel, half-animal flying squirrels, and drinking deep draughts of the love of nature from the cool, solacing oaks." [1]

Lanier was undoubtedly influenced by the life in Macon ; positively influenced in that much of this life became a part of his own, and negatively in that he reacted against many conditions and ideals that prevailed there. All the time there was developing in him his own genius. He did not remember a time when he could not play upon almost any musical instrument. "When he was seven years old he made his first effort at music upon an improvised reed cut from the neighboring river bank, with cork stopping the ends and a mouth hole and six finger holes extemporized at the side. With this he sought the woods to emulate the trills and cadences of the song birds." Santa Claus's gift one year took the form of a small, yellow, one-keyed flute, on which simple instrument he would "practice with the passion of a virtuoso." Like Schumann, he organized an orchestra among his friends and young playmates. Simultaneously he was receiving his first initiation into the joy of literature. He would frequently retire from playing with his brother and other companions to the library of his father, where he followed with absorbing interest the stories of Sir Walter Scott,

[1] Article by Clifford Lanier, in *Gulf States Historical Magazine*, July, 1903.

the romances of Froissart, the adventures of Gil Blas, and other stories that his boyish mind delighted in. He was already producing among his playmates a sense of the distinction of his personality, that caused them to reverence him as one above them.

CHAPTER II

COLLEGE DAYS

JANUARY 6, 1857, Lanier entered the sophomore
class in Oglethorpe University, situated at Midway, Ga. — two miles from Milledgeville, which
was then the capital of the State. It would be
difficult to imagine a greater contrast than that
between the sleepy town of Milledgeville and
progressive Macon, or between Oglethorpe and
the better colleges of the South at the present
time. The essentially primitive life of the college is seen in an act which was passed by the
legislature making it unlawful for any person to
" establish, keep, or maintain any store or shop
of any description for vending any species of
merchandise, groceries or confectioneries within
a mile and a half of the University." It was a
denominational college established by the Presbyterian Church, and belonged to the synods of
South Carolina and Georgia. Like many other
denominational colleges throughout the South,
it arose in response to a demand that attention
should be given in education to the cultivation of a strong religious faith in the minds

SIDNEY LANIER AT THE AGE OF FIFTEEN

From an ambrotype in the possession of the family

of students. The older State universities were supposed to be dominated by the aristocratic class and by political parties, and there was a tendency in them towards a more liberal view of religion than comported with an orthodox faith. The origin of the denominational colleges was similar to that of Princeton and the smaller colleges of New England. Many of them, with small endowments and a small number of men in the faculty, did much to foster intellectual as well as spiritual growth; their place in the history of Southern life has not been fully appreciated. Before the public-school system of later days was established, they did much to educate the masses of the people.

Oglethorpe, at the time when Lanier became a student, was presided over by Rev. Samuel K. Talmage, originally of New Jersey, a graduate of Princeton and a tutor there for three years. He was a warm personal friend of Alexander H. Stephens, and was known throughout Georgia as a preacher of much power, "foremost in the councils of his church." Another member of the small faculty was Charles W. Lane, of the department of mathematics, of whom one of his friends wrote that he was "the sunniest, sweetest Calvinist that ever nestled close to the heart of Arminians and all else who loved the Master's image when they saw it. His cottage at Midway was a Bethel; it was God's house and heaven's gate."

The piety of such men confirmed in Lanier a natural religious fervor. But the man who was destined to have a really formative influence over him was James Woodrow, of the department of science. A native of England and during his younger days a citizen of Pennsylvania, he had studied at Lawrence Scientific School under Agassiz, and had just returned from two years' study in Germany when Lanier came under his influence. Circumstances were such that he never became an investigator in his special line of work, but he was a thorough scholar who kept abreast with the knowledge of his subject. He afterwards became professor of science in the Presbyterian Theological Seminary at Columbia, S. C., and later the president of the University of South Carolina. In 1873 and 1874 he was the champion of science against those who called the church " to rise in arms against Physical Science as the mortal enemy of all the Christian holds dear, and to take no rest until this infidel and atheistic foe has been utterly destroyed." [1] Dr. Woodrow maintained that the science of theology, as a science, is equally human and uninspired with the science of geology. He cited

[1] *An Examination of Certain Recent Assaults on Physical Science.* By James Woodrow. Columbia, 1873.

illustrations from the long warfare of science and theology to show that the church would make a great mistake if it attempted to shut off the human intellect from the search of truth as reverent investigators in the realms of geology and biology might find it. Comparing scientific truth to a great ocean, he speaks of an opponent of science as " brandishing his mop against each succeeding wave, pushing it back with all his might, but the ocean rolls on, and never minds him ; science is utterly unconscious of his opposition." This point of view, maintained even to the point of accepting the theory of evolution, led eventually to his trial and condemnation by the Southern Presbyterian Church. Throughout the whole controversy he maintained a calm and moderate temper and never abated in the least his acceptance of the fundamental ideas of the Christian religion. Such a man, coming into the life of Lanier at a formative period, influenced him profoundly. He set his mind going in the direction which he afterwards followed with great zest, the value of science in modern life and its relation to poetry and religion. He also revealed to him the meaning of genuine scholarship.

Teacher and pupil became intimate friends. In a letter addressed to the writer, Professor Woodrow says : " When he graduated I caused him to be appointed tutor in the University, so that I became better acquainted with him, and liked him better and better. I was professor of natural science, and often took him to ramble with me, observing and studying whatever we saw, but also talking about everything either of us cared for. About the same time I was licensed to preach, and spent my Saturdays and Sundays in preaching to feeble churches and in school-houses, court houses, and private houses, within forty or more miles of the college; trying to make my Sunday night services come within twenty-five miles of home, so that I could drive to the college in time for my Monday morning sunrise lecture. Every now and then I would invite Lanier to go with me. During such drives we were constantly engaged without interruption in our conversation. In these ways, and in listening frequently to his marvelous flute-playing, we were much together. We were both young and fond of study."

The first letter written by Lanier to his father from college announces his admission to the sophomore class: "I have just done studying to-night my first lesson, to wit, forty-five lines of Horace, which I 'did' in about fifteen minutes." Other letters show that he was a very hard student and intensely conscientious. At one time having violated one of his father's regulations, that he was not under any circumstances to borrow money from his college mates, he wrote: "My father, I have sinned. With what intensity of thought, with what deep and earnest reflection have I contemplated this lately! My heart throbs with the intensity of its anguish. . . . If by hard study and good conduct I can atone for that, God in heaven knows that I shall not be found wanting. . . . Not a night passes but what the supplication, God bless my parents, ascends to the great mercy seat." At another time he writes for the following books: Olmsted's Philosophy, Blair's Rhetoric, Cicero de Oratore, and an Analytical Geometry. He already has some Greek tragedies which he is to study. Contemplating his junior year, he writes: "I feel quite enthusiastic on the subject of studying. . . . The very name of Junior has something of study-inspiring and energy-exciting to me."

Lanier pursued the limited curriculum of the college with zeal and with mastery. From his letters it is seen that he read such of the Greek and Latin classics as were generally studied in American colleges at that time. He mastered mathematics beyond any man of his class, and became interested in philosophy and science. His alert mind and energy enabled him to take at once a position of leadership in the college. He joined a secret literary society, of which he wrote to his father: "I have derived more benefit from that, than any one of my collegiate studies. We meet together in a nice room, read compositions, declaim, and debate upon interesting subjects."

His contact with these specially intimate friends was a thoroughly healthy one. He took part in their sports and mischief-making as well as in their more serious pastimes. " I shall never forget," says one of his companions, " those moonlight nights at old Oglethorpe, when, after study hours, we would crash up the stairway and get out on the cupola, making the night merry with music, song, and laughter. Sid would play upon his flute like one inspired, while the rest of us would listen in solemn silence."

Besides being a faithful student, Lanier was an omnivorous reader in the wide fields of English literature, sharing his tastes with some of his companions who with him lived in " an atmosphere of ardent and loyal friendship." " I can recall," says Mr. T. F. Newell, his classmate and room-mate,[1] " those Attic nights, for they are among the dearest and tenderest recollections of my life, when with a few chosen companions we would read from some treasured volume, it may have been Tennyson or Carlyle or Christopher North's ' Noctes Ambrosianae,' or we would make the hours vocal with music and

[1] Quoted from Baskervill's *Southern Writers*, p. 149.

song ; those happy nights, which were veritable
refections of the gods. . . . On such occasions I
have seen him walk up and down the room and
with his flute extemporize the sweetest music
ever vouchsafed to mortal ear. At such times it
would seem as if his soul were in a trance, and
could only find existence, expression, in the
ecstasy of tone, that would catch our souls with
his into the very seventh heaven of harmony.
Or, in merry mood, I have seen him take a banjo,
for he could play on any instrument, and as
with deft fingers he would strike some strange
new note or chord, you would see his eyes
brighten, he would begin to smile and laugh as
if his very soul were tickled, while his hearers
would catch the inspiration, and an old-fashioned
' walk-round' and ' negro breakdown,' in which all
would participate, would be the inevitable result.
At other times, with our musical instruments,
we would sally forth into the night and 'neath
moon and stars and under ' Bonny Bell window
panes' — ah, those serenades ! were there ever
or will there ever be anything like them again ?
— when the velvet flute notes of Lanier would
fall pleasantly upon the night."

Speaking further of his reading and of the
way in which he shared his delight with others,
the same writer says : " I recall how he delighted in the quaint and curious of our old

literature. I remember that it was he who introduced me to that rare old book, Burton's ' Anatomy of Melancholy,' whose name and size had
frightened me as I first saw it on the shelves,
but which I found to be wholly different from
what its title would indicate; and old Jeremy
Taylor, ' the poet-preacher;' and Keats's ' En-
dymion,' and ' Chatterton,' the ' marvelous boy
who perished in his pride.' Yes, I first learned
the story of the Monk Rowley and his wonderful
poems with Lanier. And Shelley and Coleridge
and Christopher North, and that strange, weird
poem of ' The Ettrick Shepherd ' of ' How Kil-
meny Came Hame,' and a whole sweet host and
noble company, ' rare and complete.' Yes,
Tennyson, with his ' Locksley Hall ' and his ' In
Memoriam ' and his ' Maud,' which last we almost
knew by heart. And then old Carlyle, with his
' Sartor Resartus,' ' Hero-Worship,' ' Past and
Present,' and his wonderful book of essays, especially the ones on Burns and Jean Paul, ' The
Only.' Without a doubt it was Carlyle who first
enkindled in Lanier a love of German literature
and a desire to know more of the language."

His flute-playing and extensive reading did
not prevent Lanier from graduating at the head
of his class in July, 1860.[1] His oration was on

---

[1] He was out of college the year 1858–9, being clerk in the
Macon post-office. The college records show that he received

the ambitious subject, " The Philosophy of History." One of the most important events in his early life was the vacation following his graduation. His grandfather had bought in the mountains of East Tennessee, at Montvale Springs, a large estate, on which had been built a beautiful hotel. During the summer his children and grandchildren — some twenty-five in all — visited him. Here they enjoyed the pleasures of hunting, fishing, and social life. There were many visitors from the Southern States to this " Saratoga of the South." " What an assemblage of facilities for enjoyment," Lanier writes, " I have up here in the mountains, — kinsfolk, men friends, women friends, books, music, wine, hunting, fishing, billiards, tenpins, chess, eating, mosquitoless sleeping, mountain scenery, and a month of idleness." This experience, somewhat idealized, is the basis of the first part of " Tiger Lilies." Here Lanier had the opportunity of seeing at its best the life of the old South just before it vanished in the cataclysm of the Civil War. Of that life he afterwards wrote : " Nothing can be more pitiable than that at the time when this amiable outcome of the old Southern civilization became known to the world at large, it became so through being laid bare by the

the highest marks in his senior year, but shared the honors of graduation with one whose record for the entire course was equal to his.

sharp spasm of civil war. There was a time
when all our eyes and faces were distorted with
passion ; none of us either saw or showed true.
Thrice pitiable, one says again, that the fairer
aspects of a social state, which though neither perfect as its violent friends preached, nor satanic as
its violent enemies denounced, yet gave rise to so
many beautiful relations of honor and fidelity,
should have now gone to the past, to remain illuminated only by the unfavorable glare of acci-
dentally associated emotions in which no man
can see clearly." [1]

But while Lanier was thoroughly identified
with this life, he was at the time dreaming of a
career which was not fostered by it — a career
in which music and poetry should be the domi-
nating figures. The scene in the first book of
" Tiger Lilies " of a band of friends gathered on
the balcony of John Sterling's house — a palace
of art reared by Lanier's imagination in the
mountains of East Tennessee — is strictly autobiographical. As they watch the sunset over
the valley, the rich notes of violin, flute, and
piano blend with the beauty of nature ; the
future of music is the theme and poetry the
comment. The various characters of that immature romance quote from Emerson, Carlyle, and
Richter. As they talk upon the theme so dear

[1] *Florida : Its Scenery, Climate, and History*, p. 232.

to their imagination twilight comes. "And so the last note floated out over the rock, over the river, over the twilight to the west."

With something of the power of Charles Egbert Craddock, Lanier writes in the same book of the mountain scenery of that region: "Here grow the strong sweet trees, like brawny men with virgins' hearts. Here wave the ferns, and cling the mosses and clamber the reckless vines. Here, one's soul may climb as upon Pisgah, and see one's land of peace, seeing Christ who made all these beautiful things." Again, it is "the trees that ever lifted their arms toward heaven, obeying the injunction of the Apostle, *praying always*, — the great uncomplaining trees, whose life is surely the finest of all lives, since it is nothing but a continual growing and being beautiful." He describes a moonlight night on the mountains: "All this time the grace of moonlight lay tenderly upon the rugged majesty of the mountains, as if Desdemona placed a dainty white hand upon Othello's brow. All this time the old priestly oaks lifted yearning arms toward the stars, and a mighty company of leaf-chapleted followers, with silent reverence, joined this most pathetic prayer of these dumb ministers of the hills."

After this enchanting and inspiring experience, he returned to Oglethorpe as tutor: it

was to be a year of hard work, especially in
Greek. He described himself at this period as
" a spare-built boy, of average height and under-
weight, mostly addicted to hard study, long
reveries, and exhausting smokes with a German
pipe." He did much miscellaneous reading and
was busy with " hints and fragments of a poetical,
musical conception, — a sort of musical drama
of the peasant uprising in France, called the
Jacquerie," which continued to interest him during the remainder of his life, but which remained unfinished at his death. If he wrote any
poetry, it has not been preserved. His brother is
of the opinion that his earliest efforts were Byron-
esque, if not Wertheresque. " I have his first
attempt at poetry," he says ; " it is characteristic,
it is not suggestive of swallow flights of song,
but of an eaglet peering up toward the empy-
rean." His mind at this time turned more especially in the direction of music. He jots down in
one of his note-books : " The point which I
wish to settle is merely by what method shall
I ascertain what I am fit for as preliminary to
ascertaining God's will with reference to me ; or
what my inclinations are, as preliminary to ascertaining what my capacities are — that is, what I
am fit for. I am more than all perplexed by this
fact : that the prime inclination — that is, natural bent (which I have checked, though) of my

nature is to music, and for that I have the greatest talent; indeed, not boasting, for God gave it me, I have an extraordinary musical talent, and feel it within me plainly that I could rise as high as any composer. But I cannot bring myself to believe that I was intended for a musician, because it seems so small a business in comparison with other things which, it seems to me, I might do. Question here: 'What is the province of music in the economy of the world?'"

But the really practical plan that formed itself in Lanier's mind was that of study in a German university, as preliminary to a professorship in an American college, which might in turn give opportunity for creative work. Young Southerners from the University of Virginia — such as Basil Gildersleeve and Thomas R. Price — had already begun their pilgrimages to the German universities. The situation in Lanier's case is an exact parallel to that of Longfellow at Bowdoin College, and one cannot but wonder what would have been Lanier's future if circumstances had allowed him to follow out the career here indicated. The best account given of him at this time is that of a young Northerner who was teaching in an academy at Midway: —

"It was during the four months immediately preceding the outbreak of the war that a kind Fate brought me into contact and companionship with Sidney Lanier. We occupied adjoining rooms at Ike Sherman's boarding-house and ate at the same table. Myself a young fellow just out of a Northern college, boasting the same number of years, conducting a boys' academy in the shadow of Oglethorpe, there was between us a bond of sympathy which led to a friendship interrupted only by the Civil War and broken only by his untimely death. Many a stroll and talk we had together among the moaning pines, beguiled by the song of the mocking-bird. Together we called on the young ladies of Midway, — as this little college community was known, — together joined in serenades, in which his flute or guitar had the place of honor, played chess together, and together dreamed day-dreams which were never to be realized. Contemporary testimony to my joy in his companionship is borne in frequent references thereto in my private correspondence of those days. 'Several students,' says a New Year's letter to a Northern friend, 'room in the hotel, as well as a young and very intellectual tutor, right back of me, which makes it very pleasant.' In a later letter : 'The tutor is a brick. I am much pleased with him and anticipate much pleasure in his company.' As to his plans for the future: 'The tutor — Lanier — is studying for a professorship; is going to remain here about two years, then go to Heidelberg, Germany, remain about two years, come back, and take a professorship somewhere.' It is needless to add that the destroying angel of war wrecked ruthlessly all these beautiful ambitions.

" Lanier's passion for music asserted itself at every opportunity. His flute and guitar furnished recreation for himself and pleasant entertainment for the friends dropping in upon him. As a master of the flute he was said to be, even at eighteen, without an equal in Georgia. ' Tutor Lanier,' I find myself recording at the time, ' is the finest flute-player you or I ever saw. It is perfectly splendid — his playing. He is far famed for it. His flute cost fifty dollars, and he runs the notes as easily as any one on the piano. Description is inadequate.' " [1]

Before he was twenty years old, then, the master passions of Lanier's soul — scholarship, music, and to a less degree poetry — had asserted themselves. He had a right to look forward to a brilliant future.

[1] " Recollections and Letters of Sidney Lanier," by Milton H. Northrup. *Lippincott's Magazine*, March, 1905.

CHAPTER III

A CONFEDERATE SOLDIER

FROM his dreams of music and poetry and from
the ideal he had formed of study at Heidelberg, Lanier was awakened by the guns of Fort
Sumter and by the agitation everywhere in
Georgia. At Milledgeville he heard some of
the great speeches made for and against secession, for, from November to January, the conflict throughout the State and especially in the
capital was a severe one. He himself, like his
father, hoped that the Union might be preserved,
but the forces of discord could not be stayed.
The people of Macon, on November 8, 1860,
passed a declaration of independence, setting
forth their grievances against the North. When
secession was declared in Charleston on December 1, a hundred guns were fired amidst the
ringing of bells and the shouts of the people. At
night there was a procession of fifteen hundred
people with banners and transparencies.[1] When
on January 16 the Georgia convention voted
to secede from the Union, Milledgeville was in

[1] Butler's *History of Macon.*

" rapturous commotion." " Tears of joy fell from many eyes, and words of congratulation were uttered by every tongue. The artillery from the capitol square thundered forth the glad tidings, and the bells of the city pealed forth the joyous welcome to the new-born Republic."

Lanier afterwards, in " Tiger Lilies," described the war fever as it swept over the South. " An afflatus of war was breathed upon us. Like a great wind it drew on, and blew upon men, women, and children. Its sound mingled with the serenity of the church organs and arose with the earnest words of preachers praying for guidance in the matter. It sighed in the half-breathed words of sweethearts, conditioning impatient lovers with war services. It thundered splendidly in the impassioned appeals of orators to the people. It whistled through the streets, it stole into the firesides, it clinked glasses in bar-rooms, it lifted the gray hairs of our wise men in conventions, it thrilled through the lectures in college halls, it rustled the thumbed book leaves of the schoolrooms. This wind blew upon all vanes of all the churches of the country and turned them one way,—toward war. It blew, and shook out, as if by magic a flag whose device was unknown to soldier or sailor before, but whose every flap and flutter made the blood bound in our veins. . . . It arrayed the sanctity of a righteous cause in the brilliant trappings of military display. . . . It offered tests to all allegiances and loyalties, — of church, of state; of private loves, of public devotion; of personal consanguinity, of social ties." [1]

It does not fall within the province of this book to discuss the issues that led to the Civil War, — the questions of secession and slavery. In 1861 they had ceased to be debated in the halls of Congress; all the Southern people were being merged into a unit. Ardent opponents of secession, like Alexander H. Stephens, threw in their lot with the new Confederacy; States like Virginia, which hesitated to disrupt a Union with which they had had so much to do, were as enthusiastic as the more ardent Southern States; old men vied with young men in their military ardor. Scotch-Irish opponents of slavery marched side by side with the Cavaliers, to whom slavery was the very corner-stone of a feudal aristocracy. The fact is, the whole South was animated by a passion for war. To young men like Lanier the Southern cause was one of liberty, of resistance to despotism and fanaticism, of the protection of homes. He who would understand their point of view must read such war lyrics as " Maryland, My Maryland " and Timrod's " Ethnogenesis," or enter sympathetically into the lives of that youthful band of Confederate soldiers all of

[1] *Tiger Lilies*, p. 119.

whom were afterwards to become distinguished
in the field of letters, — Timrod, Hayne, Cable,
Maurice Thompson, and Lanier.

It was not given to many men on either side
to divine the true issues of the war. Lanier afterwards rejoiced in the overthrow of slavery,
and knew that it was the belief in the soundness
and greatness of the American Union among
the millions of the North and of the great
Northwest which really conquered the South.
" As soon as we invaded the North," he said,
" and arrayed this sentiment against us, our
swift destruction followed." In a note-book of
1867 he pointed out with touches of humor the
folly of many of the ideas formerly held by himself and other Southerners. He is writing an
essay on the Devil's Bombs, " some half-dozen of
which were exploded between the years 1861 and
1865 over the Southern portion of North America with widespread and somewhat sad results :
namely, a million of men slain and maimed ; a
million of widows and orphans created ; several
billions of money destroyed ; several hundred
thousand of ignorant schoolboys who could not
study on account of the noise made by the
shells ; and a large miscellaneous mass of poverty,
starvation, recklessness, and ruin precipitated so
suddenly upon the country that many were buried
beneath it beyond hope of being extricated."

This universal tragedy he attributes in part to the conceit of the Southern people. He himself became " convinced of his ability to whip at least five Yankees. The author does not know now and did not then, by what course of reasoning he arrived at this said conviction ; in the best of the author's judgment he did not reason it out at all, rather absorbed it, from the press of surrounding similar convictions. The author, however, was also confident, not only that he personally could whip five Yankees, but *any* Southern boy could do it. The whole South was satisfied it could whip five Norths. The newspapers said we could do it ; the preachers pronounced anathemas against the man that did n't believe we could do it ; our old men said at the street corners, if they were young they could do it, and by the Eternal, they believed they could do it anyhow (whereat great applause and ' Hurrah for ole Harris ! ') ; the young men said they 'd be blanked if they could n't do it, and the young ladies said they would n't marry a man who could n't do it. This arrogant perpetual invitation to draw and come on, this idea which possessed the whole section, which originated no one knows when, grew no one knows how, was a devil's own bombshell, the fuse of which sparkled when Mr. Brooks struck Mr. Sumner upon the head with a cane.

" Of course we laugh at it *now*,— laugh in the hope that our neighbors will attribute the redness of our cheeks to that and not to our shame. . . . The conceit of an individual is ridiculous because it is powerless. . . . The conceit of a whole people is terrible, it is a devil's bombshell, surcharged with death, plethoric with all foul despairs and disasters."

So Lanier spoke in the sober maturity of his manhood of the great tragedy through which he with his section passed. But during the war there was but one idea in his mind, and that was that he might take part in the establishment of a Confederacy. He dreamed with his people of a nation that might be the embodiment of all that was fine in government and in society, that the " new Confederacy was to enter upon an era of prosperity such as no other nation, ancient or modern, had ever enjoyed, and that the city of Macon, his birthplace and home, was to become a great art centre." In this hope, soon after finishing the year's work at Oglethorpe,[1] he volunteered for service and went to Virginia to join the Macon Volunteers, who had left Georgia early in April — the first company that went out of the

[1] The faculty and students almost to a man enlisted in the army; and the college buildings were afterwards used for barracks and hospitals. President Talmage lost his mind by reason of the conflict between his affection for his native and for his adopted section.

State to Virginia. It was an old company that
had won distinction in the Mexican War, and was
the special pride of the city of Macon. The
company was stationed for several months near
Norfolk, where Lanier experienced some of the
joys of city life in those early days when war was
largely a picnic — a holiday time it was — " the
gay days of mandolin and guitar and moonlight
sails on the James River."

In the main, however, they played " Marsh-
Divers and Meadow-Crakes," their principal
duties being to picket the beach, and their " pleasures and sweet rewards-of-toil consisting in agues
which played dice with our bones, and blue-
mass pills that played the deuce with our livers." [1]
The company was sent in 1862 to Wilmington, N.
C., where they experienced a pleasant change in
the style of fever, " indulging for two or three
months," continues Lanier, " in what are called
the ' dry shakes of the sand hills,' a sort of brilliant, tremolo movement, brilliantly executed
upon 'that pan-pipe, man,' by an invisible but very
powerful performer." From here, where they
were engaged in building Fort Fisher, they were
called to Drewry's Bluff ; and from there to the
Chickahominy, participating in the seven days'

[1] The account of Lanier's war experiences is based on the
poet's letters to Northrup, the reminiscences of Clifford Lanier,
Lanier's unpublished letters to his father, *Tiger Lilies,* and
the *Official Records of the War of the Rebellion.*

fighting around Richmond. Just before the battle
of Malvern Hill they marched all night through
drenching rain, over torn and swampy roads.
These were the only important battles in which
Lanier took part. Soon afterwards he was in a
little gunboat fight or two on the south bank of
the James River. On August 26 they were sent
to Petersburg to rest. While there he enjoyed
the use of the city library. He and his brother
and two friends were transferred to the signal
corps, which was considered at that time the most
efficient in the Southern army, and, becoming
soon proficient in the system, attracted the attention of the commanding officer, who formed them
into a mounted field squad and attached them
to the staff of Major-General French. " Often
Lanier and a friend," says the latter officer,
" would come to my quarters and pass the evenings with us, where the ' alarums of war ' were lost
in the soft notes of their flutes, for Lanier was
an excellent musician." [1] Lanier tells in a letter
written to his father at that time of four Georgia
privates with one general, six captains, and one
lieutenant, serenading the city.

One of the most precious memories of Lanier's
war career was that of General Lee attending
religious services in Petersburg. The height of
every Confederate soldier's ambition was to get a

[1] *A History of Two Wars*, by Samuel G. French.

glimpse of the beloved general, who was the idol
of his soldiers. Lanier reverenced him as one of
the greatest of men. In later years he gave his
ideal of what a great musician ought to be. " A
great artist," he said, " should have the sensibility and expressive genius of Schumann, the calm
grandeur of Lee, and the human breadth of
Shakespeare, all in one." In his " Confederate
Memorial Address " he speaks of Lee as " stately
in victory, stately in defeat; stately among the
cannon, stately among the books ; stately in soli-
tude, stately in society ; stately in form, in soul,
in character, and in action." Fortunately he
had the chance to see him under specially interesting circumstances. He afterwards related
the incident to the Confederate veterans in
Macon : " The last time that I saw with mortal eyes — for, with spiritual eyes, many, many
times have I contemplated him since — the scene
was so beautiful, the surroundings were so rare,
nay, time and circumstance did so fitly frame
him, as it were, that I think the picture should
not be lost. . . . It was at fateful Petersburg,
on one glorious Sunday morning, whilst the
armies of Grant and Butler were investing our
last stronghold there. It had been announced,
to those who happened to be stationed in the
neighborhood of General Lee's headquarters,
that religious services would be conducted on

that morning by Major-General Pendleton. At the appointed time I strolled over to Dunn's Hill, where General Lee's tent was pitched, and found General Pendleton ensconced under a magnificent tree, and a small party of soldiers, with a few ladies from the dwelling near by, collected about him. In a few moments, General Lee appeared with his camp chair, and sat down. The services began. That terrible battery, Number Five, was firing, very slowly, each report of the great guns making the otherwise profound silence still more profound. I sat down on the grass and gazed, with such reverence as I had never given to mortal man before, upon the grand face of General Lee. He had been greatly fatigued by loss of sleep.

" As the sermon progressed, and the immortal words of Christian doctrine came to our hearts and comforted us, sweet influences born of the liberal sunlight which lay warm upon the grass, of the moving leaves and trembling flowers, seemed to steal over the General's soul. Presently his eyelids gradually closed, and he fell gently asleep. Not a muscle of him stirred, not a nerve of his grand countenance twitched; there was no drooping of the head, nor bowing of the figure. . . . As he slumbered so, sitting erect, with arms folded upon his chest, in an attitude of majestic repose, such as I never saw assumed by mortal

man before; as the large and comfortable word
fell from the preacher's lips; as the lazy cannon
of the enemy anon hurled a screaming shell to
within a few hundred yards of where we sat, as
finally a bird flew into a tree overhead and sat
and piped small blissful notes in unearthly contrast with the roar of the war engines; it seemed
to me as if the present earth floated off through
the sunlight, and the antique earth returned out
of the past, and some majestic god sat on a hill,
sculptured in stone, presiding over a terrible yet
sublime contest of human passion."

A pleasant interlude in Lanier's soldier life
was a two weeks' visit to Macon in the spring of
1863. The city had not yet felt any of the calam-
ities of war, although high prices prevailed. Mrs.
Clay, wife of Senator Clement C. Clay, was a
visitor in the city at that time, waiting for a sum-
mons to join her husband in Richmond. She
writes, in recalling those days: " Spring was in
its precious beauty. Gardens glowed with brilliant blossoms. Thousands of fragrant odors
mingled in the air, the voices of myriad birds
sang about the foliaged avenues." [1] It was then
that Lanier met Miss Mary Day, at the home
of their friend, Miss Lamar. Her father was a
prominent business man in Macon. She had lived
for the first few years of her life in Macon, but

[1] *A Belle of the Fifties*, p. 194.

had been since 1851 studying music in New York, and living with cultivated people at Saratoga and West Point. In an atmosphere of romance, music, and love Lanier spent his vacation.

On their return to the Virginia battlefields the two brothers were accompanied by Mrs. Clay and her sister-in-law. Mrs. Clay had been a popular belle in Washington in the fifties, and was well acquainted with leading men and women throughout the country. She had heard and met in social circles Charlotte Cushman, Jenny Lind, Thackeray, Lord Napier, and other notabilities. Lanier, eager always to hear of the larger world outside of his own limited life, was much attracted by her reminiscences of well-known men and women. Returning to Suffolk, Va., Clifford Lanier wrote to her: "What a transition is this — from the spring and peace of Macon to this muddy and war-distracted country! Going to sleep in the moonlight and soft air of Italy, I seem to have waked embedded in Lapland snow." Sidney wrote: "Have you ever wandered, in an all night's dream, through exquisite flowery mosses, through labyrinthine grottoes, 'full of all sparkling and sparry loveliness,' over mountains of unknown height, by abysses of unfathomable depth, all beneath skies of an infinite brightness caused by no sun; strangest of all, — wandered about in wonder, as if you had lived an eternity

in the familiar contemplation of such things? If
you have dreamed, thought, and felt so, you can
realize the imbecile stare with which I gaze on
all of this life which goes on around me here.
Macon was my two weeks' dream." [1]

During 1863 and a large part of 1864 the
two brothers served as scouts in Milligan's Corps
along the James River. The duties were unusu-
ally dangerous and onerous, from the fact that
their movements had to be concealed, and that
they were in constant danger of being captured.
In this work of hard riding Lanier displayed
a cool and collected courage; he was untiring
in his energy, prudent and cautious. Notwithstanding the dangers and hardships, he looked
upon the period of life at Fort Boykin on Burwell's Bay — their headquarters — as " the most
delicious period of his life in many respects."
Writing of it later he said: " Our life was as
full of romance as heart could desire. We had
a flute and a guitar, good horses, a beautiful
country, splendid residences inhabited by friends
who loved us, and plenty of hairbreadth 'scapes
from the roving bands of Federals who were
continually visiting that Debatable Land. . . .
Cliff and I never cease to talk of the beautiful women, the serenades, the moonlight dashes
on the beach of fair Burwell's Bay, and the

[1] *A Belle of the Fifties*, p. 200.

SIDNEY LANIER IN 1866

From a " carte de visite " photograph owned by Milton H. Northrup

spirited brushes of our little force with the
enemy." [1]

This is the period of his life which he describes in the second part of "Tiger Lilies."
His brother Clifford also made it the basis of
his novel, "Thorn-Fruit." The effect produced
by the young poet and musician on the people
who lived in the stately mansions along the
James River has been told by one who knew him
well at this time : " The two brothers were in-
separable; slender, gray-eyed youths, full of enthusiasm, Clifford grave and quiet, Sidney, the
elder, playful with a dainty mirthfulness. . . .
How often did we sit on the moonlight nights
enthralled by the entranced melodies of his
flute! Always the longing for the very highest
pervaded his life, and child though I was, in
listening to him as he paced the long galleries of
my old home, or as we rode in the sweet green
wood, I felt even then that we sat ' in the aurora
of a sunrise which was to put out all the stars.' " [2]

This period of his army life is important also
from the fact that here at Fort Boykin he defi-
nitely began to contemplate a literary life as his
probable vocation. He was studying hard, reading English poetry, and writing to his father to
" seize at any price " editions of the German

[1] Letter to Northrup, June 11, 1866.
[2] *Southern Bivouac*, May, 1887.

poets, Uhland, Lessing, Schelling, and Tieck.
Thus at a time when other Southerners were, as
Professor Gildersleeve has said, getting out their
classics to reread them, Lanier was voyaging
into strange fields of thought alone. Once, when
the little camp was captured, he lost several of
his choicest treasures, — a volume containing
the poems of Coleridge, Shelley, and Keats, a
German glossary, Heine's poems, and "Aurora
Leigh." In a letter to his father, January 18,
1864, he says : " Gradually I find that my whole
soul is merging itself into this business of writing, and especially of writing poetry. I am going
to try it ; and am going to test, in the most rigid
way I know, the awful question whether it is
my vocation." He sends his father a number of
poems, that they may be criticised. He has a
sense of his own deficiencies as a writer, — deficiencies which he never fully overcame, — for he
writes : " I have frequently noticed in myself a
tendency to a diffuse style ; a disposition to push
my metaphors too far, employing a multitude of
words to heighten the patness of the image, and
so making of it a *conceit* rather than a meta-
phor, a fault copiously illustrated in the poetry
of Cowley, Waller, Donne, and others of that
ilk."

The tendency is seen in a poem written at
Boykin's Bluff on, perhaps, his twenty-first birth-

day. Notable also is the sense of the dawn of manhood : —

> So Boyhood sets: comes Youth,
> A painful night of mists and dreams,
> That broods till Love's exquisite truth,
> The star of a morn-clear manhood, beams.

In this dawn of his manhood — not yet morn-clear, however, — he began " Tiger Lilies," writing those parts having to do with his experience in the mountains, some passages of which have already been quoted.

But Lanier's literary career was not to be begun as soon as he hoped. He was, in August, 1864, transferred to Wilmington, N. C., where he became a signal officer on the blockade-runners. Wilmington was the port which, late in the war, was the scene of the most brilliant successes of these swift vessels and the most strenuous efforts of the blockaders. " Long after every other port was closed, desperate, but wary sea pigeons would evade the big and surly watchers on the coast . . . and ho! for the open sea." This was a service of keen excitement and constant danger, demanding a clear head and iron nerves. In the latter part of 1864 it became more and more difficult for the blockade-runners to make their way to Bermuda. On November 2, a stormy night, Lanier was a signal officer on the Lucy, which made its way out of the harbor, but fourteen hours later was captured in the Gulf Stream by the Federal cruiser Santiago-de-Cuba. He was taken to Point Lookout prison, where he spent four months of dreary and distressing life. To this prison life Lanier always attributed his breakdown in health. In " Tiger Lilies " he afterwards attempted to give a description of the prison and the life led by prisoners, but turned with disgust from the harrowing memories. The few pages he did write serve as a counterpart to Walt Whitman's strictures on Southern prisons in his " Specimen Days in America."

And yet, under these loathsome conditions he read German poetry, translating Heine's " The Palm and the Pine " and Herder's " Spring Greeting." Here, too, he found comfort for himself and his companions in the flute which he had carried with him during the entire war. One of his comrades gives the following account of Lanier's playing: " Late one evening I heard from our tent the clear sweet notes of a flute in the distance, and I was told that the player was a young man from Georgia who had just come among us. I forthwith hastened to find him out, and from that hour the flute of Sidney Lanier was our daily delight. It was an angel imprisoned with us to cheer and console us. Well I remember his improvisations, and how the young artist stood there in the twilight.

(It was his custom to stand while he played.) Many a stern eye moistened to hear him, many a homesick heart for a time forgot its captivity. The night sky, clear as a dewdrop above us, the waters of the Chesapeake far to the east, the long gray beach and the distant pines, seemed all to have found an interpreter in him.

" In all those dreary months of imprisonment, under the keenest privations of life, exposed to the daily manifestations of want and depravity, sickness and death, his was the clear-hearted, hopeful voice that sang what he uttered in after years."

The purity of Lanier's soul was never better attested than in a letter written by a fellow-prisoner, Mr. John B. Tabb, to Charles Day Lanier, the oldest son of the poet, trying to impress upon his mind the character of his father as exhibited in this prison life at Point Lookout :

" To realize what our surroundings were, one must have lived in a prison camp. There was no room for pretense or disguise. Men appeared what they really were, noble or low-minded, pure or depraved ; and there did one trait of your father's character single him out. In all our intercourse I can remember no conversation or word of his that an angel might not have uttered or listened to. Set this down in your memory. . . . It will throw light upon other points, and prove the truth of Sir Galahad's words, ' My strength is as the strength of ten, because my heart is pure.' "

Lanier secured his release from prison through some gold which a friend of his had smuggled into the prison in his mouth. He came out " emaciated to a skeleton, down-hearted for want of news from home, down-headed for weariness." On his voyage to Fortress Monroe an incident occurred which, although told in somewhat over-wrought language, is a fitting climax to his career as a soldier.

The story of his rescue from death, says Baskervill, is graphically told by the lady herself who was the good Samaritan on this occasion. " She was an old friend from Montgomery, Ala., returning from New York to Richmond; and her little daughter, who had learned to call him Brother Sid, chanced to hear that he was down in the hold of the vessel dying. On application to the colonel in command permission was promptly given to her to minister to his necessity, and she made haste to go below. ' Now my friends in New York,' continued she, ' had given me a supply of medicines, for we had few such things in Dixie, and among the remedies were quinine and brandy. I hastily took a flask of brandy, and we went below, where we were led to the rude stalls provided for cattle, but now

crowded with poor human wretches. There in
that horrible place dear Sidney Lanier lay
wrapped in an old quilt, his thin hands tightly
clinched, his face drawn and pinched, his eyes
fixed and staring, his poor body shivering now
and then in a spasm of pain. Lilla fell at his side,
kissing him and calling : ' Brother Sid, don't you
know me ? Don't you know your little sister ?'
But no recognition or response came from the
sunken eyes. I poured some brandy into a spoon
and gave it to him. It gurgled down his throat
at first with no effort from him to swallow it. I
repeated the stimulant several times before he
finally revived. At last he turned his eyes slowly
about until he saw Lilla, and murmured : ' Am I
dead ? Is this Lilla ? Is this heaven ?' . . .
To make a long story short, the colonel assisted
us to get him above to our cabin. I can see his
fellow prisoners now as they crouched and assisted
to pass him along over their heads, for they were
so packed that they could not make room to carry
him through. Along over their heads they tenderly
passed the poor, emaciated body, so shrunken
with prison life and benumbed with cold. We
got him into clean blankets, but at first he could
not endure the pain from the fire, he was so
nearly frozen. We gave him some hot soup and
more brandy, and he lay quiet till after mid-
night. Then he asked for his flute and began

playing. As he played the first few notes, you should have heard the yell of joy that came up from the shivering wretches down below, who knew that their comrade was alive. And there we sat entranced about him, the colonel and his wife, Lilla and I, weeping at the tender music, as the tones of new warmth and color and hope came like liquid melody from his magic flute." [1]

Thus closes his war period. His name does not appear in any of the official records, but no private soldier had a more varied experience.[2] One scarcely knows which to admire most, — the soldier, brave and knightly, the poet, preparing his wings for a flight, or the musician, inspiriting his fellow-soldiers in camp and in prison.

[1] *Southern Writers*, p. 169.

[2] It is said that he refused promotion several times in order to be with his brother. In a memorandum on the photograph herewith presented he refers to himself as "captain" in the late Confederate army. I have been unable to reconcile these statements.

CHAPTER IV

SEEKING A VOCATION

LANIER reached Macon March 15, after a long
and painful journey through the Carolinas. Immediately upon his arrival, losing the stimulus
which had kept him going so long, he fell dan-
gerously ill, and remained so for nearly two
months. Early in May, just as he was conva-
lescing, General Wilson captured Macon, and
Jefferson Davis and Clement C. Clay were
brought to the Lanier House, whence they were
to start on their way as prisoners to Fortress
Monroe. Clifford Lanier reached home May 19.
He had, after the blockade was closed at Wilmington, gone to Cuba. From there he sailed
to Galveston and walked thence to Macon. He
arrived just in time to see his mother, who a
few days after died of consumption. She had
kept herself alive for months by " a strong conviction, which she expressed again and again, that
God would bring both her boys to her before she
died." Sidney spent the summer months with his
father and his sister, ministering to them in their
sorrow. In September he began to tutor on a

large plantation nine miles from Macon. With thirty classes a day and failing health, he whose brain was " fairly teeming with beautiful things " was shut up to the horrible monotony of the " tear and tret " of the schoolroom. He spent the winter at Point Clear on Mobile Bay, where he was greatly invigorated by the sea breezes and the air of the pine forests.

After these months of sorrow and struggle he settled in Montgomery, Ala., as clerk in the Exchange Hotel, the property of his grandfather and his uncles. His first feeling as he faces the new conditions which he is trying to explain to Northrup, his Northern friend, is one of bewilderment, — the immense distance between the beginning and the end of the war : —

" So wild and high are the big war-waves dashing between '61 and '66, as between two shores, that, looking across their ' rude, imperious surge,' I can scarcely discern any sight or sound of those old peaceful days that you and I passed on the ' sacred soil' of M——. The sweet, half-pastoral tones that *should* come from out that golden time, float to me mixed with battle cries and groans. It was our glorious spring : but, my God, the flowers of it send up sulphurous odors, and their petals are dabbled with blood.

" These things being so, I thank you, more than I can well express, for your kind letter. It comes

to me, like a welcome sail, from that old world
to this new one, through the war-storms. It
takes away the sulphur and the blood-flecks, and
drowns out the harsh noises of battle. The two
margins of the great gulf which has divided you
from me seem approaching each other : I stretch
out my hand across the narrowing fissure, to grasp
yours on the other side. And I wish, with all
my heart, that you and I could spend this inef-
fable May afternoon under that old oak at Whit-
taker's and ' talk it all over.' " [1]

In another letter (June 29, 1866) he en-
closes a photograph [2] and comments on the life
in Montgomery : —

"The cadaverous enclosed is supposed to represent the face of your friend, together with a
small portion of the Confederate gray coat in
which enwrapped he did breast the big wars.

"I have one favor to entreat ; and that is, that
you will hold in consideration the very primitive
state of the photographic art in this section, and
believe that my mouth is not so large, by some
inches, as this villainous artist portrays it.

"I despair of giving you any idea of the mortal stagnation which paralyzes all business here.
On our streets, Monday is very like Sunday :

[1] This and the following letter were printed in *Lippincott's
Magazine*, March, 1905. A few changes are made to conform
to the original copies.

[2] See p. 54.

they show no life, save late in the afternoon, when
the girls come out, one by one, and shine and
move, just as the stars do an hour later. I don't
think there's a man in town who could be in-
duced to go into his neighbor's store and ask him
how's trade; for he would have to atone for such
an insult with his life. Everything is dreamy,
and drowsy, and drone-y. The trees stand like
statues; and even when a breeze comes, the
leaves flutter and dangle idly about, as if with a
languid protest against all disturbance of their
perfect rest. The mocking-birds absolutely refuse to sing before twelve o'clock at night, when
the air is somewhat cooled: and the fireflies
flicker more slowly than I ever saw them before.
Our whole world here yawns, in a vast and sul-
try spell of laziness. An 'exposition of sleep'
is come over us, as over Sweet Bully Bottom;
we won't wake till winter. Himmel, my dear
Boy, you are all so alive up there, and we are
all so dead down here! I begin to have serious
thoughts of emigrating to your country, so that
I may live a little. There's not enough attrition
of mind on mind here, to bring out any sparks
from a man."

Into this strange new world — "the unfamiliar avenue of a new era" — Lanier passed with
unfaltering courage. He was to show that "fortitude is more manly than bravery, for noble

and long endurance wins the shining love of
God ; whereas brilliant bravery is momentary, is
easy to the enthusiastic, and only dazzles the admiration of the weak-eyed." Did any young man
ever have to begin life under more disadvantageous circumstances ? Cherishing in his heart
the ideal long since formed of the scholar's or the
artist's life, he looked around on the blankest
world one could imagine. It is perhaps in a later
letter to Bayard Taylor that Lanier came nearest
to expressing the situation that confronted him
at the end of the war. " Perhaps you know that
with us of the younger generation of the South,
since the war, pretty much the whole of life has
been merely not dying."

Added to his own poverty and sickness, was
that of his family. His grandfather had been
compelled to leave his estate in East Tennessee
in 1863, and was now in old age deprived of his
negroes and much of his land and money. His
father, weighed down with sorrow, had to take up
the practice of law from the start. Some members
of his family, " who used to roll in wealth, are
every day," he writes, " with their own hands
plowing the little patch of ground which the war
has left them, while their wives do their cooking
and washing."

Moreover, the entire South — and to those who
had shared the hopes of a Southern republic it

was still the land they loved — was in a state of despair. Middle Georgia had lost through Sherman's march to the sea $100,000,000.[1] In the wake of Sherman's armies Richard Malcom Johnston had lost his estate of $50,000, Maurice Thompson's home was in ashes, and Joel Chandler Harris, who had begun life on the old Turner plantation under such favorable auspices, was forced to seek an occupation in New Orleans. Only those who lived through that period or who have imaginatively reproduced it, can realize the truth of E. L. Godkin's statement: "I doubt much if any community in the modern world was ever so ruthlessly brought face to face with what is sternest and hardest in human life." It was not simply the material losses of the war, — these have often been commented on and statistics given, — it was the loss of libraries like those of Simms and Hayne, the burning of institutions of learning like the University of Alabama, the closing of colleges, like Lanier's own alma mater. It was the passing away of a civilization which, with all its faults, had many attractive qualities — a loss all the more apparent at a time when a more democratic civilization had not yet taken its place. The South was

Wandering between two worlds — one dead,
The other powerless to be born.

[1] Rhodes's *History of the United States*, v, 22.

Even States like Georgia, which soon showed signs
of recuperation and rejuvenation, suffered with
their more unfortunate sisters, South Carolina
and Louisiana, where the ravages of war were
terrific. There was confusion in the public mind
— uncertainty as to the future. The memories
of these days are suggested here, not for the purpose of awakening in any mind bitter memories,
but that some idea may be given of the tremendous obstacles that confronted a young man like
Lanier.

It is no wonder that under these circumstances men went to other countries, and that some
of those who did not go cherished the project of
transporting the people of various States to other
lands, where the spirit of the civilization that
had passed away might be preserved.[1] Many
men whose names are now lost passed out to the
States of the West. Business men, scholars, and
men of all professions, who have since become
famous in other States, were as complete a loss
to the South as those who died on the battle-
field. And when to all these are added the men
and women who died broken-hearted at the losses
of war, some idea may be conceived of the dis-
advantages under which the South began her
work.

[1] See the *Life and Letters of R. L. Dabney*, for a plan in
which many Virginians were interested.

The work of those men who remained in the
South and set about to inaugurate a new era cannot be too highly estimated, — a work made all
the more difficult by strong men who resisted the
march of events, and who refused to accept the
conditions that then prevailed. The readjustment
came soon to more men than some have thought.
Lanier, writing in 1867, before the pressure of
reconstruction government had been felt, said,
in commenting on the growing lack of restraint in modern political life : " At the close
of that war, three armies which had been fighting on the Southern side, and which numbered
probably forty thousand men, were disbanded.
These men had for four years been subjected to
the unfamiliar and galling restrictions of military
discipline, and to the most maddening privations.
. . . At the same time four millions of slaves,
without provisions and without prospect of labor
in a land where employers were impoverished,
were liberated. . . . The reign of law at this
thrilling time was at an end. The civil powers
of the States were dead ; the military power of
the conquerors was not yet organized for civil
purposes. The railroad and the telegraph, those
most efficient sheriffs of modern times, had fallen
in the shock of war. All possible opportunities
presented themselves to each man who chose to
injure his neighbor with impunity. The country

was sparsely settled, the country roads were intricate, the forests were extensive and dense,
the hiding-places were numerous and secure, the
witnesses were few and ignorant. Never had
crime such fair weather for his carnival. Serious apprehensions had long been entertained by
the Southern citizens that in the event of a dis-
astrous termination of the war, the whole army
would be frenzied to convert itself, after disin-
tegration, into forty thousand highwaymen. . . .
Moreover, the feuds between master and slave,
alleged by the Northern parties in the contest to
have been long smouldering in the South, would
seize this opportunity to flame out and redress
themselves. Altogether, regarding humanity from
the old point of view, there appeared to many
wise citizens a clear prospect of dwelling in [the]
midst of a furious pandemonium for several
years after an unfavorable termination of the
war; but was this prospect realized? Where
were the highway robberies, the bloody ven-
geances, the arsons, the rapine, the murders,
the outrages, the insults? They *were*, not any-
where. With great calmness the soldier cast
behind him the memory of all wrongs and hardships and reckless habits of the war, embraced
his wife, patched his cabin-roof, and proceeded
to mingle the dust of recent battles yet lingering on his feet with the peaceful clods of his

cornfield. What restrained these men? Was it
fear? The word cannot be spoken. Was he who
had breasted the storms of Gettysburg and
Perryville to shrink from the puny arm of a
civil law that was more powerless than the
shrunken muscle of Justice Shallow? And what
could the negro fear when his belief and assurance
were that a conquering nation stood ready to support him in his wildest demands? It was the
spirit of the time that brought about these things.
. . . A thousand Atlantic Cables and Pacific
Railroads would not have contributed cause for
so earnest self-gratulation as was afforded by
this one feature in our recent political convulsion." [1]

Many Southerners were ready, like Lee, to
forget the bitterness and prejudice of the war —
all but the hallowed memories. Lanier, at the
close of a fanciful passage on the blood-red
flower of war which blossomed in 1861, said : —

"It is supposed by some that the seed of
this American specimen (now dead) yet remain
in the land ; but as for this author (who, with
many friends, suffered from the unhealthy odors
of the plant), he could find it in his heart
to wish fervently that these seed, if there be
verily any, might perish in the germ, utterly
out of sight and life and memory and out of

[1] *Retrospects and Prospects*, p. 29.

the remote hope of resurrection, forever and forever, no matter in whose granary they are cherished!" [1]

In this spirit Lanier began his work in Montgomery, Ala. As has been seen, he had extended the hand of fellowship to his Northern
friend, thus laying the basis for the spirit of reconciliation afterwards so dominant in his poetry.
Uncongenial as was his work, he went about it
with a new sense of the " dignity of labor." His
aunt, Mrs. Watt, who had in the more prosperous times before the war traveled much in the
North, and had graced the brilliant scenes of the
opening of the Confederate Congress in Montgomery, becoming the intimate friend of Jefferson Davis and Stephens, now threw around her
nephews — Clifford was also working in the
hotel — the charm of the olden days. They
found pleasure in social life: close to Montgomery lived the Cloptons and Ligons, who on
their plantations enjoyed the gifts of " Santa
Claus Cotton," just after the war. Lanier writes
to his sister, September 26, 1866 : " I have just
returned from Tuskegee, where I spent a pleasant
week. . . . They fêted me to death, nearly. . . .
Indeed, they were all so good and so kind to me,
and the fair cousins were so beautiful, that I
came back feeling as if I had been in a week's

[1] *Tiger Lilies*, p. 116.

dream of fairyland." The two brothers, eager
for more intellectual companionship, organized a
literary club, for the meetings of which Sidney
prepared his first literary exercises after the
war. He played the pipe-organ in the Presbyterian church in Montgomery. He writes to a
friend about some one who was in a state of
melancholy : " She is right to cultivate music,
to cling to it ; it is the only *reality* left in the
world for her and many like her. It will revolutionize the world, and that not long hence. Let
her study it intensely, give herself to it, enter
the very innermost temple and sanctuary of it.
. . . The altar steps are wide enough for all the
world." To another friend he writes at the
same time : " Study Chopin as soon as you become able to play his music ; and get his life by
Liszt. 'T is the most enjoyable book you could
read."

Most of the leisure time of the brothers, however, was spent in literary work, with even
more ardor than while they had plenty of time
to devote to it. By May 12 Clifford had finished his novel, " Thorn-Fruit," and Sidney was
at work on " Tiger Lilies," the novel begun
at Burwell's Bay in 1863 and retouched at different times since then. They were planning,
too, a volume of poems, although with the exception of their father they had not been able

" to find a single individual who sympathized in such a pursuit enough to warrant them in showing him their production, — so scarce is general cultivation here; but," Sidney adds, "we work on, and hope to become at least recognized as good orderly citizens in the fair realm of letters yet." Indeed, they planned to go North in the fall " with bloody literary designs on some hapless publisher." [1]

In order to find out what was going on in the world of letters, Lanier subscribed to the "Round Table," which was then an important weekly paper of New York — indeed, it was more like the London " Spectator " than any paper ever published on this side the water— a journal, said the New York " Times," which " has the genius and learning and brilliancy of the higher order of London weeklies, and which at the same time has the spirit and the instincts of America." Moncure D. Conway was at that time writing letters of much interest from England and Justin Winsor from Cambridge, while Howells, Aldrich, Stedman, and Stoddard were regular contributors. The reviews of books were thoroughly cosmopolitan, and the editorials setting forth the interpretation of contemporary events were characterized by sanity and breadth.

In addition to the fact that Lanier's first

[1] Letters to Northrup.

poems were published in this journal,[1] it is to be
noted that it exerted considerable influence over
him — especially in two directions. Its broad
national policy — more sympathetic than that of
the " Nation " even — was evidence to him that
there were Northern people who were magnanimous in their attitude to Southern problems. He
was especially impressed with an editorial on the
" Duties of Peace " (July 7, 1866) as " the most
sensible discussion " he had seen of the whole
situation. In it were these striking words : "The
people of the South are our brothers, bone of
our bone and flesh of our flesh. They have
courage, integrity, honor, patriotism, and all the
manly virtues as well as ourselves. . . . Can we
realize that our duty now is to heal, not to pun-
ish ? . . . Consider their dilapidated cities, their
deserted plantations, their impoverished country,
their loss of personal property by thousands of
millions ; far more than this, their buried dead
and desolate hearts. . . . No one with a heart can
realize the truth of their condition without feeling
that the punishment has been terrific. We should
address ourselves to the grave task of restoring
the disrupted relations of the two sections by

[1] " In the Foam," " Barnacles," " The Tournament," " Resurrection," " Laughter in the Senate " (not in his collected
poems), " A Birthday Song," " Tyranny," and " Life and
Song" were published in the *Round Table* during 1867 and
1868.

acts of genuine kindness, truthfulness, fairness, and love. . . . In a word, let the era of blood be followed by another era of good feeling." The whole editorial is in accordance with the previously announced policy of the paper : " The Rebellion extinguished, the next duty is to extinguish the sectional spirit, and to seek to create fraternal feeling among all the States of the Union."

In discussing literary questions the " Round Table " showed the same national spirit, manifesting a healthy interest in those few Southern writers who were left after the deluge. The words found in two editorials, calling for a more vigorous and original class of writers, must have appealed to Lanier. An editorial, May 12, 1866, entitled a " Plain Talk with American Writers," said : " In fact the literary field was never so barren, never so utterly without hope or life. . . . The era of genius and vigor that seemed ready to burst upon us only a few months ago has not been fulfilled. There is a lack of boldness and power. Men do not seem to strike out in new paths as bravely as of old. . . . We have very little strong, original writing. Who will waken us from this sleep? Who will first show us the first signs of a genuine literary reviving ? " And again, July 14, 1866, " We look to see young men coming forward who shall inaugurate a

better literature. . . . If ever there was a time
when a magnificent field opened to young aspir-
ants for literary renown, that time is the present.
Every door is wide open. . . . All the graces of
poesy and art and music stand waiting by, ready
to welcome a bold new-comer. . . . Who will
come forward and inaugurate a new era of bold,
electrical, impressive writing ? "

With some such ambition as this in his mind,
Lanier gave up his work in Montgomery in the
spring of 1867 and went to New York with the
completed manuscript of " Tiger Lilies." [1]   He
was there for more than a month, finally arran-
ging for its publication with Hurd & Houghton,
the predecessors of the present firm of Houghton, Mifflin & Co. He was enabled to publish
his book by the generous help of Mr. J. F. D.
Lanier. Some of his experiences on this, his first
visit to the metropolis, are significant. He is
somewhat dazed by the life of the big city. " I
tell you," he writes to a friend, " the Heavens are
alien to this town, and if it were anybody else
but the Infinite God that owned them, he would
n't let them bend so blue over here." In a letter
to his father, April 16, he describes the view of

[1] William Gilmore Simms was there at about the same time
trying to get started again in his literary work, and Edward
Rowland Sill was making his first venture into the literary
world.

the city from Trinity Church steeple and tells
a characteristic incident: " The grand array of
houses and ships and rivers and distant hills did
not arrest my soul as did the long line of men
and women, which at that height seemed to writhe
and contort itself in its narrow bed of Broadway
as in a premature grave. . . . I have not seen
here a single eye that knew itself to be in front
of a heart — but one, and that was a blue one,
and a child owned it. 'T was the very double of
Sissa's [the name for his sister] eye, so I had no
sooner seen it than I made love to it, with what
success you will hear. On Saturday I dined with
J. F. D. Lanier. We had only a family party.
. . . Last and best little Kate Lanier, eight
years old, pearly cheeked, blue eyed, broad of
forehead, cherried i' the lip. About the time that
the champagne came on I happened to mention
that I had been in prison during the war.

" ' Poor fellow ! ' says little Katie, ' and how did
the rebels treat you ? '

" ' Rebels,' said I, ' I am a rebel myself, Kate ! '

" ' What ! ' she exclaimed, and lifted up her
little lilies (when I say lilies I mean hands), and
peered at me curiously with all her blue eyes
astare. ' A live Reb ! '

" This phrase in Katie's nursery had taken the
time-honored place of bugaboos, and hobgob-
lins, and men under the bed. She could not

realize that I, a smooth-faced, slender, ordinary mortal, in all respects like a common man, should be a live reb. She was inclined to hate me, as in duty bound.

" I will not describe the manner of the siege I laid to her : suffice it that when I rose to take leave, Katie stood up before [me], and half blushed, and paused a minute.

" With a coquetry I never saw executed more prettily, ' I know,' said she, ' that you are dying for a kiss, and you 're ashamed to ask for it. You may take one.' . . . And so in triumph, and singing poems to all blue eyes, I said good night."

Leaving "Tiger Lilies " in the hands of the publishers, he returned to Macon, where in September we find him reading the proof of the same. The novel appeared in October and was reviewed somewhat at length in the " Round Table." [1] The review refers to Lanier as " the author of some quaint and graceful verses published from time to time in the ' Round Table.' " " His novel goes a long way to confirm the good opinion which his poems suggested. We have, indeed, seldom read a first book more pregnant with promise, or fuller of the faults which, more surely than precocious perfection, betoken talent. . . . His errors seem to be entirely errors of

---

[1] *Round Table*, December 14, 1867.

youth and in the right direction." " Exuberance
is more easily corrected than sterility." " His
dialogue reads too often like a catalogue *raisonné*
of his library." The critic finds traces of a
scholarly and poetic taste, but withal a straining
after novelty and " an affectation of quaintness
so marked as to be often unpleasant." He objects to long abstract disquisitions on metaphysics and music. He commends it, however,
for being " unmarred by the bad taste of its
contemporaries in fanning a senseless and profit-
less sectional rancor."

With this review the reader of " Tiger Lilies "
at the present time must agree. It is seldom that
one finds a bit of contemporary criticism that
hits the mark so well as this. As a story it is
a failure — the plot is badly managed and the
work is strikingly uneven. Lanier was aware
of its defects, and yet pointed out its value to
any student of his life. In a letter to his father
from Montgomery, July 13, 1866, he says : " I
have in the last part adopted almost exclusively
the dramatic, rather than the descriptive, style
which reigns in the earlier portions, interspersed
with much high talk. Indeed, the book which I
commenced to write in 1863 and have touched
at intervals until now, represents in its change
of style almost precisely the change of tone
which has gradually been taking place in me all

the time. So much so, that it has become highly interesting to me : I seem to see portions of my old self, otherwise forgotten, here preserved."

The note sounded in the preface is characteristic. He professes " a love, strong as it is humble, for what is beautiful in God's Nature and in man's Art." He utters a plea against "the horrible piquancies of quaint crimes and of white-handed criminals, with which so many books have recently stimulated the pruriency of men; and begs that the following pages may be judged only as registering a faint cry, sent from a region where there are few artists to happier lands that own many; calling on these last for more sunshine and less night in their art, more virtuous women and fewer Lydian Guelts, more household sweetness and less Bohemian despair, clearer chords and fewer suspensions, broader quiet skies and shorter grotesque storms; since there are those, even here in the South, who still love beautiful things with sincere passion."

The story may be briefly indicated. The background of the first book is, as has been seen, the mountain scenery of East Tennessee. A party of hunters — including Philip Sterling and Paul Rübetsahl, two young transcendentalists — are on a stand waiting for deer. Philip Sterling — with " large gray poet's eyes, with a dream in each and a sparkle behind it " — is living in the mountains with his father John Sterling and his sister Felix — their home a veritable palace of art. Rübetsahl is from Frankfort, Germany, whence he brings an enthusiasm for music and philosophy, into which he inducts his newly found friends. Another companion is John Cranston, a Northerner who had also lived in Frankfort, where he had often been compared to Goethe in his youth. He had Lucifer eyes, he spoke French and German ; he " walked like a young god, he played people mad with his violin." These lovers of music and poetry furnish much amusement to the native mountaineers, one of whom, Cain Smallin, becomes one of the prominent characters in the latter part of the book. It is worthy of note that in this character and his brother, who turns out to be a villain, Lanier anticipated some of the sketches by Charles Egbert Craddock. The merry party of hunters retire to Sterling's house, where they enjoy the blessings of good friendship and of music and high thought. They, with other friends from all parts of the South, plan a masquerade party, in which they represent the various characters of Shakespeare's plays and the knights of the Round Table. After a scene of much merriment and good humor, Cranston and Rübetsahl fight a duel — both of them being in love with Felix Sterling, each knowing the other's history at Frankfort. In the mean time Ottilie with her maid comes from Germany to Chilhowee. She was formerly the lover of Rübetsahl, and was betrayed by Cranston. She becomes identified with the Sterling family, she herself being a musician, and naturally finding her place among these music-loving people.

The first book is filled with "high talk" on music, poetry, philosophy, and nature. These conversations and masquerade parties, however, are interrupted by war. The author omits the breaking out of the war and the first three years of it. The action is resumed at Burwell's Bay, where we meet the hero again with " a light rifle on his shoulder, with a good horse bounding along under him, with a fresh breeze that had in it the vigor of the salt sea and the caressing sweetness of the spring blowing upon him." With him are " five friends, tried in the tempests of war, as well as by the sterner tests of the calm association of inactive camp life." The story here is strictly autobiographical, and is filled with some stirring incidents taken from Lanier's life as a scout. Perhaps the most striking scene in the book is the one in which Cain Smallin finds out that his brother is a deserter. Never did Lanier come so near creating a scene of real dramatic power.[1] " We was poor. We

[1] Part ii, chapter vi.

ain't never had much to live on but our name,
which it was as good as gold. And now it ain't no
better 'n rusty copper; hit 'll be green and pi-
senous. An' whose done it? Gorm Smallin! My
own brother, Gorm Smallin!" When he finds
his brother he says to him: "Ef ye had been
killed in a fa'r battle, I mought ha' been able to
fight hard enough for both of us; for every time
I cried a-thinkin' of you, I 'd ha' been twice as
strong, an' twice as clear-sighted as I was buf-
fore. But — sich things as these burns me an'
weakens me and hurts my eyes that bad that
I kin scarcely look a man straight furard in
the face. Hit don't make much difference to
me now whether we whips the Yanks or they
whips us. . . . We is kin to a deserter! . . .
I cain't shoot ye hardly. The same uns raised
us and fed us. I cain't do it; an' I am sorry
I cain't." He then makes him swear a vow:
" God A'mighty 's a-lookin at you out o' the stars
yon, an' he 's a-listenin' at you out o' the sand
here, and he won't git tired by mornin'."

The coming of gunboats up the river scatters
the party in all directions, some to prison and
others to the final scenes around Richmond, with
the burning of which the story closes, not, however, before the palace in the mountains — where
John Sterling and his wife, Felix and Ottilie,
have spent the intervening time — is set fire to

by Gorm Smallin. The story is scarcely significant enough to follow all the threads.

"Tiger Lilies" has the same place in Lanier's life that "Hyperion" has in Longfellow's. They are both failures as novels or romances, but they are valuable as autobiographies. Instead of laying the scene in Germany, which he had never seen and yet yearned for, Lanier brings Germany to America. There are long disquisitions on the place of music and science in the modern world, many crude fancies, some striking descriptions of nature, some of which have already been quoted. Above all, there is Lanier's idea of what a musician or a poet ought to be, — a study, therefore, of himself.

Perhaps the best single passage on music is that describing Phil's playing of the flute. "It is like walking in the woods, amongst wild flowers, just before you go into some vast cathedral. For the flute seems to me to be peculiarly the woods-instrument: it speaks the gloss of green leaves or the pathos of bare branches; it calls up the strange mosses that are under dead leaves; it breathes of wild plants that hide and oak fragrances that vanish; it expresses to me the natural magic of music. Have you ever walked on long afternoons in warm, sunny spots of the woods, and felt a sudden thrill strike you with the half fear that a ghost would rise out of the sedge, or dart from behind the next tree, and confront you?"[1]

Two passages may be cited to show the author's tendency to use personifications and his insight into the "burthen of the mystery of all this unintelligible world:"—

"A terrible mêlée of winged opposites is forever filling the world with a battle din which only observant souls hear: Love contending with Impurity; Passion springing mines under the calm entrenchment of Reason; scowling Ignorance thrusting in the dark at holy-eyed Reverence; Romance deathfully encountering Sentimentality on the one side and Commonplace on the other; young Sensibility clanging swords with gigantic maudlin Conventionalities. . . . I have seen no man who did not suffer from the shock of these wars, unless he got help from that One Man whom it is not unmanly to acknowledge our superior."[2]

"Nature has no politics. She'll grow a rose as well for York as Lancaster, and mayhap beat both down next minute with a storm!

"She has no heart; else she never had rained on Lear's head.

"She has no eyes; for, seeing, she could never have drowned that dainty girl, Ophelia.

"She has no ears; or she would hear the wild

[1] *Tiger Lilies*, p. 28.   [2] *Ibid.* p. 41.

Sabian hymns to Night and prayers to Day that
men are uttering evermore.

"O blind, deaf, no-hearted Beauty, we cannot
woo thee, for thou silently contemnest us; we
cannot force thee, for thou art stronger than
we; we cannot compromise with thee, for thou
art treacherous as thy seas; what shall we do,
we, unhappy, that love thee, coquette Nature?"[1]

When "Tiger Lilies" appeared it was very favorably received. Lanier writes to his brother of
the "continual heavy showers of compliment and
congratulation" that he has received in Macon;
that the Macon paper had an editorial on his
novel, and that a book firm in the town had
already disposed of a large number of copies.
Writing to Northrup, March 8, 1868, he says:
"My book has been as well received as a young
author could have expected on his first plunge,
and I have seen few criticisms upon it which are
not on the whole favorable. My publishers have
just made me an offer to bring out a second
edition on very fair terms; from which I infer
that the sale of the article is progressing."[2] At
twenty-five, then, he was recognized as one of the
promising writers of the South; a biographical
article referring to his recent success, the "Tiger
Lilies," was written by J. Wood Davidson for

[1] *Tiger Lilies*, p. 178.
[2] There was never a second edition, however.

his " Living Writers of the South," which appeared in 1869, and his name was sought by
ambitious editors of mushroom magazines that
sprang up in abundance after the war.

Lanier was not destined, however, to begin his
literary career as yet, nor was the South to have
such an easy way out of her disaster as he had
hoped. He had made only one reference to politics in his romance, and that was his manly utterance in behalf of Jefferson Davis, who was then
confined in prison under rather disagreeable circumstances at Fortress Monroe. He said, " If
there was guilt in any, there was guilt in nigh
all of us, between Maryland and Mexico; Mr.
Davis, if he be termed the ringleader of the Rebellion, was so, not by virtue of any instigating
act of his, but purely by the unanimous will and
appointment of the Southern people; and the
hearts of the Southern people bleed to see how
their own act has resulted in the chaining of Mr.
Davis, who was as innocent as they, and in the
pardon of those who were guilty as he."

The Davis incident was an indication that
forces other than those which one might have
hoped to see were in the air. By the fall of 1867
the reaction against the magnanimous policy of
Lincoln had come in the North. Reconstruction
governments were being inaugurated throughout
the South. This was due in part to the lack of

wisdom displayed by Southern legislatures under the Johnson governments, — a "disposition on the part of the Southern States to claim rights instead of submitting to conditions," and harsh laws of Southern legislatures concerning the freedmen. It must be confessed that the extreme men of the South were in some localities as rash, unreasonable, and impracticable as the radicals of the North. The magnanimous spirit of Lincoln and the heroic, chivalric spirit of Lee could not prevail in the two sections; hence followed a direful period in American history. As E. L. Godkin said, " That the chapter which tells the story of reconstruction should have followed in American history the chapter which tells the story of the war and emancipation, is something over which many a generation will blush."

Again it must be said, as was said of the effect of the war on the South, that reconstruction was something more than excessive taxation, grinding and unjust as that was, something more than the fear of black domination, as unthinkable as that is. There was the uncertainty of the situation, the sense of despair that rankled in the hearts of men, with the knowledge that nothing the South could do could have any influence in deciding its fate. It was the closing of institutions of learning, or running them under such circumstances that the better element of the South could have nothing to do with them. Lanier, writing about a position in the University of Alabama which he very much desired, said: " The trustees, who are appointees of the State, are so hampered by the expected change of State government that nothing can be certainly predicated as to their action."

Lanier felt the effect of reconstruction at every point, — he was baptized with the baptism of the Southern people. The weight of that sad time bore heavily upon him. As he had during the war touched the experience of his people at every point, so now he went down with them into the Valley of Humiliation.

Under these circumstances his friend Northrup wrote him, inviting him to go to Germany with him. He replied: " Indeed, indeed, y'r trip-to-Europe invitation finds me all *thirsty* to go with you; but, alas, how little do you know of our wretched poverties and distresses here, — that you ask me such a thing. . . . It spoils our dreams of Germany, ruthlessly. I 've been presiding over eighty-six scholars, in a large Academy at Prattville, Ala., having two assistants under me ; 't is terrible work, and the labor difficulties, with the recent poor price of cotton, conspire to make the pay very slim. I think y'r people can have no idea of the slow terrors with which this winter has invested our life in the

South. Some time I'm going to give you a few simple details, which you must publish in your paper."

Prattville, where he spent the winter of 1867–68, was a small manufacturing town, with all the crudeness of a new industrial order and without any of the refinement to which Lanier had been accustomed in Macon and elsewhere. Perhaps there was never a time when drudgery so weighed upon him, although his usual playfulness is seen in the remark: "There is but one man in my school who could lick me in a fair fight, and he thinks me at once a Samson and a Solomon." He worked for people who thought that he was defrauding them if he did not work from "sun up to sun down," as one of his patrons expressed it. It was here, too, that he suffered from his first hemorrhages. His poetry written at this time was an expression of the despair which prevailed throughout the South. He whom the Civil War had not inspired to speech, and who had kept silent under the suffering of the days after the war, now gave expression to his disgust and his indignation. It is not great poetry, for Lanier was not adapted to that kind of poetry, and consequently neither he nor his wife ever collected all the poems. "Laughter in the Senate," published in the "Round Table," is typical of

a group, several of which he left in an old
ledger : —

> Comes now the Peace, so long delayed ?
> Is it the cheerful voice of aid ?
> Begins the time, his heart has prayed,
>   When men may reap and sow ?
>
> Ah, God ! back to the cold earth's breast!
> The sages chuckle o'er their jest!
> Must they, to give a people rest,
>   Their dainty wit forego ?
>
> The tyrants sit in a stately hall;
> They gibe at a wretched people's fall;
> The tyrants forget how fresh is the pall
>   Over their dead and ours.
>
> Look how the senators ape the clown,
> And don the motley and hide the gown,
> But yonder a fast rising frown
>   On the people's forehead lowers.

To the same effect he wrote in unpublished
poems, " Steel in Soft Hands " and " To Our
Hills : " —

> We mourn your fall into daintier hands
>   Of senators, rosy fingered,
> That wrote while you fought,
>   And afar from the battles lingered.

And again in " Raven Days " and " Tyranny : " —

> Oh, Raven days, dark Raven days of sorrow,
>   Will ever any warm light come again ?
> Will ever the lit mountains of To-morrow
>   Begin to gleam athwart the mournful plain ?

Young Trade is dead,
And swart Work sullen sits in the hillside fern
And folds his arms that find no bread to earn,
And bows his head.

In a letter to his father, January 21, 1868, he wrote: "There are strong indications here of much bad feeling between the whites and blacks, especially those engaged in the late row at this place; and I have fears, which are shared by Mr. Pratt and many citizens here, that some indiscretion of the more thoughtless among the whites may plunge us into bloodshed. The whites have no organization at all, and the affair would be a mere butchery. . . . The Canton imbroglio may precipitate matters." Writing of laws passed by Congress, he said: "Who will find words to express the sorrowful surprise at their total absence of philosophical insight into the age which has resulted in those hundreds of laws recently promulgated by the reigning body in the United States; laws which, if from no other cause, at least from sheer multiplicity, are wholly at variance with the genius of the time and of the people, laws which have resulted in such a mass of crime and hatred and bitterness as even the four terrible years of war have entirely failed to bring about." [1]

He recognized the need of some great man.

[1] *Retrospects and Prospects*, p. 31.

A pilot, God, a pilot ! for the helm is left awry.

Years later, when the end of the reconstruction period had come, he described a type of man that was needed for this emergency : whether he realized it or not, it was a wish that Abraham Lincoln might have been spared to meet the situation. " I have been wondering where we are going to get a *Great Man*, that will be tall enough to see over the whole country, and to direct that vast undoing of things which has got to be accomplished in a few years. It is a situation in which mere cleverness will not begin to work. The horizon of cleverness is too limited ; it does not embrace enough of the heart of man, to enable a merely clever politician, such as those in which we abound, to lead matters properly in this juncture. The vast generosities which whirl a small revenge out of the way, as the winds whirl a leaf ; the awful integrities which will pay a debt twice rather than allow the faintest flicker of suspicion about it ; the splendid indignations which are also tender compassions, and will in one moment be hustling the money-changers out of the Temple, and in the next be preaching Love to them from the steps of it, — where are we to find these ? It is time for a man to arise who is a man." [1]

This state of affairs here set forth in Lanier's

[1] Letter to Judge Logan E. Bleckley, Nov. 15, 1874.

words caused many to leave the South in absolute despair of its future. It drove Maurice Thompson from Georgia to Indiana, and the Le Conte brothers from Columbia to California. It caused the middle-aged Lamar to stand sorrowfully at his gate in the afternoons in Oxford, Mississippi, gazing wistfully into the west, while young men like Henry Grady — naturally optimistic and buoyant — wondered what could be the future for them. There is no better evidence of the heroism of Lanier than the way in which he met the situation that confronted him. He found refuge in intellectual work. In a letter to his father he urges him to send him the latest magazines and books. June 1, 1868, he writes from Prattville: "I shall go to work on my essays, and on a course of study in German and in the Latin works of Lucretius, whom I have long desired to study." In another letter he said: "I have been deeply engaged in working out some metaphysical ideas for some time, — an application which goes on all the time, whether I sit at desk or walk the streets." The volume of essays referred to was never published, but we have some of them in the essays "Retrospects and Prospects," "Nature-Metaphors," and some unpublished ones in an old ledger in which he wrote at this time, such as "The Oversight of Modern Philosophy," "Cause and Effect," "Time and Space," "The

Solecisms of Mathematics," " Devil's Bombs,"
and other essays, which reveal Lanier's tendency
to speculative philosophy and his exuberant
fancy. In this same ledger he wrote down many
quotations, which show that at the time he was
not only keeping up with contemporary literature,
but continuing his reading in German poetry.

In the meantime, December 21, 1867, Lanier
had married Miss Mary Day. " Not even the wide-
mouthed, villainous-nosed, tallow-faced drudger-
ies of my eighty-fold life," he wrote his father,
" can squeeze the sentiment out of me." From
the worldly standpoint it was a serious mistake
to marry, with no prospect of position and in the
general upheaval of society about them. But to
the two lovers no such considerations could appeal, and with his marriage to this accomplished
woman came one of the greatest blessings of
Lanier's life. It was " an idyllic marriage, which
the poet thought a rich compensation for all
the other perfect gifts which Providence denied
him." She was a sufferer like himself, but her
accuracy and alertness of mind, her rare appreciation of music, and her deep divining of his
own powers, made her the ideal wife of the poet.
Those who know " My Springs " and the series
of sonnets which he wrote to her during their
separation when he was spending the winters in
Baltimore, need not be told of the part that this

love played in his life. Perhaps there are no two single lines in American poetry which express better the deeper meaning of love than these : —

> I marvel that God made you mine,
> For when He frowns 't is then ye shine.

In his later lectures at the Peabody Institute in Baltimore, contrasting the heroines of epic poetry with the lyric woman of modern times, — the patient wife in the secure home, — he said: " But the daily grandeurs which every good wife, no matter how uneventful her lot, must achieve, the secret endurances which not only have no poet to sing them, but no human eye even to see them, the heroism which is as fine and bright at two o'clock in the morning as it is at noonday, all those prodigious fortitudes under sorrows which one is scarcely willing to whisper even to God Almighty, and of which probably every delicate-souled woman knows, either by intuition or actual experience, — this lyric heroism, altogether great and beautiful as it is, does not appear, save by one or two brief glimpses, in the early poetry of our ancestors." [1] He could not have described better his own wife and all that she was to be in the years to come. Her fame is linked with his as is Clara Schumann's with that of the great German musician.

---

[1] *Shakspere and his Forerunners*, i, 99.

MARY DAY LANIER IN 1873

CHAPTER V

LAWYER AND TRAVELER

UNABLE to secure a position in a Southern college or to make a living by literary work, Lanier decided at the end of 1868 to take up the profession of law. He was led to do so by the earnest solicitation of his father. With his mind once made up in that direction, he went to the work with characteristic zeal. He displayed a business-like and methodical spirit which at once attracted attention. On November 19, 1869, he wrote to his brother, who was urging him to go into the cotton-mill business : " I have a far more feasible project, which I have been long incubating : let us go to Brunswick. We know something of the law, and are rapidly knowing more ; it is a business which is far better than that of any salaried officer could possibly be. . . . It is best that you and I make up our minds immediately to be lawyers, *nothing but lawyers, good* lawyers, and *successful* lawyers ; and direct all our energies to this end. We are too far in life to change our course now ; it would be greatly disadvantageous to both of us. Therefore, to the

law, Boy. It is your vocation; stick to it: It
will presently reward you for your devotion."
The scheme did not materialize, however; he
remained at Macon in the office of Lanier and
Anderson. He writes to Northrup, who has
again held out to him a plan for going to Germany: —

"As for my sweet old dreams of studying in
Germany, *eheu !* here is come a wife, and by'r
Lady, a boy, a most rare-lung'd, imperious, world-
grasping, blue-eyed, kingly Manikin; [1] and the
same must have his tiring-woman or nurse, mark
you, and his laces and embroideries and small carriage, being now half a year old: so that, what with
mine ancient Money-Cormorants, the Butcher
and the Baker and the Tailor, my substance is
like to be so pecked up that I must stick fast
in Georgia, unless litigation and my reputation
should take a simultaneous start and both grow
outrageously. For, you must know, these Southern colleges are all so poor that they hold out
absolutely no inducement in the way of support
to a professor: and so last January I suddenly
came to the conclusion that I wanted to make
some money for my wife and my baby, and in-
continently betook me to studying Law : wherein
I am now well advanced, and, D. V., will be admitted to the Bar in May next. My advantages

[1] Charles Day Lanier. See poem, " Baby Charley."

are good, since my Father and uncle (firm of
Lanier and Anderson) are among the oldest
lawyers in the city and have a large practice, into
which I shall be quickly inducted.

" I have not, however, ceased my devotion to
letters, which I love better than all things in my
heart of hearts ; and have now in the hands of
the Lit. Bureau in N. Y. a vol. of essays. I 'm
(or rather have been) busy, too, on a long poem,
yclept the ' Jacquerie,' on which I had bestowed
more *real work* than on any of the frothy things
which I have hitherto sent out ; tho' this is
now necessarily suspended until the summer
shall give me a little rest from the office business with which I have to support myself while
I am studying law." [1]

Lanier's work as a lawyer was that of the
office, as he never practiced in the courts. To the
accuracy and fidelity of this work the words of
his successor, Chancellor Walter B. Hill of the
University of Georgia, bear testimony : —

" About 1874 or 1875 I became associated as
partner with the firm of Lanier and Anderson, in
whose office Sidney Lanier practiced law up to
the time he left Macon [1869–1873] — I do not
know whether he was a partner in the firm or
whether he merely used the same office. At any
rate, it seems that the greater part of his work

[1] *Lippincott's Magazine*, March, 1905.

consisted in the examination of titles. The firm
of Lanier and Anderson represented several
building and loan associations and had a large
business in this line of work. To examine a title,
as you know, requires a visit to what Oliver Wen-
dell Holmes calls ' that cemetery of dead transactions,' the place for the official registry of deeds
and other muniments of title, called in Georgia
the office of the Clerk of the Superior Court.
One cannot imagine work that is more dry-as-
dust in its character than going over these records
for the purpose of tracing the successive links in
a chain of title. When I came into the firm I
had occasion frequently to examine the letter-
press copybook in which Lanier's ' abstracts ' or
reports upon title had been copied. Not only
were the books themselves models of neatness,
but all his work in the examination of titles
showed the utmost thoroughness, patience, and
fidelity. The law of Georgia in regard to the
registration of titles was by no means perfect at
that time ; so imperfect, indeed, that I have known
prominent lawyers to refuse to engage in the
work on account of the risk of error involved.
I remained a member of the firm for some time
afterwards, but during the whole period of my
residence in Macon I never heard any question
raised as to the correctness and thoroughness of
Lanier's work in this difficult and intricate de-

partment of practice. In going over some of his
work I have often keenly felt the contrast between
such toil and that for which Lanier's genius fit-
ted him. To find that the poet spent many laborious days in such uninspiring labor was as
great an anomaly as it would be to see a foun-
tain spring from a bed of sawdust and 'shake
its loosened silver in the sun.' " [1]

While engaged in the practice of law, Lanier
now and then made public addresses. The most
important of these was the Confederate Memorial Address, April 26, 1870.[2] The spirit and
the language of it are equally admirable. He who
had suffered all that any man could suffer during the Civil War and during the reconstruction
period shows that he has risen above all bitterness and prejudice. There is no threshing over
of dead issues. The spirit of the address is more
like that seen in the letters of Robert E. Lee
than any other thing written by Southerners during this period. Lanier is not yet national in his
point of view, but he represents the best attitude
of mind that could be held by the most liberal
of Southerners at that time. Standing in the
cemetery at Macon, — one of the most beautiful
in the Southern States, — he begins: " In the
unbroken silence of the dead soldierly forms that

[1] Letter to the author.
[2] *Retrospects and Prospects*, p. 94.

lie beneath our feet ; in the winding processions
of these stately trees ; in the large tranquillity of
this vast and benignant heaven that overspreads
us ; in the quiet ripple of yonder patient river,
flowing down to his death in the sea ; in the
manifold melodies drawn from these green leaves
by wandering airs that go like Troubadours singing in all the lands ; in the many-voiced memories
that flock into this day, and fill it as swallows
fill the summer, — in all these, there is to me so
voluble an eloquence to-day that I cannot but
shrink from the harsher sounds of my own human voice." Taking these as a text, he comments
first on the necessity for silence in an age when
" trade is the most boisterous god of all the false
gods under heaven." The clatter of factories,
the clank of mills, the groaning of forges, the
sputtering and laboring of his water power, are
all lost sight of in contemplating the august
presence of the dead, who speak not. He speaks
next of the stateliness of the trees, which suggests
to him the stateliness of the two great heroes of
the Confederacy, Robert E. Lee and Stonewall
Jackson, — " bright, magnificent exemplars of
stateliness, — those noble figures that arose and
moved in splendid procession across the theatre
of our Confederate war ! " The patience of the
river suggests the soldiers who walked their life of
battle, " patient through heat and cold, through

rain and drought, through bullets and diseases, through hunger and nakedness, through rigor of discipline and laxity of morals, ay, through the very shards and pits of hell, down to the almost inevitable death that awaited them."

The most significant passage, however, is his appeal to the men and women of the South to rise to the plane of tranquillity and magnanimity: —

"I spoke next of the tranquillity of the overspanning heavens. This, too, is a noble quality which your Association tends to keep alive. Who in all the world needs tranquillity more than we? I know not a deeper question in our Southern life at this present time, than how we shall bear our load of wrong and injury with the calmness and tranquil dignity that become men and women who would be great in misfortune; and believe me, I know not where we will draw deeper inspirations of calm strength for this great emergency than in this place where we now stand, in the midst of departed heroes who fought against these things to death. Why, yonder lies my brave, brilliant friend, Lamar; and yonder, genial Robert Smith; and yonder, generous Tracy, — gallant men, all, good knights and stainless gentlemen. How calmly they sleep in the midst of it! Unto this calmness shall we come, at last. If so, why should we disquiet our souls for the

petty stings of our conquerors ? There comes a
time when conqueror and conquered shall alike
descend into the grave. In that time, O my
countrymen, in that time the conqueror shall be
ashamed of his lash, and the conquered shall be
proud of his calm endurance ; in that time the
conqueror shall hide his face, and the conquered
shall lift his head with an exultation in his tranquil fortitude which God shall surely pardon !

" For the contemplation of this tranquillity, my
friends of this Association, in the name of a land
stung half to madness, I thank you.

.   .   .   .

" To-day we are here for love and not for hate.
To-day we are here for harmony and not for
discord. To-day we are risen immeasurably
above all vengeance. To-day, standing upon the
serene heights of forgiveness, our souls choir
together the enchanting music of harmonious
Christian civilization. To-day we will not dis-
turb the peaceful slumbers of these sleepers with
music less sweet than the serenade of loving
remembrances, breathing upon our hearts as the
winds of heaven breathe upon these swaying
leaves above us."

Lanier did not abandon altogether his ideal
of doing literary work. He was much encouraged at this time by a sympathetic correspondence
with Paul Hamilton Hayne, who, after the Civil

War, had settled in a little cottage near Augusta. His beautiful home in Charleston had been burned to the ground and his large, handsome library utterly lost. With heroic spirit at a time when, as Lanier said of him, " the war of secession had left the South in a condition which appeared to render an exclusively literary life a hopeless impossibility, he immured himself in the woods of Georgia and gave himself wholly to his pen." When Simms visited him here in 1866, the poet had for supplies " a box of hard tack, two sides of bacon, and fourscore, more or less, of smoked herring, a frying-pan and a gridiron." He and his wife lived as simply as the Hawthornes did in the Old Manse. His writing desk was a carpenter's work-bench. He wrote continually for the magazines, corresponded with the poets of England and New England, received visitors, with whom he talked about the old days in Charleston when he and Timrod and Simms had projected " Russell's Magazine," and held out to young Southern writers the encouragement of an older brother.

It was this man who, at a critical time in Lanier's life, inspired him to believe that he might succeed in a literary career. " I have had constantly in mind the kindly help and encouragement which your cheering words used to bring me when I was even more obscure than I am now," wrote the younger poet at a later time. He did not have time, however, to act on this encouragement. He wrote now and then a dialect poem which was printed in the Georgia dailies and attracted attention by its humor and its insight into contemporary life, and occasionally an exquisite lyric like " Nirvâna." In the main he had to say : —

" I have not put pen to paper in a literary way in a long time. How I thirst to do so, — how I long to sing a thousand various songs that oppress me, unsung, — is inexpressible. Yet the mere work that brings me bread gives me no time. I know not, after all, if this is a sorrowful thing. Nobody likes my poems except two or three friends, — who are themselves poets, and can supply themselves ! " And yet he writes, " It gives me great encouragement that you think I might succeed in the literary life ; for I take it that you are in earnest in saying so, believing that you love Art with too genuine affection to trifle with her by bringing to her service, through mere politeness, an unworthy worker." [1]

Hayne was impressed with Lanier's intimate knowledge of Elizabethan and older English literature, as displayed in his letters of this period. He says : —

" He had steeped his imagination from boy-

[1] *Letters*, passim.

hood in the writings of the earlier English an-
nalists and poets,— Geoffrey of Monmouth, Sir
Thomas Mallory, Gower, Chaucer, and the whole
bead-roll of such ancient English worthies. I
was of course a little surprised during our earlier
epistolary communion to perceive, not only his un-
usually thorough knowledge of Chaucer, for example, whose couplets flowed as trippingly from his
pen as if ' The Canterbury Tales ' and ' The Ro-
maunt of the Rose ' were his daily mental food,
but to find him quoting as naturally and easily
from ' Piers Plowman ' and scores of the half-
obsolete ballads of the English and Scottish
borders.

" He gloried in antiquarian lore and antiquarian literature. Hardly ' Old Monkbarns ' himself could have pored over a black-letter volume
with greater enthusiasm. Especially he loved the
tales of chivalry, and thus, when the opportunity
came, was fully equipped as an interpreter of
Froissart and ' King Arthur ' for the benefit of
our younger generation of students. With the
great Elizabethans Lanier was equally familiar.
Instead of skimming Shakespeare, he went down
into his depths. Few have written so subtly
of Shakespeare's mysterious sonnets. Through
all Lanier's productions we trace the influence
of his early literary loves ; but nowhere do the
pithy quaintnesses of the old bards and chron-

iclers display themselves more effectively — not only in the illustrations, but through the innermost warp and woof of the texture of his ideas and his style — than in some of his familiar epistles." [1]

That Lanier kept in touch, too, with contemporary literature is shown by an acute criticism of Browning's "The Ring and the Book," then recently published: "Have you seen Browning's 'The Ring and the Book?' I am confident that, at the birth of this man, among all the good fairies who showered him with magnificent endowments, one bad one — as in the old tale — crept in by stealth and gave him a constitutional twist i' the neck, whereby his windpipe became, and has ever since remained, a marvelous tortuous passage. Out of this glottis-labyrinth his words won't, and can't, come straight. A hitch and a sharp crook in every sentence bring you up with a shock. But what a shock it is! Did you ever see a picture of a lasso, in the act of being flung? In a thousand coils and turns, inextricably crooked and involved and whirled, yet, if you mark the noose at the end, you see that it is directly in front of the bison's head, there, and is bound to catch him! That is the way Robert Browning catches you. The first sixty or seventy pages of 'The Ring and the Book'

[1] *Letters*, p. 220.

are altogether the most doleful reading, in point
either of idea or of music, in the English language; and yet the monologue of Giuseppe
Caponsacchi, that of Pompilia Comparini, and
the two of Guido Franceschini, are unapproach-
able, in their kind, by any living or dead poet,
me judice. Here Browning's jerkiness comes in
with inevitable effect. You get lightning glimpses
— and, as one naturally expects from lightning,
zigzag glimpses — into the intense night of the
passion of these souls. It is entirely wonderful
and without precedent. The fitful play of Guido's
lust, and scorn, and hate, and cowardice, closes
with a master stroke: —

> "Christ ! Maria ! God ! . . .
> *Pompilia, will you let them murder me?*

"Pompilia, mark you, is dead, by Guido's own
hand; deliberately stabbed, because he hated
her purity, which all along he has reviled and
mocked with the Devil's own malignant inge-
nuity of sarcasm." [1]

On account of ill health Lanier frequently
had to leave Macon and go to places better suited
to his physical temperament. At Brunswick,
Georgia, — the scene of the Marsh poems, — at
Alleghany Springs in Virginia, and at Lookout
Mountain in Tennessee, he spent successive sum-
mers. In all of these places he reveled in the

[1] *Letters*, p. 206; letter to Hayne, April 13, 1870.

beauty and grandeur of the scenery. His letters written to his wife and his father during his absences from Macon are evidence that he was at this time developing steadily in that subtle appreciation of nature which was afterwards to play such an important part in his poetry. In fact, the letters themselves, when published, as they will be some time, show artistic growth when compared with the writings already noted. He was all his life a prolific letter-writer — and a great one. Writing from Alleghany Springs, July 12, 1872, he says to his wife : —

" How necessary is it that one should occasionally place oneself in the midst of those more striking forms of nature in which God has indulged His fantasy! It is very true that the flat land, the bare hillside, the muddy stream comes also directly from the creative hand : but these do not bring one into the sweetness of the heartier moods of God ; in the midst of them it is as if one were transacting the business of life with God : whereas, when one has but to lift one's eyes in order to receive the exquisite shocks of thrilling form and color and motion that leap invisibly from mountain and groves and stream, then one feels as if one had surprised the Father in his tender, sportive, and loving moments.

"To the soul then, weak with the long flesh fight and filled with a sluggish languor by those wearisome disappointments which arise from the constant contemplation of men's weaknesses, and from the constant back-thrusting of one's consciousness of impotence to strengthen them — thou, with thy nimble fancy, canst imagine what ethereal and yet indestructible essences of new dignity, of new strength, of new patience, of new serenity, of new hope, new faith, and new love, do continually flash out of the gorges, the mountains, and the streams, into the heart, and charge it, as the lightnings charge the earth, with subtle and heavenly fires.

" A bewildering sorcery seems to spread itself over even those things which are commonplace. The songs and cries of birds acquire a strange sound to me : I cannot understand the little spontaneous tongues, the quivering throats, the open beaks, the small bright eyes that gleam with unknown emotion, the nimble capricious heads that twist this way and that with such bizarre unreasonableness.

" Nor do I fathom this long unceasing monotone of the little shallow river that sings yonder over the rocks in its bosom as a mother crooning over her children ; it is but one word the stream utters : but as when we speak a well-known word over and over again until it comes to have a frightful mystery in it, so this familiar stream-sound fills me with indescribable wonder.

" Nor do I comprehend the eloquence of the mountains which comes in a strange *patois* of two tongues; for the mountains speak at once the languages of repose and of convulsion, two languages which have naught in common.

" Wondering therefore, from day to night, with a good wonder which directs attention not to one's ignorance but to God's wisdom, stricken, but not exhausted, by continual tranquil surprises; surrounded by a world of enchantments which, so far from being elusive, are the most substantial of realties, — thou knowest that nature is kind to me."

He went to New York in 1869, 1870, and 1871, now on business and now to consult medical experts. In May, 1869, we find him trying to make the sale of some property on which iron was supposed to be. He writes his father that he has been down on Wall Street all day. There is — now as compared with his 1867 visit — a certain fascination for him in the intense spirit of hurry which displays itself on every side. He finds himself in competition with many Southerners who were at that time projecting similar enterprises. He is also visiting the clients of Lanier and Anderson, and is anxious to extend the firm's name. He is given much social attention,

— " teas, dinners, calls, visits, business " con-
sume his time. He visits the superb villa of his
cousin on the Hudson near Poughkeepsie. He
writes, on May 15, that he is beginning " to feel
entirely unflurried in the crowd and to go about
business deliberately." He is in New York again
in 1871, when the Tweed ring is being exposed,
and he cannot but compare the situation there
with the reconstruction government that prevails
in his own State. " Somehow this is n't a good
day for thieves," he says. " Would n't it be a
curious and refreshing phenomenon if Tweed,
Hall, Bullock,[1] and that ilk should all continue
in the service of the State — only changing the
scene of their labors from the office to the peni-
tentiary ? "

Most of all, however, Lanier was interested in
the music which he heard on these trips to the
metropolis. He had kept up his flute-playing
while busy with his law work, frequently playing
at charity concerts in Macon and other cities of
Georgia. In New York he reveled in the singing
of Nilsson, in religious music at St. Paul's
Church, but above all in Theodore Thomas's
orchestra, then just beginning its triumphant
career. He writes, August 15, 1870 : " Ah, how
they have belied Wagner ! I heard Theodore
Thomas's orchestra play his overture to ' Tann-

[1] Governor of Georgia during reconstruction days.

häuser.' The ' Music of the Future ' is surely thy music and my music. Each harmony was a chorus of pure aspirations. The sequences flowed along, one after another, as if all the great and noble deeds of time had formed a procession and marched in review before one's *ears* instead of one's *eyes*. These 'great and noble deeds' were not deeds of war and statesmanship, but majestic victories of inner struggles of a man. This unbroken march of beautiful-bodied Triumphs irresistibly invites the soul of a man to create other processions like it. I would I might lead a so magnificent file of glories into heaven ! " [1]

And again, in 1871 : " And to-night I come out of what might have been heaven. . . .

" 'T was opening night of Theodore Thomas's orchestra, at Central Park Garden, and I could not resist the temptation to go and bathe in the sweet amber seas of the music of this fine orchestra, and so I went, and tugged me through a vast crowd, and, after standing some while, found a seat, and the *bâton* tapped and waved, and I plunged into the sea, and lay and floated. Ah ! the dear flutes and oboes and horns drifted me hither and thither, and the great violins and small violins swayed me upon waves, and overflowed me with strong lavations, and sprinkled glisten-

[1] *Letters*, p. 68.

ing foam in my face, and in among the clarinetti, as among waving water-lilies with flexile stems, I pushed my easy way, and so, even lying in the music-waters, I floated and flowed, my soul utterly bent and prostrate." [1]

In November, 1872, Lanier went to San Antonio in quest of health. In letters to his father giving an account of his trip from New Orleans to Galveston and thence to Austin, he shows keen insight into the life of that State. He sketches many types of character and scenes — sketches that show at once his knowledge of human nature and his ability as a reporter. It may be said here that Lanier always took an interest in the passing show, — he was not a detached dreamer. He arrived at San Antonio in November. On account of his ill health he could write but few letters, although he is " fairly reeking with all manner of quips and quiddities which I yearn to spread for the delectation of such a partial set of people as a home set always is." He writes to his sister : " To-day has been as lovely as any day can hope to be this side of Millennium ; and I have been out strolling morning and afternoon, far and wide, ever tempted onward by the delicious buoyant balm in the air and pleasantly surprised in finding what a distance I could accomplish without over fatigue."

[1] *Letters*, p. 70.

He rode horseback a great deal — a form of
exercise he was especially fond of all his life.

In a letter to his father he refers to some work
he is doing in the library: "I have also managed to advance very largely my conceptions of
the Jacquerie through a history which I secured
from the Library of the Alamo Literary Society,
— a flourishing institution here which is now
building a hall to cost some thirteen thousand
dollars, and of which I have become a literary
member." He has been reading Michelet's " History of France " which " gives him the essence of
an old book which he had despaired of ever seeing, but which is the only authority extant, —
save Froissart and a few others equally unreli-
able ; it is the chronicle of the ' Continuator of
Guillaume de Nangis.' " With Olmsted's book
of travels as a model, he planned a series of
articles for a New York paper.

The only result, however, from these plans
was a picturesque sketch of San Antonio,[1] afterwards published in the " Southern Magazine."
This sketch is at once a history of San Antonio
and a description of the scenery and the people
of that quaint city. " Over all the round of aspects in which a thoughtful mind may view a city,"
he says in a typical passage, " it bristles with striking idiosyncrasies and *bizarre* contrasts. Its his-

[1] *Retrospects and Prospects*, p. 34.

tory, population, climate, location, architecture, soil, water, customs, costumes, horses, cattle, all attract the stranger's attention, either by force of intrinsic singularity or of odd juxtapositions. It was a puling infant for a century and a quarter, yet has grown to a pretty vigorous youth in a quarter of a century; its inhabitants are so varied that the ' go slow ' directions over its bridges are printed in three languages, and the religious services in its churches held in four; the thermometer, the barometer, the vane, the hygrometer, oscillate so rapidly, so frequently, so lawlessly, and through so wide a meteorological range, that the climate is simply indescribable, yet it is a growing resort for consumptives; it stands with all its gay prosperity just in the edge of a lonesome, untilled belt of land one hundred and fifty miles wide, like *Mardi Gras* on the austere brink of Lent; it has no Sunday laws, and that day finds its bar-rooms and billiard-saloons as freely open and as fully attended as its churches; its buildings, ranging from the Mexican *jacal* to the San Fernando Cathedral, represent all the progressive stages of man's architectural progress in edifices of mud, of wood, of stone, of iron, and of sundry combinations of those materials; its soil is in wet weather an inky-black cement, but in dry a floury-white powder; it is built along both banks of two limpid streams,

yet it drinks rain water collected in cisterns; its
horses and mules are from Lilliput, while its
oxen are from Brobdingnag." In the same vivid
style he sketches the various characteristics of
the city and its people. His account of a Texas
"norther," his descriptions of the San Fernando
Cathedral and of the Mission San José de
Aquayo are especially good.

It was on this visit to San Antonio that Lanier
resolved finally to devote himself to an artist's
career. He came in contact with some of the
German musicians of the city and played before
the Maennerchor, which received his flute-playing with enthusiastic applause.

Last night at eight o'clock came Mr. Scheidemantel, a genuine lover of music and a fine pian-
ist, to take me to the Maennerchor, which meets
every Wednesday night for practice. Quickly
we came to a hall, one end of which was occupied
by a minute stage with appurtenances, and a
piano; and in the middle thereof a long table,
at which each singer sat down as he came in.
Presently, seventeen Germans were seated at the
singing-table, long-necked bottles of Rhine-wine
were opened and tasted, great pipes and cigars
were all afire; the leader, Herr Thielepape, —
an old man with long, white beard and mustache,

formerly mayor of the city, — rapped his tuning-fork vigorously, gave the chords by rapid arpeggios of his voice (a wonderful, wild, high tenor, such as thou wouldst dream that the old Welsh harpers had, wherewith to sing songs that would cut against the fierce sea-blasts), and off they all swung into such a noble, noble old German full-voiced *lied*, that imperious tears rushed into my eyes, and I could scarce restrain myself from running and kissing each one in turn and from howling dolefully the while. And so . . . I all the time worshiping . . . with these great chords . . . we drove through the evening until twelve o'clock, absorbing enormous quantities of Rhine-wine and beer, whereof I imbibed my full share. After the second song I was called on to play, and lifted my poor old flute in air with tumultuous, beating heart; for I had no confidence in that or in myself. But, *du Himmel!* Thou shouldst have heard mine old love warble herself forth. To my utter astonishment, I was perfect master of the instrument. Is not this most strange? Thou knowest I had never learned it; and thou rememberest what a poor muddle I made at Marietta in playing difficult passages; and I certainly have not practiced; and yet there I commanded and the blessed notes obeyed me, and when I had finished, amid a storm of applause, Herr Thielepape arose and ran to me and grasped my hand, and declared that he hat never heert de flude accompany itself pefore! I played once more during the evening, and ended with even more rapturous bravos than before, Mr. Scheidemantel grasping my hand this time, and thanking me very earnestly.

My heart, which was hurt greatly when I went into the music-room, came forth from the holy bath of concords greatly refreshed, strengthened, and quieted, and so remaineth to-day. I also feel better than in a long time before.[1]

Again he played for "an elegant-looking company of ladies and gentlemen" in a private home. "I had not played three seconds," he says, "before a profound silence reigned among the people, seeing which, and dreaming wildly, and feeling somehow in an eerie and elfish, and half-uncanny mood, I flew off into all manner of trills, and laments, and cadenza-monstrosities for a long time, but finally floated down into 'La Mélancolie,' which melted itself forth with such eloquent lamenting that it almost brought my tears — and, to make a long story short, when I allowed the last note to die, a simultaneous cry of pleasure broke forth from men and women that almost amounted to a shout." [2] Two weeks later he wrote: "I have writ the most beautiful piece, 'Field-larks and Blackbirds,' wherein I

---

[1] *Letters*, p. 71.   [2] *Letters*, p. 73.

have mirrored Mr. Field-lark's pretty eloquence so that I doubt he would know the difference betwixt the flute and his own voice." [1]

Inspired by the sympathy of people in whose judgment he had confidence, and impelled by his own genius asserting itself, and realizing that his hold upon life was but slight, he went from San Antonio in April, 1873, with the fixed purpose to give the remainder of his life to music and poetry. The resolution is all the more significant when it is remembered that the year 1873 was one of financial distress, especially in the South. "It was then," says Joel Chandler Harris, "that the effects of war and waste were fully felt, and then that the stoutest heart was tried, labor was restless and hard to control, the planter was out of funds and interest was high, . . . the farmers were almost at the point of desperation."

The formation of this resolution to devote himself •to artistic work marks an epoch in Lanier's life so important as to call for further comment. For twelve years he had been deflected out of his true orbit. For seven years he had given his time and talent to pursuits which he did not cherish — writing only now and then with his left hand. Everything had been against him. To preserve unspotted the ideal of his

[1] *Letters*, p. 47.

youth — through all the changes and struggles of these years — and now to give himself to it meant heroism of a rare type. It meant that he must seem disobedient to a father with whom his relation had been peculiarly intimate, that he would go in the face of the opinion of friends and relatives, and that he must for a while at least leave behind his family, whom he loved with an unparalleled affection. He was to enter upon a career the future of which was not certain. In spite of all these obstacles, he deliberately made up his mind to give the remainder of his life to the work that he loved. Once again, after he had settled down in Baltimore, his father made a determined effort to induce him to change his mind, but to no avail. Lanier's answer to his father's letter, written November 29, 1873, is really his declaration of independence — the vow of consecration : —

"I have given your last letter the fullest and most careful consideration. After doing so I feel sure that Macon is not the place for me. If you could taste the delicious crystalline air, and the champagne breeze that I've just been rushing about in, I am equally sure that in point of climate you would agree with me that my chance for life is ten times as great here as in Macon. Then, as to business, why should I, nay, how *can* I, settle myself down to be a third-rate

struggling lawyer for the balance of my little
life, as long as there is a certainty almost absolute that I can do some other thing so much
better? Several persons, from whose judgment
in such matters there can be no appeal, have
told me, for instance, that I am the greatest
flute-player in the world; and several others, of
equally authoritative judgment, have given me
an almost equal encouragement to work with my
pen. (Of course I protest against the necessity
which makes me write such things about myself.
I only do so because I so appreciate the love and
tenderness which prompt you to desire me with
you that I will make the fullest explanation possible of my course, out of reciprocal honor and
respect for the motives which lead you to think
differently from me.) My dear father, think
how, for twenty years, through poverty, through
pain, through weariness, through sickness,
through the uncongenial atmosphere of a farcical
college and of a bare army and then of an exact-
ing business life, through all the discouragement
of being wholly unacquainted with literary people and literary ways, — I say, think how, in
spite of all these depressing circumstances, and
of a thousand more which I could enumerate,
these two figures of music and of poetry have
steadily kept in my heart so that I could not
banish them. Does it not seem to you as to

me, that I begin to have the right to enroll myself among the devotees of these two sublime arts, after having followed them so long and so humbly, and through so much bitterness?" [1]

The letter just quoted needs to be read with caution. It sets in too sharp antagonism his life up to this point and that of his later years. Previous chapters of this book have been written in vain if they have not revealed the fact that Lanier was a much more highly developed man when he left Georgia than the letter would indicate. He wrote it in the first flush of enthusiasm at finding himself among artists. But it is misleading. For instance, he speaks of the " farcical college ; " yet in his last days, when he saw his life in its proper perspective, he said that he owed to Dr. Woodrow the strongest and most valuable stimulus of his early life. He was not a raw provincial ; he had traveled extensively, had been associated with people of culture, if not of letters, and he had read widely and wisely. His inheritance from Southern people, — their temperament and their civilization, — and his indebtedness to Southern scenery will be the more apparent in later chapters of this book. All the while his genius had been steadily growing. When the time came he was a prepared man —

[1] Quoted by William Hayes Ward in his Introduction to Lanier's *Poems*.

ready to seize with avidity every opportunity that presented itself.

Furthermore, the very struggle he had to maintain his ideal, and it will not do to minimize this struggle, had strengthened and enlarged his soul. One may as well lament Milton's absorption in the conflicts of his country as Lanier's participation in the war and in the stirring events of reconstruction. After the fortitude and endurance manifested in this period of his life, his later sufferings were the more easily borne. One of his favorite theories was that antagonism or opposition either in art or morals is to be welcomed, for out of it comes a finer art and a larger manhood. He developed somewhat at length this theory in his admirable study of Shakespeare's growth. In a passage evidently autobiographical he traces Shakespeare's progress in the three periods of his life, the Dream Period, the Real or Hamlet Period, and the Ideal Period. Lanier, too, passed through his Dream Period, — the college days and the early years of the war. He passed through his Hamlet Period — the years from 1865 to 1873 — years in which he felt the shock of the real, the twist and cross of life. There had been suffering from poverty, drudgery, and disease ; there had been also something of the storm and stress of religious and philosophic doubt. With the beginning of his

artistic life he passes into his Ideal Period, when
by reason of the terrific shock of the real he was
able to realize " a new and immortally fine reconstruction of his youth." He was to know what
suffering meant in the future ; but the serenity
and joy of his life from this point are apparent
to all who may study it.

> Of fret, of dark, of thorn, of chill,
>   Complain no more ; for these, O heart,
> Direct the random of the will
>   As rhymes direct the rage of art.

CHAPTER VI

A MUSICIAN IN BALTIMORE

WITH his purpose firmly fixed in his mind he
started for New York, which was then fast becoming the musical and literary centre of the
country. For three months and more he gave himself unstintedly to the work of perfecting himself
in playing the flute, and attended regularly the
great concerts then being given by Theodore
Thomas. It was an opportune time. The day of
the Italian opera, for which Lanier did not care,
was past, and orchestral music was beginning its
triumphant career in this country. These were
months, then, of education in the very music for
which Lanier had yearned. He at once attracted
musical critics and made a stir in some of the
churches and concert-rooms of the city. He had
brought along with him two of his own compositions, "Swamp Robin" and "Blackbirds;" and
there were some who did not hesitate to pro-
phesy a brilliant career for him as "the greatest
flute-player in the world." Lanier did not rely
on inspiration, however, nor was he satisfied with
the applause of popular audiences; he knew that

his course must be one of "straightforward behavior and hard work and steady improvement."
He would be satisfied only with the judgment
of Thomas or Dr. Leopold Damrosch, then conductor of the Philharmonic Society.

On his way to New York he had stopped at
Baltimore, and on the advice of his friend Henry
Wysham had played for Asger Hamerik, who
was at that time making efforts to have the Peabody Institute establish an orchestra. Hamerik
was so attracted by Lanier's playing, both of
masterpieces and of his own compositions, that
he invited him to become first flute in the prospective orchestra. With even this promise in
view, Lanier had written to his wife: "It is
therefore a *possibility* . . . that I may be first
flute in the Peabody Orchestra, on a salary of
$120 a month, which, with five flute scholars,
would grow to $200 a month, and so . . . we
might dwell in the beautiful city, among the
great libraries, and midst of the music, the religion, and the art that we love — and I could
write my books and be the man I wish to be." [1]
Hamerik did succeed in getting the orchestra
established and Lanier accepted the position —
for far less money, however. Lanier settled in
Baltimore, in December, and at once attracted the
attention of the patrons of the orchestra. In the

[1] *Letters*, p. 75.

Baltimore " Sun " of December 8, 1873, his
playing was mentioned as one of the features
of the opening symphony concert. In the same
paper of January 25 occurs this note : " Lanier
and Stubbs could not have acquitted themselves
better, nor done more justice to their very difficult parts." And so throughout the winter there
is contemporary evidence that this " raw provincial, without practice and guiltless of instruction," was holding his own with the finely trained
Germans and Danes of Hamerik's Orchestra.

The fact is, Lanier was a musical genius. In
playing the flute he combined deftness of hand
and quick intuitiveness of soul. The director of
the Peabody Orchestra, who had been a pupil of
Von Bülow, and was a composer of distinction,
has left the most authoritative account of Lanier
as a performer : —

" To him as a child in his cradle Music was
given, the heavenly gift to feel and to express
himself in tones. His human nature was like an
enchanted instrument, a magic flute, or the lyre
of Apollo, needing but a breath or a touch to send
its beauty out into the world. It was indeed irresistible that he should turn with those poetical
feelings which transcend language to the penetrating gentleness of the flute, or the infinite
passion of the violin ; for there was an agreement,
a spiritual correspondence between his nature

and theirs, so that they mutually absorbed and expressed each other. In his hands the flute no longer remained a mere material instrument, but was transformed into a voice that set heavenly harmonies into vibration. Its tones developed colors, warmth, and a low sweetness of unspeakable poetry ; they were not only true and pure, but poetic, allegoric as it were, suggestive of the depths and heights of being and of the delights which the earthly ear never hears and the earthly eye never sees. No doubt his firm faith in these lofty idealities gave him the power to present them to our imaginations, and thus by the aid of the higher language of Music to inspire others with that sense of beauty in which he constantly dwelt. His conception of music was not reached by an analytic study of note by note, but was intuitive and spontaneous ; like a woman's reason : he felt it so, because he felt it so, and his delicate perception required no more logical form of reasoning. His playing appealed alike to the musically learned and to the unlearned — for he would magnetize the listener ; but the artist felt in his performance the superiority of the momentary living inspiration to all the rules and shifts of mere technical scholarship. His art was not only the art of art, but an art above art. I will never forget the impression he made on me when he played the flute concerta of Emil Hartmann at a Peabody symphony concert, in 1878, — his tall, handsome, manly presence, his flute breathing noble sorrows, noble joys, the orchestra softly responding. The audience was spellbound. Such distinction, such refinement! He stood, the master, the genius!"[1]

He made the same impression on every other artist he ever played for. Badger called his flute-playing "astonishing;" Wehner, the first flute in Thomas's Orchestra, sought every opportunity to play with him. Theodore Thomas planned to have him in his orchestra at the time when Lanier's health failed in 1876; Dr. Damrosch said he played "Wind-Song" like an artist, — that "he was greatly astonished and pleased with the poetry of the piece and the enthusiasm of its rendering."

His own compositions, too, appealed to men. At times the "fury of creation" was upon him. During the first winter in Baltimore he wrote a midge dance, the origin of which he thus gives in a letter to his wife: "I am copying off — in order to try the publishers therewith — a 'Danse des Moucherons' (midge dance), which I have written for flute and piano, and which I think enough of to let go forward as Op. 1. Dost thou remember one morning last summer, Charley and I were walking in the upper part of the yard,

---

[1] Quoted in Ward's Introduction to *Poems*.

before breakfast, and saw a swarm of gnats, of whose strange evolutions we did relate to thee a marvelous tale ? I have put the grave oaks, the quiet shade, the sudden sunlight, the fantastic, contrariwise, and ever-shifting midge movements, the sweet hills afar off, . . . all in the piece, and thus *I* like it; but I know not if others will, I have not played it for anybody. "[1]

During this winter and the succeeding one Lanier gave almost his entire time to music. He practiced assiduously, took every opportunity to play with the best musicians, — both those of his own orchestra and of Theodore Thomas's, — and often spent evenings with three or four of the choicest spirits he could command. Hamerik was of special inspiration to him, bringing to him as he did much of the spirit of music that prevailed in German cities. Lanier studied the technique of the flute, mastering his new silver Boehm, which "begins to feel me," he writes. "How much I have learned in the last two months!" he exclaims. "I am not yet an art-ist, though, on the flute. The technique of the instrument has many depths which I had not thought of before, and I would not call myself a virtuoso within a year." He suffers agony because he does not attain a point in harmony which the audience did not notice. Writing of

[1] *Letters*, p. 98.

3rd Flute
Arran. by S. C. Lanier
Dec. 1861.
Huldegung der Britischen Nation
Labitzky
ritard.do

the temptation of flute soloists, he once said :
" They have rarely been able to resist the fatal
facility of the instrument, and have usually addressed themselves to winning the applause of concert audiences by the execution of those brilliant
but utterly trifling and inane variations which
constitute the great body of existing solos for
the flute." [1] He fretted because " the flute had
been the black beast in the orchestra." With
his mastery of its technique and his own marvelous ability to bring new results from it, he looked
forward to the time when it would have a far
more important place therein.

Lanier played not only for the Peabody
Orchestra, but for the Germania Männerchor
Orchestra, — one of the many companies of
Germans who did so much to develop music in
different parts of the country, — the Concordia
Theatre, charity concerts, churches, and in private homes. He was very popular in Baltimore.
Most of the musicians were Germans, but Lanier
was an American and a Southerner, who had
graces of manner and goodness of soul. He was
a close friend of the Baltimore musicians, such
as Madame Falk-Auerbach, a pupil of Rossini's
and a teacher in the Conservatory of Music, " a
woman who plays Beethoven with the large conception of a man, and yet nurses her children all

[1] *Music and Poetry*, p. 38.

day with a noble simplicity of devotion such as I have rarely seen," said Lanier. Outside of musical circles he had access to the homes of the most prominent people of Baltimore, in which he frequently played the flute or piano, while members of the family accompanied him. " Memory pictures," says one of his admirers, " that frail, slender figure at the piano, touching with white, shapely hands the chords of Chopin's ' Nocturne.' " " He was a frequent visitor to our house," says another, " and would often play for us on his beautiful silver flute. The image of him standing in his rapt passion, while he poured forth the entrancing sound, I remember most distinctly."

And while he grew in his mastery of the flute he grew, too, in discriminating study of the orchestra. His first interpretations of orchestral music are rather impulsive — he goes off into raptures without restraint, even when the occasion is not really of the highest sort. It is altogether unfair to him to confuse his earlier with his later letters. As in every other respect, Lanier was growing in intellectual power. " I am beginning," he writes, " in the midst of the stormy glories of the orchestra, to feel my heart sure, and my soul discriminating. Not less do I thrill to ride upon the great surges ; but I am growing calm enough to see the star that should light

the musician, and presently my hand will be
firm enough to hold the helm and guide the ship
that way. *Now* I am very quiet; I am waiting."[1] And again, after he has heard Thomas's
Orchestra; "I can preserve my internal dignity in great measure, free from the dreadful
distractions of solicitude, and thus my soul revels
in the midst of the heaven of these great symphonic works with almost unobstructed freedom."[2]

One of the plans proposed by Lanier for help-
ing people to understand better the meaning of
orchestral music should be mentioned in this connection. He was always anxious to take every
one with him into his kingdom of beauty. He
proposed that, for people living in cities of from
three to twenty thousand inhabitants, there should
be organized " a Nonette Club, consisting of himself for flute, oboe, clarionet, bassoon, and French
horn, and a string quartette. This club would
travel through the smaller cities, performing
original compositions as well as excerpts from the
greatest symphonic orchestral works, and thus
educating the masses to an understanding of orchestral tonal color, and the relations, in an analytical form, which the wood wind instruments
bore to the stringed family. . . . It was his purpose, after each movement of a composition, to

[1] *Letters*, p. 91.   [2] *Letters*, p. 110.

lecture on the same, with special reference to the function performed by each instrument, and in the formation of harmonious tonal color." [1]

While Lanier was giving his time to the perfection of his flute-playing and to the study of the orchestra, he became interested in the science of music. Helmholtz's recent discoveries in acoustics inspired him to make research in that direction. He ransacked the Peabody Library for books on the subject, many of them yet not unpacked.

While few people ever appreciated more the art of music and its spiritual message to men, he realized that there was a science of music as well, "embodying a great number of classified facts, and presenting a great number of scientific laws which are as thoroughly recognized among musicians as are the laws of any other sciences among their professors. There is a science of harmony, a science of composition, a science of orchestration, a science of performance upon stringed instruments, a science of performance upon wind instruments, a science of vocalization; not a branch of the art of music but has its own analogous body of classified facts and general laws. Music is so much a science that a man may be a thorough musician who has never written a tune and who cannot play upon any

[1] Letter from Mr. F. H. Gottlieb to the author.

instrument." [1] Some of these investigations he afterwards used to good effect in his " Science of English Verse."

Furthermore, Lanier became interested in the history of music. In his valuable monograph on " Music in Shakespeare's Time " [2] he shows a minute knowledge of Elizabethan music, — madrigals, dances, catches, and other forms of instrumental and vocal music. He took great delight in following out through Shakespeare's plays the dramatist's knowledge and appreciation of the art of music. Indeed, all the people of that time were " enthusiastic lovers of the art. There were professorships of music in the universities, and multitudes of teachers of it among the people. The monarch, the lord, the gentleman, the merchant, the artisan, the rustic clown, all ranks and conditions of society, from highest to lowest, cultivated the practice of singing or of playing upon some of the numerous instruments of the time." For the class to which he was then lecturing in the Peabody Institute he was able to point out and illustrate various forms of music and to give biographical sketches of the English musicians of Shakespeare's age.

Lanier was most of all interested, however, in the development of modern music, and especially

[1] *Music and Poetry*, p. 50.
[2] *Shakspere and His Forerunners*, vol. ii, p. 1.

in orchestral music. He underrated some of the classical composers, notably Mozart. He was familiar with the biographies of Chopin, Beethoven, Schumann, and Wagner. He left behind a translation of Wagner's " Rheingold." His poems on Beethoven and Wagner indicate his appreciation of their music, while his essays " From Bacon to Beethoven " and " The Modern Orchestra " show minute knowledge of their work and of the significance of the orchestra in modern life. A better description of Theodore Thomas as the leader of an orchestra has not been written than Lanier's : —

" To see Thomas lead . . . is music itself ! His *bâton* is alive, full of grace, of symmetry ; he maketh no gestures, he readeth his score almost without looking at it, he seeth everybody, heareth everything, warneth every man, encourageth every instrument, quietly, firmly, marvelously. Not the slightest shade of nonsense, not the faintest spark of affectation, not the minutest grain of *effect* is in him. He taketh the orchestra in his hand as if it were a pen, — and writeth with it." [1]

If Lanier had been only a successful virtuoso with the flute, the tradition of his playing would have lingered in the minds of at least two generations. Through the reminiscences of college

[1] *Letters*, p. 92.

mates, of soldiers and of frequenters of the Peabody concerts, the memory of this genius with
the flute would have remained like that of some
troubadour of the Middle Ages. It is unfortunate
that he left no compositions to indicate a musical
power sufficient to give him a place in the history
of American music. It cannot be controverted,
however, that he is the one man of letters in
America who has had an adequate appreciation
of the value of music in the culture of the modern world. To him music was a culture study as
much as the study of literature. It was an education to him to hear the adequate representation
of modern orchestral works. Hamerik's plan of
giving separate nights to the music of various
nationalities was calculated to emphasize this
phase of musical culture. To Lanier, who had
never traveled abroad and who did not have time
to read the literatures of foreign nations, such musical programmes had the effect of enabling him
to divine the places and the life from which the
music had come. " I am just come from Venice,"
he says, " and have strolled home through the
moonlight, singing serenades. . . . I have been
playing 'Stradella' and I am full of gondellieds,
of serenades, of balconies with white arms leaning over the balustrades thereof, of gleaming
waters, of lithe figures in black velvet, of sting-
ing sweet coquetries, of diamonds, daggers, and

desperadoes. . . . I cannot tell the intense delight which these lovely conceptions of Flotow gave me. The man has put Venice, lovely, romantic, wicked-sweet Venice, into music, and the melodies breathe out an eloquence that is at once sentimental and powerful, at once languid and thrilling." [1]

A description of the " Hunt of Henry IV " shows how Lanier associated nature, music, and poetry with each other. He was an ardent advocate of " programme-music." He saw music as he heard poetry. He felt the musical effects in poetry and the poetical effects in music : " Then, the ' Hunt of Henry IV ' ! . . . It openeth with a grave and courteous invitation, as of a cavalier riding by some dainty lady, through the green aisles of the deep woods, to the hunt, — a lovely, romantic melody, the first violins discoursing the man's words, the first flute replying for the lady. Presently a fanfare ; a sweet horn replies out of the far woods ; then the meeting of the gay cavaliers ; then the start, the dogs are unleashed, one hound gives tongue, another joins, the stag is seen — hey, gentlemen ! away they all fly through the sweet leaves, by the great oaks and beeches, all a-dash among the brambles, till presently, bang ! goeth a pistol (it was my veritable old revolver loaded with blank

[1] *Letters*, p. 98.

cartridge for the occasion, the revolver that hath lain so many nights under my head), fired by *Tympani* (as we call him, the same being a nervous little Frenchman who playeth our drums), and then the stag dieth in a celestial concord of flutes, oboes, and violins. Oh, how far off my soul was in this thrilling moment! It was in a rare, sweet glen in Tennessee; the sun was rising over a wilderness of mountains, I was standing (how well I remember the spot!) alone in the dewy grass, wild with rapture and with expectation. Yonder came, gracefully walking, a lovely fawn. I looked into its liquid eyes, hesitated, prayed, gulped a sigh, then overcome with the savage hunter's instinct, fired; the fawn leaped convulsively a few yards, I ran to it, found it lying on its side, and received into my agonized and remorseful heart the reproaches of its most tender, dying gaze. But luckily I had not the right to linger over this sad scene; the conductor's *bâton* shook away the dying pause; on all sides shouts and fanfares and gallopings 'to the death,' to which the first flute had to reply in time, recalled me to my work, and I came through brilliantly." [1]

Because of its culture value, Lanier believed that music should have its place in every college and university. As far back as 1867 — in " Tiger

[1] *Letters*, p. 85.

Lilies " — he had advocated the appointment of professors of music in American colleges of equal dignity with other specialists. He himself hoped that he might be appointed to such a chair, first in the College of Music in New York and later in Johns Hopkins University. It is easy to conceive that he might have become an expert teacher in the science of music, but it is more probable that if he had held a chair in an academic institution he would have forwarded the work that has now become a distinct feature of all the larger universities. He would have made an excellent " literary " teacher of music, interesting men in the biographies of great musicians, and interpreting for them the mysteries of orchestra and opera. He conceived of music as one of the humanities, and would have agreed with President Eliot that " music is a culture study, if there is one in the world." In his life it took the place that travel and many literatures held in the lives of Longfellow and Lowell. He believed with Theodore Thomas that Beethoven's music is " something more than mere pleasure ; it is education, thought, emotion, love, and hope."

Furthermore, Lanier believed in the religious value of music ; it was a " gospel whereof the people are in great need, — a later revelation of all gospels in one." " Music," he says, " is to be the Church of the future, wherein all creeds will unite like the tones in a chord." He was one of " those fervent souls who fare easily by this road to the Lord." Haydn's inscription, "Laus Deo," was in Lanier's mind whenever he listened to great music ; for it tended to " help the emotions of man across the immensity of the known into the boundaries of the Unknown." He would have composers to be ministers of religion. He could not understand the indifference of some leaders of orchestras, who could be satisfied with appealing to the æsthetic emotions of an audience, while they might " set the hearts of fifteen hundred people afire." The final meaning of music to him was that it created within man " a great, pure, unanalyzable yearning after God."

Holding this exalted view of music, he believed that its future was immense and that in America its triumphs were to be greater than they had been elsewhere. At a time when musical culture was rare in this country, he looked forward with hope and expectation to the time when America would become a patron of the best music. " When Americans," he said, " shall have learned the supreme value and glory of the orchestra, . . . then I look to see America the home of the orchestra, and to hear everywhere the profound messages of Beethoven and Bach to men." And again : "All the signs of the times seem to point to this country as the scene of the future development of music. . . . It only needs direction, artistic atmosphere, and technique in order to fill the land with such orchestras as the world has never heard. When our so-called conservatories and music schools, instead of straining every nerve to outdo each other in turning out hosts of bad piano-players, shall address themselves earnestly to the education of performers upon all the orchestral instruments ; when our people shall have become aware of the height and glory of the orchestra, as the only instrument for the deepest adorations in man ; . . . when our young women shall ask themselves for any serious reason why they should all, with one accord, devote themselves to the piano instead of to the flute, the violin, the hautboy, the harp, the viola, the violoncello, the horn instruments which pertain to women fully as much as to men, and some of which actually belong by nature to those supple, tactile, delicate, firm, passionate, and tender fingers with which the woman is endowed ; when our young men shall have discovered that the orchestral player can so exercise his office as to make it of far more dignity and worth than any political place in the gift of the people, and that the business of making orchestral music may one

day become far higher in nobility than the ig-
noble sentinelship over one's pocket to which
most lawyers are reduced, or the melancholy
slaveries of the shop and the counting-room and
the like ' business ' which is now paramount in esteem ; when — I will not say when we have a new
music to perform, but when we shall have played
Beethoven's symphonies as they should be played,
and shall have revealed to us all the might,
all the faith, all the religion, the tenderness, the
heavenly invitation, the subtle excursions down
into the heart of man, the brotherhood, the freedom, the exaltation, the whisperings of sorrow
unto sorrow, the messages of God which these
immortal and yet unmeasured compositions em-
body," [1] then will America give to music the place
it deserves. Music will be one of the redeemers
of the people from crass commercialism.

While Lanier held before the American people
the vision of what they might accomplish in
music, he held up to musicians the high ideal of
what they should be. In the essay just quoted, he
indorses the saying of Mazzini's that "musicians
may become a priesthood and ministry of moral
regeneration. . . . Why rest contented with
stringing notes together — mere trouvères of a
day — when it remains with you to consecrate

---

[1] An uncollected essay by Lanier, " Mazzini on Music," *The
Independent*, June 27, 1878.

yourselves, even on earth, to a mission such as in the popular belief only God's angels know?" With his high ideal of what a musician should be, he could not but be disgusted at times with the Bohemianism of the men who played with him, and with the loose moral life of many more eminent musicians. "Ah, these heathenish Germans!" he exclaims, as he sees some of the orchestra at a church service making fun of the communion service: "Double-bass was a big fellow, with a black mustache, to whom life was all a joke, which he expressed by a comical smile, and Viola was a young Hercules, so full of beer that he dreamed himself in heaven, and Oboe was a young sprig, just out from Munich, with a complexion of milk and roses, like a girl's, and miraculously bright spectacles on his pale blue eyes, and there they sat — Oboe and Viola and Double-bass — and ogled each other, and raised their brows, and snickered behind the columns, without a suspicion of interest either in the music or the service. Dash these fellows, they are utterly given over to heathenism, prejudice, and beer." [1]

The best expression of his ideal of what a great composer should be, is in a letter written to his wife just after he had read the life of Robert Schumann: —

[1] *Letters*, p. 88.

NEW YORK, Sunday, October 18, 1874.

I have been in my room all day; and have just concluded a half-dozen delicious hours, during which I have been devouring, with a hungry ferocity of rapture which I know not how to express, "The Life of Robert Schumann," by his pupil, von Wasielewski. This pupil, I am sure, did not fully comprehend his great master. I think the key to Schumann's whole character, with all its labyrinthine and often disappointing peculiarities, is this : That he had no mode of self-expression, or, I should rather say, of self-expansion, besides the musical mode. This may seem a strange remark to make of him who was the founder and prolific editor of a great musical journal, and who perhaps exceeded any musician of his time in general culture. But I do not mean that he was confined to music for self-expression, though indeed, the sort of critical writing which Schumann did so much of is not at all like poetry in its tranquillizing effects upon the soul of the writer. What I do mean is that his sympathies were not *big* enough, he did not go through the awful struggle of genius, and lash and storm and beat about until his soul was grown large enough to embrace the whole of life and the All of things, that is, large enough to appreciate (if even without understanding) the magnificent designs of God, and tall enough to stand in the trough of the awful cross-waves of circumstance and look over their heights along the whole sea of God's manifold acts, and deep enough to admit the peace that passeth understanding. This is, indeed, the fault of all German culture, and the weakness of all German genius. A great artist should have the sensibility and expressive genius of Schumann, the calm grandeur of Lee, and the human breadth of Shakespeare, all in one.

Now in this particular, of being open, unprejudiced, and unenvious, Schumann soars far above his brother Germans; he valiantly defended our dear Chopin, and other young musicians who were struggling to make head against the abominable pettiness of German prejudice. But, withal, I cannot find that his life was great, as a whole; I cannot see him caring for his land, for the poor, for religion, for humanity; he was always a restless soul; and the ceaseless wear of incompleteness finally killed, as a maniac, him whom a broader Love might have kept alive as a glorious artist to this day.

The truth is, the world does not require enough at the hands of genius. Under the special plea of greater sensibilities, and of consequent greater temptations, it excuses its gifted ones, and even sometimes makes "a law of their weakness." But this is wrong: the sensibility of genius is just as much greater to high emotions as to low ones; and whilst it subjects to stronger temptations, it at the same time interposes — if it *will* — stronger considerations for resistance.

These are scarcely fair things to be saying *apropos* of Robert Schumann; for I do not think he was ever guilty of any excesses of genius — as they are called: I only mean them to apply to the *unrest* of his life.

And yet, for all I have said, how his music does burn in my soul! It stretches me upon the very rack of delight; I know no musician that fills me so full of heavenly anguish, and if I had to give up all the writers of music save one, my one should be Robert Schumann. — Some of his experiences cover some of my own as aptly as one half of an oyster shell does the other half.[1]

---

[1] *Letters*, p. 103.

CHAPTER VII

THE BEGINNING OF A LITERARY CAREER

DURING the winter of 1873–74, the first winter in Baltimore, Lanier had, as has been seen, given his entire time to music. The only poetry he had written had been inspired by love for his absent wife, — poems breathing of the deepest and tenderest affection. Scarcely less poetical were the letters written to her giving expression to his joy in the large new world into which he was entering, and at the same time to his sense of loneliness and pain at their separation. To her and his boys he went as soon as his engagement with the Peabody Orchestra was ended. In one of his letters he had spoken of himself as "an exile from his dear Land, which is always the land where my loved ones are." He found delight during this summer, as in the following ones, in the renewal of home ties, and in the enjoyment of the natural scenery of Macon and Brunswick, to whose beauty he never ceased to be sensitive.

It was in August, 1874, that he received a fresh impulse towards poetry, or, at least, towards the writing of more important poems than those he had heretofore written. While visiting at Sunnyside, Georgia, some sixty miles from Macon, he was struck at once with the beauty of cornfields and the pathos of deserted farms. Hence arose his first poem that attracted attention throughout the country. He took it to New York with him in the fall. Writing to his friend, Judge Logan E. Bleckley, now Chief Justice of Georgia, who during this summer spoke encouraging words to him about the faith he had in his literary future, he inclosed his recently finished poem with these words : —

195 Dean St., Brooklyn, N.Y.
October 9, 1874.

My dear Sir, — I could never tell you how sincerely grateful I am to you, and shall always be, for a few words you spoke to me recently.

Such encouragement would have been pleasant at any time, but this happened to come just at a critical moment when, although I had succeeded in making up my mind finally and decisively as to my own career, I was yet faint from a desperate struggle with certain untoward circumstances which it would not become me to detail.

Did you ever lie for a whole day after being wounded, and then have water brought you? If so, you will know how your words came to me.

I inclose the manuscript of a poem in which I have endeavored to carry some very prosaic matters up to a loftier plane. I have been struck with alarm in seeing the number of old, deserted homesteads and gullied hills in the older counties of Georgia; and though they are dreadfully commonplace, I have thought they are surely mournful enough to be poetic. Please give me your judgment on my effort, *without reserve ;* for if you should say you do not like it, the only effect on me will be to make me write one that you do like.

Believe me always your friend,

SIDNEY LANIER.

The answer to this letter, giving a detailed criticism of the poem, was very helpful to Lanier. Judge Bleckley is a man of much cultivation, and is widely known throughout Georgia as at once one of the leading lawyers of the State and a man who can in his leisure moments engage in literary work which, though not published, gives evidence of imagination and taste. Lanier was wise enough to accept most of his criticism : the revised form of the poem compared with the first form shows a great many changes, and is striking evidence of Lanier's power to improve his work. Judge Bleckley's characterization of " Corn " so accurately describes it that his words may be quoted here : " It presents four pictures ; three of them landscapes and one a portrait. You paint the woods, a cornfield, and a worn-out hill. These are your landscapes. And your portrait is the likeness of an anxious, unthrifty cotton-planter, who always spends his crop before he has made it, borrows on heavy interest to carry himself over from year to year, wears out his land, meets at last with utter ruin, and migrates to the West. Your second landscape is turned into a vegetable person [the cornstalk is Lanier's symbol of the poet], and you give its poetry with many touches of marvel and mystery in vegetable life. Your third landscape takes for an instant the form and tragic state of King Lear ; you thus make it seize on our sympathies as if it were a real person, and you then restore it to the inanimate, and contemplate its possible beneficence in the distant future." [1]

The poem was published in " Lippincott's Magazine," February, 1875, and at once attracted the attention of some discriminating readers of magazines, notably Mr. Gibson Peacock, the editor of the Philadelphia " Evening Bulletin," who reviewed it in a most sympathetic manner, and became one of the poet's best friends during the remainder of his life. It is noteworthy that the scenery of the poem should

[1] Quoted in Callaway's *Select Poems of Lanier*, p. 61.

be so distinctively and realistically Southern.
There is in the first part all of Lanier's love
of the Southern forest: the shimmering forms
in the woods, the leaves, the subtlety of mighty
tenderness in the embracing boughs, the long
muscadines, the mosses, ferns, and flowers, are all
delicately felt and described — with a suggestion
of Keats. As he wanders from this forest to the
zigzag-cornered fence, his fieldward-faring eyes
take in the beauty of the cornfield, "the heaven of blue inwoven with a heaven of green."
One tall corn captain becomes to his mind the
symbol of the poet-soul sublime, who takes
from all that he may give to all. The picture
of the thriftless and negligent Southern farmer,
"a gamester's cat'spaw and a banker's slave,"
shows Lanier's keen insight into Southern conditions, which he had, while living in Macon,
studied with much care and which he now lifted
into the realm of poetry. The red hills of
Georgia, deserted and barren, are presented with
true pathos. Nevertheless, like a genuine prophet, the poet looks forward to a better day : —

Yet shall the great God turn thy fate,
And bring thee back into thy monarch state
        And majesty immaculate.
    Lo, through hot waverings of the August morn,
    Thou givest from thy vasty sides forlorn
    Visions of golden treasuries of corn —
Ripe largesse lingering for some bolder heart

That manfully shall take thy part,
    And tend thee,
    And defend thee,
With antique sinew and with modern art.

This vision of the South's restored agriculture
was one that remained with Lanier to the end.
He did not properly appreciate the development
of manufacturing in the South, but he believed
that the redemption of the country would come
through the development of agriculture — not
the restoration of the large plantations of the
old régime, but the large number of small farms
with diversified products. On a later visit to the
South he exclaimed to his brother, " My countrymen, why plant ye not the vineyards of the
Lord ? " and later he wrote in his essay on the
" New South " of the actual fulfillment of his
prophecy in " Corn."

Encouraged by the success of " Corn," Lanier,
while giving a large part of his time to music
during the winter of 1874–75, looked more
and more in the direction of poetry. He writes
again to Judge Bleckley, November 15, 1874 :
" Your encouraging words give me at once
strength and pleasure. I hope hard and work
hard to do something worthy of them some day.
My head and my heart are both so full of poems
which the dreadful struggle for bread does not
give me time to put on paper, that I am often

driven to headache and heartache purely for
want of an hour or two to hold a pen." He then
proceeds to outline what is to be his first *magnum
opus*, " a long poem, founded on that strange
uprising in the middle of the fourteenth century
in France, called ' The Jacquerie.' It was the
first time that the big hungers of *the People* appear in our modern civilization ; and it is full of
significance. The peasants learned from the merchant potentates of Flanders that a man who
could not be a lord by birth, might be one by
wealth ; and so Trade arose, and overthrew Chivalry. Trade has now had possession of the civilized world for four hundred years : it controls all
things, it interprets the Bible, it guides our national and almost all our individual life with its
maxims ; and its oppressions upon the moral
existence of man have come to be ten thousand
times more grievous than the worst tyrannies of
the Feudal System ever were. Thus in the re-
versals of time, it is *now* the *gentleman* who must
rise and overthrow Trade. That chivalry which
every man has, in some degree, in his heart ;
which does not depend upon birth, but which is
a revelation from God of justice, of fair dealing,
of scorn of mean advantages ; which contemns
the selling of stock which one *knows* is going to
fall, to a man who *believes* it is going to rise, as
much as it would contemn any other form of

rascality or of injustice or of meanness — it is this which must in these latter days organize its insurrections and burn up every one of the cunning moral castles from which Trade sends out its forays upon the conscience of modern society. — This is about the plan which is to run through my book : though I conceal it under the form of a pure novel." [1]

Lanier never finished this poem, but he was soon hard at work on another which was based on the same idea, "The Symphony." Writing to his newly acquired friend, Mr. Peacock, March 24, 1875, he says : "About four days ago, a certain poem which I had vaguely ruminated for a week before took hold of me like a real James River ague, and I have been in a mortal shake with the same, day and night, ever since. I call it ' The Symphony : ' I personify each instrument in the orchestra, and make them discuss various deep social questions of the times, in the progress of the music. It is now nearly finished ; and I shall be rejoiced thereat, for it verily racks all the bones of my spirit." The poem was published in " Lippincott's Magazine," June, 1875 ; and besides confirming the good opinion of Mr. Peacock, won the praise of Bayard Taylor, George H. Calvert, Elizabeth Stuart Phelps, and Charlotte Cushman, and was

[1] Quoted in part in Callaway's *Select Poems of Lanier*, p. 65.

copied in full in Dwight's "Journal of Music."

As in his first poem Lanier had pointed out a defect in Southern life, so in his second long poem he struck at one of the evils of national life. In the South he felt that there was not enough of the spirit of industry ; looking at the nation as a whole, however, he exclaims : —

> " O Trade ! O Trade ! would thou wert dead !
> The time needs heart — 't is tired of head :
> We are all for love," the violins said.

The germ of this poem is found perhaps in a letter written from Wheeling, West Virginia, where he went with some of his fellow musicians to give a concert, April 16, 1874. It is a realistic picture of a city completely dominated by factory life. What he afterwards called " the hell-colored smoke of the factories " created within him a feeling of righteous indignation akin to that of Ruskin, although it must be said in justice to Lanier that, in combating the evils of industrial life, he never went to the extreme of eccentric passion displayed by the English writer. Nor, on the other hand, could he say with Walt Whitman: "I hail with joy the oceanic, variegated, intense practical energy, the demand for facts, even the business materialism, of the current age. . . . I perceive clearly that the extreme business energy and this almost maniacal appetite for wealth prevalent in the United States are parts of a melioration and progress, indispensably needed to prepare the very results I demand."

Lanier's poem is more applicable to the conditions that prevail to-day than to those of his own time. He shows himself a prophet, the truth of whose words is realized by many of the finer minds of the country. He lets the various instruments of the orchestra utter their protest against the evils of modern trade. The violin, speaking for the poor who stand wedged by the pressing of trade's hand and "weave in the mills and heave in the kilns," protests against the spirit of competition that says even when human life is involved, "Trade is only war grown miserly."

> Alas, for the poor to have some part
> In yon sweet living lands of art.

Then the flute — Lanier's own flute, summing up the voices of nature, "all fair forms, and sounds, and lights" — echoes the words of the Master, "All men are neighbors." Trade, the king of the modern days, will not allow the poor a glimpse of "the outside hills of liberty." The clarionet is the voice of a lady who speaks of the merchandise of love and yearns for the old days of chivalry before trade had withered up love's sinewy prime : —

If men loved larger, larger were our lives;
And wooed they nobler, won they nobler wives.

To her the bold, straightforward horn answers,
"like any knight in knighthood's morn." He
would bring back the age of chivalry, when there
would be "contempts of mean-got gain and hates
of inward stain." He voices, too, the idea long
ago expressed by Milton that men should be as
pure as women : —

> Shall woman scorch for a single sin,
> That her betrayer may revel in,
> And she be burnt, and he but grin
>   When that the flames begin,
>   Fair lady ?
>
> Shall ne'er prevail the woman's plea,
> *We maids would far, far whiter be*
> *If that our eyes might sometimes see*
>   *Men maids in purity.*

Then the hautboy sings, "like any large-eyed
child," calling for simplicity and naturalness in
this modern life. And all join at the last in a
triumphant chant of the power of love to heal
all the ills of life : —

> And ever Love hears the poor-folks' crying,
> And ever Love hears the women's sighing,
> And ever sweet knighthood's death-defying,
> And ever wise childhood's deep implying,
> But never a trader's glozing and lying.
>
> And yet shall Love himself be heard,
> Though long deferred, though long deferred :

O'er the modern waste a dove hath whirred :
Music is Love in search of a word.

By this time Lanier was hard at work for the publishers. Although he never lost his love for music — he could not —he began to see that his must be a literary career. In a letter of March 20, 1876, he says to Judge Bleckley that he has had a year of frightful overwork. " I have been working at such a rate as, if I could keep it up, would soon make me the proverb of fecundity that Lope de Vega now is." He refers to the India papers written for "Lippincott's." "The collection of the multitudinous particulars involved in them cost me such a world of labor among the libraries of Boston, New York, Philadelphia, and Baltimore as would take a long time to describe. . . . In addition to these I have written a number of papers not yet published, and a dozen small poems which have appeared here and there.

" Now, I don't work for bread ; in truth, I suppose that any man who, after many days and nights of tribulation and bloody sweat, has finally emerged from all doubt into the quiet and yet joyful activity of one who *knows* exactly what his Great Passion is and what his God desires him to do, will straightway lose all anxiety as to what he is working *for*, in the simple glory of doing that which lies immediately before him. As for me, life has resolved simply into a time

during which I must get upon paper as many as
possible of the poems with which my heart is
stuffed like a schoolboy's pocket." He quotes
from " that simple and powerful sonnet of dear
old William Drummond of Hawthornden : " —

Know what I list, this all cannot me move,
But that, O me ! — I both must write and love.

He had to give much of his time, however, to
hack work. During the summer of 1875 he was
engaged in writing a book on Florida for the
Lippincotts. It is, as he wrote to Paul Hamilton
Hayne, " a sort of spiritualized guide-book " to
a section which was then drawing a large number of visitors. " The thing immediately began
to ramify and expand, until I quickly found I
was in for a long and very difficult job : so long,
and so difficult, that, after working day and night
for the last three months on the materials I had
previously collected, I have just finished the book,
and am now up to my ears in proof-sheets and
wood-cuts which the publishers are rushing
through in order to publish at the earliest possible moment, the book having several features
designed to meet the wants of winter visitors
to Florida." It is filled with facts in regard to
climate and scenery, practical hints for travelers,
and other things characteristic of a guide-book ;
but it is more than that. Like everything else
that Lanier ever did, — even the dreariest hack

work, — he threw himself into it with great zest. It has suggestions to consumptives born out of his own experience. There are allusions to music, literature, and philosophy. There are descriptions and historical anecdotes of the cities of South Carolina and Georgia; above all, there are descriptions of the Florida country which only a poet could write. Two passages are characteristic : —

"And now it is bed-time. Let me tell you how to sleep on an Ocklawaha steamer in May. With a small bribe persuade Jim, the steward, to take the mattress out of your berth and lay it slanting just along the railing that incloses the lower part of the deck in front and to the left of the pilot-house. Lie flat on your back down on the mattress, draw your blanket over you, put your cap on your head, on account of the night air, fold your arms, say some little prayer or other, and fall asleep with a star looking right down on your eye. When you wake in the morning you will feel as new as Adam."

"Presently we abandoned the broad highway of the St. Johns, and turned off to the right into the narrow lane of the Ocklawaha. This is the sweetest water-lane in the world, a lane which runs for more than one hundred and fifty miles of pure delight betwixt hedge-rows of oaks and cypresses and palms and magnolias and mosses and vines; a lane clean to travel, for there is never a speck of dust in it save the blue dust and gold dust which the wind blows out of the flags and lilies."

In the discussion of " The Symphony," emphasis was laid upon Lanier's national point of view. The opportunity soon came to him of giving expression to his love of the Union. At Bayard Taylor's suggestion he was appointed by the Centennial Commission to write the words for a cantata to be sung at the opening exercises of the exposition in Philadelphia. Taylor, in announcing the fact, on December 28, 1875, said : " I have just had a visit from Theodore Thomas and Mr. Buck, and we talked the whole matter over. Thomas remembers you well, and Mr. Buck says it will be especially agreeable to him to compose for the words of a Southern poet. I have taken the liberty of speaking for you, both to them and to General Hawley, and you must not fail me. . . .

" Now, my dear Lanier, I am sure you *can* do this worthily. It's a great occasion, — not especially for poetry as an art, but for Poetry to assert herself as a power."[1] To this letter Lanier replied : " If it were a cantata upon your goodness, . . . I am willing to wager I could write a stirring one and a grateful withal.

" Of course I will accept — when 't is offered.

[1] *Letters*, p. 136.

I only write a hasty line now to say how deeply I am touched by the friendly forethought of your letter." [1]

He announces the fact to his wife in a jubilant letter of January 8, 1876 : " Moreover, I have a charming piece of news which — although thou art not yet to communicate it to any one except Clifford — I cannot keep from thee. The opening ceremonies of the Centennial Exhibition will be very grand; and among other things there are to be sung by a full chorus (and played by the orchestra, under Thomas's direction) a hymn and a cantata. General Hawley, President of the Centennial Commission, has written inviting me to write the latter (I mean the *poem ;* Dudley Buck, of New York, is to write the music). Bayard Taylor is to write the hymn.[2] This is very pleasing to me ; for I am chosen as representative of our dear South ; and the matter puts my name by the side of very delightful and honorable ones, besides bringing me in contact with many people I would desire to know.

" Mr. Buck has written me that he wants the poem by January 15, which as I have not yet had the least time for it, gives me just seven days to write it in. I would much rather have had seven

---

[1] *Letters*, p. 137.
[2] Whittier wrote this hymn and Bayard Taylor wrote the Ode for the Fourth of July celebration.

months ; but God is great. Remember, thou and
Cliff, that this is not yet to be spoken of at all." [1]

With enthusiasm the poet entered upon the
task assigned him. The progress of the Cantata
from the time when it first presented itself to
his mind to the time when he completed it, may
be traced in the letters to Bayard Taylor and
Gibson Peacock, which have already been published.[2] Writing to Mr. Dudley Buck, January
15, 1876, he said : —

DEAR MR. BUCK, — I send you herewith the
complete text for the Cantata. I have tried to
make it a genuine Song, at once full of fire and
of large and artless simplicity befitting a young
but already colossal land.

I have made out a working copy for you, with
marginal notes which give an analysis of each
movement (or rather *motive*, for I take it the
whole will be a continuous progression ; and I
only use the word " movement " as indicating the
entire contrast which I have secured between
each two adjacent *motives*), and which will, I
hope, facilitate your labor by presenting an outline of the tones characterizing each change of
idea. One movement is placed on each page.

Mr. Thomas was kind enough to express him-

[1] Quoted in Baskervill's *Southern Writers*, p. 200.
[2] See *Letters*, passim.

self very cordially as to the ideas of the piece;
and I devoutly trust that they will meet your
views. I found that the projection which I had
made in my own mind embraced all the substantial features of the Scheme which had occurred to
you, and therefore, although greatly differing in
details, I have not hesitated to avail myself of
your thoughtful warning against being in any
way hampered. It will give me keen pleasure
to know from you, as soon as you shall have
digested the poem, that you like it.

God send you a soul full of colossal and simple chords, — says

Yours sincerely,

SIDNEY LANIER.

In another letter, of February 1, 1876, he
wrote : " I will leave the whole matter of the
publication of the poem in the hands of Mr.
Thomas and yourself ; only begging that the
inclosed copy be the one which shall go to the
printer. The truth is, I shrank from the criticism which I fear my poem will provoke, — not
because I think it unworthy, but because I have
purposely made it absolutely free from all melo-
dramatic artifice, and wholly simple and artless ;
and although I did this in the full consciousness
that I would thereby give it such a form as would
inevitably cause it to be disappointing on the first

reading to most people, yet I had somewhat the same feeling (when your unexpected proposition to print first came) as when a raw salt spray dashes suddenly in your face and makes you duck your head. As for my own private poems, I do not even see the criticisms on them, and am far above the plane where they could possibly reach me; but this poem is *not* mine, it is to represent the people, and the people have a right that it should please them."

In this letter Lanier anticipates the criticism that was sure to come upon the poem when printed without the music. It was at once received with ridicule in all parts of the country. The leading critical journal of America exclaimed: " It reads like a communication from the spirit of Nat Lee, rendered through a bedlamite medium, failing in all the ordinary laws of sense and sound, melody and prosody." It urged the commissioners to " save American letters from the humiliation of presenting to the assembled world such a farrago as this." For several weeks Lanier could not pick up a newspaper without seeing his name held up to ridicule, the Southern papers alone, out of purely sectional pride and with " no understanding of the *principles* involved," coming to his rescue. The spirit in which he received this criticism may be seen in a letter written to his brother: —

This is the sixth letter I've written since nine o'clock to night, and it is like saying one's prayers before going to bed, to have a quiet word with you.

Your letter came to-day, and I see that you have been annoyed by the howling of the critics over the Cantata. I was greatly so at first, before I had recovered from my amazement at finding a work of art received in this way, sufficiently to think, but now the whole matter is quite plain to me and gives me no more thought, at all. . . .

The whole agitation has been of infinite value to me. It has taught me, in the first place, to lift my heart absolutely above all *expectation* save that which finds its fulfillment in the large consciousness of beautiful devotion to the highest ideals in art. This enables me to work in tranquillity.

In the second place, it has naturally caused me to make a merciless arraignment and trial of my artistic purposes ; and an unspeakable content arises out of the revelation that they come from the ordeal confirmed in innocence and clearly defined in their relations with all things. . . .

The commotion about the Cantata has not been unfavorable, on the whole, to my personal interests. It has led many to read closely what

they would otherwise have read cursorily, and I
believe I have many earnest friends whose liking
was of a nature to be confirmed by such opposition. . . .

And now, dear little Boy, may God convoy
you over to the morning across this night, and
across all nights,   Prays your

                                                S. L.

That the poem was misjudged cannot be denied. Lanier's defense published in the New
York " Tribune " must be taken as a justification,
in part at least, of the principles he had in mind.[1]
It was not written as a poem, — and Mrs. Lanier
has wisely put it as an appendix to her edition
of the poems, — but as the words of a musical
composition to be rendered by a large orchestra
and chorus. It compares, therefore, with a lyric
very much as one of the librettos of a Wagner
drama would compare with a genuine drama. It
serves merely to give the ideas which were to
be interpreted emotionally through the forms of
music. Lanier knew well the requirements of
an orchestra. He knew the effect of contrasts
and of short, simple words which would suggest
the deeper emotions intended by the author. He
thought of Beethoven's " large and artless forms "
rather than that of formal lyric poetry. He had

[1] *Music and Poetry,* p. 80.

heard Von Bülow conduct the Peabody Orchestra in a symphony based on one of Uhland's poems, in which only the simple elemental words were retained, "leaving all else to his hearers' imaginations." This served as a model for his Cantata.

That the Cantata was a success is borne out by contemporary evidence. The very paper which had criticised Lanier most severely said, in giving an account of the opening exercises, " The rendering of Lanier's Cantata was exquisite, and Whitney's bass solo deserves to the full all the praise that has been heaped upon it." Ex-President Gilman thus writes of the effect produced on the vast audience assembled in Philadelphia :

" As a Baltimorean who had just formed the acquaintance of Lanier (both of us being strangers at that time in a city we came to love as a most hospitable and responsive home), — I was much interested in his appointment. It was then true, though Dr. Holmes had not yet said it, that Baltimore had produced three poems, each of them the best of its kind: the 'Star-Spangled Banner' of Key, 'The Raven,' of Poe, and 'Maryland, My Maryland,' by Randall. Was it to produce a fourth poem as remarkable as these ? Lanier's Cantata appeared in one of the daily journals, prematurely. I read it as one reads newspaper articles, with a rapid glance, and could make no sense of it. I heard the comments of other bewildered critics. I read the piece again and again and again, before the meaning began to dawn on me. Soon afterwards, Lanier's own explanation, and the dawn became daylight. The ode was not written 'to be read.' It was to be sung — and sung, not by a single voice, with a piano accompaniment, but in the open air, by a chorus of many hundred voices, and with the accompaniment of a majestic orchestra, to music especially written for it by a composer of great distinction. The critical test would be its rendition. From this point of view the Cantata must be judged.

" I remember well the day of trial. The President of the United States, the Emperor of Brazil, the governors of States, the judges of the highest courts, the chief military and naval heroes, were seated on the platform in the face of an immense assembly. There was no pictorial effect in the way they were grouped. They were a mass of living beings, a crowd of black-coated dignitaries, not arranged in any impressive order. No cathedral of Canterbury, no Sanders Hall, no episcopal or academic gowns. The oratory was likewise ineffective. There were loud voices and vigorous gestures, but none of the eloquence which enchants a multitude. The devotional exercises awakened no sentiment of reverence. At length came the Cantata. From the overture to the closing cadence it held the attention of the vast throng of listeners, and when it was concluded loud applause rang through the air. A noble conception had been nobly rendered. Words and music, voices and instruments, produced an impression as remarkable as the rendering of the Hallelujah Chorus in the nave of Westminster Abbey. Lanier had triumphed. It was an opportunity of a lifetime to test upon a grand scale his theory of verse. He came off victorious." [1]

The most important thing, however, about the writing of the Cantata was that it gave expression to a strong faith in the nation as felt by one who had been a Confederate soldier. The central note of the poem is the preservation of the Union. In spite of all the physical obstacles that had hindered the early settlers, in spite of the distinct individualities of the various people of the sections, in spite of sectional misunderstandings which had led in the process of time to a bloody civil war, the nation had survived. All of these had said, " No, thou shalt not be."

> Now praise to God's oft-granted grace,
> Now praise to man's undaunted face,
> Despite the land, despite the sea,
> I was : I am : and I shall be.

[1] *South Atlantic Quarterly*, April, 1905.

Lanier desired, however, to avoid anything like spread-eagleism, and so after the chorus of jubilation just quoted, there is a note of doubt as to how long the nation will last. The answer, sung by the Boston soloist, Myron D. Whitney, was particularly impressive : —

> Long as thine Art shall love true love,
> Long as thy Science truth shall know,
> Long as thine Eagle harms no Dove,
> Long as thy Law by law shall grow,
> Long as thy God is God above,
> Thy Brother every man below,
> So long, dear Land of all my love,
> Thy name shall shine, thy fame shall glow !

Soon after finishing the Centennial Cantata, Lanier started upon a much longer centennial poem which, as the " Psalm of the West," was published in " Lippincott's Magazine," June, 1876, and for which he received $300. " By the grace of God," he writes to Bayard Taylor, April 4, 1876, " my centennial Ode is finished. I now only know how divine has been the agony of the last three weeks, during which I have been rapt away to heights where all my own purposes as to a revisal of artistic forms lay clear before me, and where the sole travail was of choice out of multitude." This poem was written with the idea of a symphony in his mind. One of the last things he planned was to write the music for it.

The poem as a whole is a musical rhapsody rather than a self-contained work of art. Although there are fancies and obscurities, the general theme, the magnificent opening lines, and the Columbus sonnets, with here and there lines of imaginative power, make it noteworthy. The poem is a passionate assertion of the triumph of freedom in America, — freedom, the Eve of this tall Adam of lands.

Her shalt thou clasp for a balm to the scars of thy breast,
Her shalt thou kiss for a calm to thy wars of unrest,
Her shalt extol in the psalm of the soul of the West.

Freedom with all its dangers is the precious heritage of Americans. "For Weakness, in freedom, grows stronger than Strength with a chain." With the aid of the God of the artist the poet reviews the history of the past, beginning with the time when in this continent "Blank was king and Nothing had his will." The coming of the Northmen, the discovery of the land by Columbus, the voyage of the Mayflower,— ship of Faith's best hope,— the battle of Lexington, the signing of the Declaration of Independence, and the opening up of the West, are all chanted in unrestrained poetry. The Civil War is described as a tournament : —

Heartstrong South would have his way,
Headstrong North hath said him nay.

They charged, they struck ; both fell, both bled;
  Brain rose again, ungloved;
Heart fainting smiled and softly said,
  My love to my Beloved.

Heart and brain ! no more be twain;
Throb and think, one flesh again !
Lo ! they weep, they turn, they run;
Lo ! they kiss : Love, thou art one.

The poem closes as it began, with the triumphant vision of the future : —

At heart let no man fear for thee :
  Thy Past sings ever Freedom's song,
Thy Future's voice sounds wondrous free ;
  And Freedom is more large than Crime,
  And Error is more small than Time.

The significance of the national spirit in these
two poems may be seen only when it is looked
at from the standpoint of the sectionalism that
prevailed in the South and in the North. At the
very time when Lanier was writing them, men in
Congress were giving exhibitions of partisanship
and prejudice that threatened to make of the
Centennial a farce. "The fate of the Centennial bill in Congress," he writes to Dudley
Buck, "reveals — in spite of its passage — a good
deal of opposition. All this will die out in a
couple of months, and *then* every one will be
in a temper to receive a poem of reconciliation.
I fancy that to print the poem *now* will be much

like making a dinner speech before the wine has been around." Indeed, there were few men in America at this time who really understood the significance of the national spirit. Southern men, smarting under reconstruction governments and bitter with the prejudice engendered by the war, had not been able, except in rare cases, to rise to a national point of view. The sectional spirit was ready to break out at any time. It was but natural. In the Centennial year a speaker at the University of Virginia said : " Not space, or time, or the convenience of any human arm, can reconcile institutions for the turbulent fanatic of Plymouth Rock and the God-fearing Christian of Jamestown. . . . You may assign them to the closest territorial proximity, with all the forms, modes, and shows of civilization, but you can never cement them into the bonds of brotherhood." On the other hand, the leading public men of the North, while protesting their love of the Union and naturally believing in the Union, which Northern armies had saved, had little of the spirit of a sympathetic realization of the South's problem and her condition. Only in a few large-minded publicists, and in editors like Godkin and poets like Lowell and Walt Whitman, did the national spirit prevail.

Lanier came forward, therefore, at a critical time to express his passionate faith in the future

of the American Union. He was not the only
Southerner, however, who felt this way. His
two friends, Senators Morgan of Alabama and
Lamar of Mississippi (formerly of Georgia), had
been stout upholders of the national idea in
Congress. As early as 1873 Lamar had paid
a notable tribute to Charles Sumner. He had
risen to the point where he could see the whole
struggle against slavery and against secession
from Sumner's standpoint. At the conclusion
of his remarkable address he said : " Bound to
each other by a common constitution, destined
to live together under a common government,
shall we not now at last endeavor to grow *toward*
each other once more in heart, as we are already
indissolubly linked in fortunes ? . . . Would
that the spirit of the illustrious dead whom we
lament to-day could speak from the grave to
both parties to this deplorable discord in tones
which should reach every heart throughout this
broad territory : My countrymen ! *Know* one
another, and you will *love* one another." In 1876
he made an extended argument for the Centennial bill, an eloquent plea *against* the old States'-
rights arguments. " He poured out," says his
biographer, " an exposition of nationalism and
constitutionalism which equaled in effect one of
Webster's masterpieces." " As a representative
of the South," Lamar said at a later time, " I

felt myself, with my Southern associates, to be a joint heir of a mighty and glorious heritage of honor and responsibility."

It was in this spirit and to voice the better sentiment of the South, that Lanier eagerly responded to the invitation to write the Centennial poems. He had fought with valor in the Confederate armies, hoping to the last that they would be victorious. He had suffered all the poverty and humiliation of reconstruction days, but he had risen out of sectionalism into nationalism. It is a striking fact that the two poets who are the least sectional of all American poets — for even Lowell never saw Southern life and Southern problems from a national point of view — were Walt Whitman and Lanier, the only two poets of first importance who took part in the Civil War. It is also significant, that in Lanier's "Psalm of the West" we have a Southerner chanting the glory of freedom, without any chance of having the slavery of a race to make the boast a paradox.

"Corn," "The Symphony," and the "Psalm of the West," with a few shorter poems, were published in a volume in the fall of 1876 (the volume bore the date 1877, however). Reserving the discussion of the merits of the volume for a future chapter, I wish now to give some idea of Lanier's widening acquaintance with men of culture and of letters. The first man of prominence to herald him as a new poet was, as has been seen, Mr. Gibson Peacock. The correspondence between them is well known to all students of Lanier.[1] Mr. Peacock "had read widely the best English literature, was familiar with the modern languages, had traveled far in this country and in Europe, and had cultivated himself not less in dramatic criticism than in books." He brought to Lanier financial aid at critical times in his life ; but more than that, his home in Philadelphia was as a second home to the poet in those years before he had settled in Baltimore, when, as he wrote Hayne, he was "as homeless as the ghost of Judas Iscariot." Mrs. Peacock — a good linguist, a highly skilled musician, and withal a most magnetic personality — joined with her husband in his hearty friendship for the newly discovered poet. She was the daughter of the Marquis de la Figanière, Portuguese minister to this country. In their home were entertained all the first-rate artistic people who came to Philadelphia, such as Salvini, Charlotte Cushman, Bayard Taylor, and others. It was a home in which music and literature were highly honored, and here Lanier met some of the most interesting people then living in Philadelphia, such as John Foster Kirk, editor

[1] See *Letters.*

of " Lippincott's Magazine," Charles Heber
Clarke — " big, heartsome, ' Max Adeler ' " —
and others.

Soon after meeting Mr. Peacock and his wife,
Lanier was sought out by Charlotte Cushman on
one of her trips to Baltimore. She had been
much interested in reading " Corn," and was so
attracted by the personality of the author (as he
was by her), that an intimate friendship sprang
up between them, growing in intensity until her
death, February 18, 1876. She had but recently
been greeted with a great ovation in New York
city, at a meeting in which Joseph Jefferson had
represented the stage and Bryant and Stoddard
the realm of letters. The ovation was repeated
in the cities of Boston and Philadelphia.
" Though coming into the circle of her friendships during the latter years of her life, when
she had become famous throughout the English-
speaking world, Lanier won for himself there a
warm and high place," says her biographer.
There was much to attract the two to each other.
Both had the highest ideals of their art; for to
Miss Cushman as to Lanier, art was a sacred
thing. " I know," she said, " He does not fail to
set me his work to do and help me to do it and
help others to help me." Furthermore, they were
both sufferers from an incurable malady, and
both victors over it in a certain serene spirit

which transcended suffering. Her words are
paralleled by many of Lanier's: " I know my
enemy; he is ever before me and he must con-
quer, but I cannot give up to him; I laugh in
his face and try to be jolly — and I am! I
declare I am even when he presses me hardest."
She talked much with him of the great men she
had known and discussed with him the ideals of
art.

Lanier threw himself into this friendship with
characteristic ardor. He gave her the manuscript
copies of his poems and dedicated the first volume
to her, greeting her as " Art's artist, Love's
dear woman, Fame's good queen." During 1875
he wrote many letters to her, letters full of chivalry and love and humility. Some of these tell
the story of his life during the months of 1875
so well, and are at the same time so characteristic,
that I quote : —

BRUNSWICK, GA., June 17, 1875.

It is only seldom, dear Miss Cushman, that I
can bring myself to such a point of daring as to
ask that you will stretch out your tired arms
merely to take one of my little roses, — you whose
hands are already filled with the best flowers this
world can grow.

Does she not (I say to myself) find them
under her feet and wear them about her brows;

may she not walk on them by day and lie on them by night, nay, does not her life stand rooted in men's regard like one pistil in a great lily?

But sometimes I really cannot help making love to you, just for one little intense minute; there is a certain Communistic temper always adhering in true love which *will* occasionally break out and behead all the Royal Proprieties and hang Law to the first lamp-post : it is even now so, my heart is a little '93, *aux armes !* Where is this minister that imprisons us, away from our friends, in the Bastile of Separation, let him die, — and as for Silence, that luxurious tyrant that collects all the dead for his taxes, behold, I am even now pricking him to a terrible death with the point of this good pen.

When one is in a state of insurrection, one makes demands : mine is that you write me, dear friend, if you are quite recovered from the fatigues of Baltimore and of Boston, and if you have not nourished yourself to new strength in feeding upon the honeys the people brought you there so freely.

.   .   .   .

Copies of " The Symphony " have been ordered sent to you and Miss Stebbins, and I have the *MS.* copy which you desired, ready to transmit to you. You will be glad to know that " The Symphony " has met with favor. The " Power of

Prayer " in " Scribner's " for June — although the
editor cruelly mutilated the dialect in some places,
turning, for instance, " Marster " (which is pure
Alabama negro) into Mah'sr (which is only Dan
Bryant negro, and does not exist in real life) —
has gone all over the land, and reappears before
my eyes in frequent heart-breaking yet comical
disguises of misprints and disfigurements. Tell
me ; *ought* one to be a little ashamed of writing
a dialect poem, — as at least one newspaper has
hinted ? And did Robert Burns prove himself
no poet by writing mostly in dialect ? And is
Tennyson's " Death of the North Country Farmer " — certainly one of the very strongest things
he ever wrote — not a poem, really ?

Mr. Peacock's friendship, in the matter of
" The Symphony," as indeed in all others, has
been wonderful, a thing too fine to speak of in
prose.

To-morrow I go to Savannah, and hope to find
there a letter from Miss Stebbins. Tell me of
her, when you write : and tell *her*, from me, how
truly and faithfully I am her and

Your friend,

SIDNEY LANIER.

PHILADELPHIA, PA., July 31, 1875.

It was so good of you, my dear friend, to write
me in the midst of your suffering, that it amounts

to a translation of pain into something beautiful; and with this thought I console myself for the fear lest your exertion may have caused you some pang that might have been spared.

I long to hear from you; though Miss Stebbins's letter brought me a good account from your physician about you. If tender wishes were but medicinal, if fervent aspirations could but cure, if my daily upward breathings in your behalf were but as powerful as they are earnest, — how perfect would be your state!

I have latterly been a shuttlecock betwixt two big battledores — New York and Florida. I scarcely dare to recall how many times I have been to and fro these two States in the last six weeks. It has been just move on, all the time: car dust, cinders, the fumes of hot axle grease, these have been my portion; and between them I have almost felt sometimes as if my soul would be asphyxiated. But I now cease to wander for a month, with inexpressible delight. To-morrow I leave here for Brooklyn, where I will be engaged in hard labor for a month, namely, in finishing up the Florida book. . . .

I am very glad to find my " Symphony " copied in full in Dwight's "Journal of Music:" and I am sure you will care to know that the poem has found great favor in all parts of the land. I have the keenest desire to see some English judg-

ment on this poem; but not the least idea how
to compass that end. Can you make me any suggestion in that behalf?

I am full curious to hear you talk about
Tennyson's " Queen Mary." Nothing could be
more astonishing than the methods of treatment
with which this production has been disposed of,
in the few criticisms I have seen upon it. One
critic declared that it was a good poem but no
drama; another avers decidedly that it is a fine
drama, but not a poem; while the " Nation " man
thinks that it is neither a poem nor a drama,
but a sort of didactic narrative intended to be in
the first place British, and, in the second place,
a warning against the advancing powers of the
Catholic Church. There is but a solitary thread
of judgment in common among these criticisms.

I cannot tell you with how much delight I
read the account of Sidney Dobell, nor with
how much loving recognition I took into my
heart all the extracts from his poems given in
the review. I am going to read all his poems
when my little holiday comes, I hope in September, and I will send you then some organized and critical thanks for having introduced
me to so noble and beautiful a soul. . . .

As for you, my dear Queen Catherine, may
this velvety night be spread under your feet even
as Raleigh's cloak was spread for *his* queen's, so

that you may walk dry shod as to all pain over
to the morning, — prays

> Your faithful   SIDNEY LANIER.

I did not dream, my dear friend, of giving you
anything in the least approaching the nature of
a worry, — in asking you for a suggestion as to
the best method of piercing the British hearts
of oak; and you must not " think about it " as
you declare you are going to do — for a single
minute. Indeed, I had, in mentioning it to you,
no more definite idea in my head than that perhaps you might know somebody who knew somebody that knew somebody that . . . etc., etc., *ad
infinitum* . . . that might . . . and then my idea
of what the somebody was to do, completely faded
into vague nothing.

It isn't *worth* thinking about, to you; and
I have not the least doubt that what I want will
finally come, in just such measure as I shall
deserve.

The publishers have limited me in time so
rigorously, *quoad* the Florida book, that I will
have to work night and day to get it ready. I
do not now see the least chance for a single day
to devote to my own devices before the fifth or
sixth of September.

And I do *so* long to see you and Miss Stebbins!

Out of the sombre depths of a bottomless sea of Florida statistics in which I am at this present floundering, pray accept, my liege Queen, in art as in friendliness, all such loyal messages and fair reports compacted of love, as may come from so dull a waste of waters; graciously resting in your mind upon nothing therein save the true faithful allegiance of your humble knight and subject,   SIDNEY L.

In November, 1875, he visited her for a week at the Parker House in Boston. Though she was at that time critically ill, she was "fairly overflowing with all manner of tender and bright and witty sayings." "Each day," he wrote, "was crowded with pleasant things which she and her numerous friends had prepared for me." On this visit to Boston Lanier spent two "delightful afternoons" with Lowell and Longfellow. Of this visit Lowell afterwards wrote President Gilman : "He was not only a man of genius with a rare gift for the happy word, but had in him qualities that won affection and commanded respect. I had the pleasure of seeing him but once, when he called on me 'in more gladsome days,' at Elmwood, but the image of his shining presence is among the friendliest in my memory."

66 Centre St.
Baltimore, Md.
Dec. 30th, 8/5.

If this New Year that approaches
you (more happy than I, who
cannot) did but know you as well
as I (more happy than he, who does
not) he would strew his days
about you even as white apple-blossoms
and his nights as blue-black heartsease;
for then he should be your true faithful-
erring lover — as am I — and
should desire — as I do — that the
general pelting of Time might
become to you only a tender rain
of such flowers as foretell fruit

and of such as make tranquil beds

But though I cannot teach this same New Year to be the servant of my fair wishes, I can persuade him to be the bearer of them ' and I trust he and these words will come to you together; giving you such report, and so freshly from my heart, as shall confirm to you that my message, though greatly briefer than my love, is yet greatly longer than I would the interval were, which stands betwixt you and your often-longing

Lanier returned from Boston and on New Year's day sent a greeting to Miss Cushman. It is quoted as an illustration of Lanier's considerate regard for his friends, which expressed itself in many delicate ways, especially on anniversaries and special seasons of the year. It is an Elizabethan sonnet in prose: —

If this New Year that approaches you (more happy than I, who cannot) did but know you as well as I (more happy than he, who does not) he would strew his days about you even as white apple-blossoms and his nights as blue-black heart's-ease; for then he should be your true faithful-serving lover — as am I — and should desire — as I do — that the general pelting of time might become to you only a tender rain of such flowers as foretell fruit and of such as make tranquil beds.

But though I cannot teach this same New Year to be the servant of my fair wishes, I can persuade him to be the bearer of them; and I trust he and these words will come to you together; giving you such report, and so freshly from my heart, as shall confirm to you that my message, though greatly briefer than my love, is yet greatly longer than I would the interval were, which stands betwixt you and your often-longing,   S. L.

Another friend that Mr. Peacock interested in
Lanier was Bayard Taylor, who was the means
of bringing the poet into the world of letters, and
became one of the most inspiring influences in his
life. Taylor had been a very prominent figure
in the literary world for over twenty-five years,
as author, translator, traveller, diplomatist, and
lecturer. To meet him was like the fulfillment
of a dream to a man who had lived all his life
outside of literary circles, and Taylor's encouraging words to Lanier were "as inspiriting as
those from a strong swimmer whom one perceives
far ahead, advancing calmly and swiftly."
Taylor, on the other hand, was glad to extend the
young poet's acquaintance among those whom
he had a right to know. Through him Lanier
attended the Goethe celebration, August 28,
1875, and was admitted to the Century Club, of
which Bryant was at that time president, and
where Taylor, Stoddard, Stedman, and "many
other good fellows" frequently met. What this
meant to Lanier is shown in the following quotation : —

"As to pen and ink, and all toil, I 've been
almost suppressed by continued illness. I can't
tell you how much I sigh for some quiet evenings
at the Century, where I might hear some of you
talk about the matters I love, or merely sit and
think in the atmosphere of the thinkers. I fancy

one can almost come to know the dead thinkers too well : a certain mournfulness of longing seems sometimes to peer out from behind one's joy in one's Shakespeare and one's Chaucer, — a sort of physical protest and yearning of the living eye for its like. Perhaps one's friendship with the dead poets comes indeed to acquire something of the quality of worship, through the very mystery which withdraws them from us and which allows no more messages from them, cry how we will, after that sudden and perilous Stoppage. I hope those are not illegitimate moods in which one sometimes desires to surround one's self with a companionship less awful, and would rather have a friend than a god." [1]

Mr. Stedman has recorded his impression of Lanier as he met him at Bayard Taylor's : " I saw him more than once in the study of our lamented Deucalion, — the host so buoyant and sympathetic, the Southerner nervous and eager, with dark hair and silken beard, features delicately moulded, pallid complexion, and hands of the slender, white, artistic type." The friendship between Lanier and Taylor was no less cherished by the older poet. He rejoiced to recognize in Lanier " a new, *true* poet — such a poet as I believe you to be — the genuine poetic nature, temperament, and *morale*." He was heartily glad

[1] *Letters*, p. 171.

to welcome him into the fellowship of authors.
He gave him some valuable criticism as to the
details of his work, and encouraged him by showing him that the struggle through which he was
passing was identical with his own. He, too, had
to resort to pot-boiling and hack work of all kinds,
and he had also been severely criticised by the
same men who now criticised Lanier. So he closed
many of his letters with the inspiriting words:
"Be of good cheer! On! be bold!" The friendship which began as a literary friendship soon
developed on Taylor's part, as well as Lanier's,
into one of deep personal regard. Taylor recognized, as did every other man who came in personal touch with Lanier, the charm and the
fineness of his personality.

By the summer of 1876 Lanier had thus established himself as a promising man of letters.
He had not only written poetry that had attracted attention, but he had found a place among
a group of artists who recognized the value of his
work and the charm of his personality. When
Charlotte Cushman died, he had the promise that
he would be employed by her family to write
her life. Upon the basis of this promise he
brought his family North, and they settled down
at Chadd's Ford, Pennsylvania. Soon afterwards,
however, he received the disappointing news that
Miss Stebbins, on account of ill health, could

not fulfill her part of the contract, namely, to go over the correspondence of Miss Cushman. This was a severe blow to him, and probably had something to do with his breakdown in health. He spent several weeks at Mr. Peacock's in Philadelphia, attended by the best physicians in the city. He was planning to go back to Baltimore to resume his place in the orchestra, when he was told that he must go at once to Florida if he wished to save his life. He went, attended by his wife, and they spent the winter there and the spring in Brunswick and Macon. The letters written by him to Mr. Peacock and Bayard Taylor are among the best he ever wrote, full as they are of sunshine and hope. A few extracts are given : [1] —

"I have found a shaggy gray mare upon whose back I thrid the great pine forests daily, much to my delight. Nothing seems so restorative to me as a good gallop."

"What would I not give to transport you from your frozen sorrows instantly into the midst of the green leaves, the gold oranges, the glitter of great and tranquil waters, the liberal friendship of the sun, the heavenly conversation of robins and mocking-birds and larks, which fill my days with delight!"

"In truth I 'bubble song' continually during

[1] *Letters* passim.

these heavenly days, and it is as hard to keep
me from the pen as a toper from his tipple."

" I have at command a springy mare, with
ankles like a Spanish girl, upon whose back I go
darting through the green overgrown woodpaths,
like a thrasher about his thicket. The whole air
feels full of fecundity: as I ride I am like one
of those insects that are fertilized on the wing, —
every leaf that I brush against breeds a poem.
God help the world when this now-hatching
brood of my Ephemeræ shall take flight and
darken the air."

" I long to be steadily writing again. I am
taken with a poem pretty nearly every day, and
have to content myself with making a note of its
train of thought on the back of whatever letter
is in my coat-pocket. I don't write it out, because I find my poetry now wholly unsatisfactory
in consequence of a certain haunting impatience
which has its root in the straining uncertainty
of my daily affairs ; and I am trying with all my
might to put off composition of all sorts until
some approach to the certainty of next week's
dinner shall remove this remnant of haste, and
leave me that repose which ought to fill the
artist's firmament while he is creating."

They returned to the North in June and spent
another summer at Chadd's Ford, — a place
of great natural beauty. " As for me," says

Lanier, "all this loveliness of wood, earth, and water makes me feel as if I could do the whole Universe into poetry; but I don't want to write anything large for a year or so. And thus I content myself with throwing off a sort of spray of little songs, whereof the magazines now have several."

Notwithstanding his illness, then, the year ending with September, 1877, was one of marked productivity. He wrote "Waving of the Corn," "Under the Cedarcroft Chestnut," "From the Flats," "The Mocking-Bird," "Tampa Robins," "The Bee," "A Florida Sunday," "The Stirrup-Cup," "To Beethoven," "The Dove," "The Song of the Chattahoochee," and "An Evening Song." He was in a fair way to realize his ambition with regard to poetry. Again, however, he was to be deflected from his course, but at the same time to find "fresh woods and pastures new."

CHAPTER VIII

STUDENT AND TEACHER OF ENGLISH
LITERATURE

WHEN Lanier returned from Florida he tried
to get various positions which might enable him
to secure a livelihood. A lectureship at Johns
Hopkins University, — about which President
Gilman had talked with him in 1876 — a libra-
rian's position in the Peabody Library, and a
place in some of the departments of the government in Washington, — all these were sought for
in vain. One of the saddest commentaries on
the condition of political life in the seventies is
that Lanier was not able to secure even a clerk-
ship in any department. The days of civil service
reform and the time when a commissioner of
civil service would urge the application for government positions by Southern men had not yet
come. "Inasmuch," Lanier says in a letter to
Mr. Gibson Peacock, June 13, 1877, "as I
had never been a party man of any sort, I did
not see with what grace I could ask any appointment; and furthermore I could not see it
to be delicate, on general principles, for me to

make *personal* application for any particular office. . . . My name has been mentioned to Mr. Sherman (and to Mr. Evarts, I believe) by quite cordially disposed persons. But I do not think any formal application has been entered, — though I do not know. I *hope* not ; for then the reporters will get hold of it, and I scarcely know what I should do if I could see my name figuring alongside of Jack Brown's and Foster Blodgett's and the others of my native State." [1] It was the same year in which Bayard Taylor was nominated as minister to Germany and Lowell as minister to Spain, but Lanier could not obtain a consulate to France or even the humblest position, " seventy-five dollars a month and the like," in any department in Washington.

Under these circumstances he wrote what are perhaps the most pathetic words in all his letters. " Altogether," he says, " it seems as if there wasn't any place for me in this world, and if it were not for May I should certainly quit it, in mortification at being so useless." [2] He did not remain in this mood long, however. He settled in Baltimore with his family in November, 1877, in four rooms arranged somewhat as a French flat, and a little later in a cottage, about which he writes enthusiastically to his friends. There is no better illustration of his playfulness and

---

[1] *Letters*, p. 43.   [2] *Letters*, p. 46.

his ability to get the most out of everything than his letter to Gibson Peacock : —

33 DENMEAD ST., BALTIMORE, MD.,
January 6, 1878.

The painters, the whitewashers, the plumbers, the locksmiths, the carpenters, the gas-fitters, the stove-put-up-ers, the carmen, the piano-movers, the carpet-layers, — all these have I seen, bargained with, reproached for bad jobs, and finally paid off : I have also coaxed my landlord into all manner of outlays for damp walls, cold bath-rooms, and other like matters : I have furthermore bought at least three hundred and twenty-seven household utensils which suddenly came to be absolutely necessary to our existence : I have moreover hired a colored gentlewoman who is willing to wear out my carpets, burn out my range, freeze out my water-pipes, and be generally useful : I have also moved my family into our new home, have had a Xmas tree for the youngsters, have looked up a cheap school for Harry and Sidney, have discharged my daily duties as first flute of the Peabody Orchestra, have written a couple of poems and part of an essay on Beethoven and Bismarck, have accomplished at least a hundred thousand miscellaneous necessary nothings, — and have *not*, in consequence of the aforesaid, sent to you and my dear

Maria the loving greetings whereof my heart has been full during the whole season. Maria's cards were duly distributed, and we were all touched with her charming little remembrances. With how much pleasure do I look forward to the time when I may kiss her hand in my own house! We are in a state of supreme content with our new home: it really seems to me as incredible that myriads of people have been living in their own homes heretofore as to the young couple with a first baby it seems impossible that a great many other couples have had similar prodigies. It is simply too delightful. Good heavens, how I wish that the whole world had a Home!

I confess I *am* a little nervous about the gas-bills, which must come in, in the course of time; and there are the water-rates, and several sorts of imposts and taxes: but then, the dignity of being liable for such things (!) is a very supporting consideration. No man is a Bohemian who has to pay water-rates and a street-tax. Every day when I sit down in my dining-room — *my* dining-room! — I find the wish growing stronger that each poor soul in Baltimore, whether saint or sinner, could come and dine with me. How I would carve out the merry thoughts for the old hags! How I would stuff the big wall-eyed rascals till their rags ripped again! There was a knight of old times who built the dining-hall of his castle

across the highway, so that every wayfarer must
perforce pass through : there the traveler, rich
or poor, found always a trencher and wherewithal
to fill it. Three times a day, in my own chair at
my own table, do I envy that knight and wish
that I might do as he did.[1]

He was soon to find another joy in the study
of Old and Middle English literature, which he
entered upon with unbounded zest and energy.
As has been seen in previous chapters, Lanier
had been all his life a reader of the best books.
Before he came to Baltimore to live he had
impressed Paul Hamilton Hayne with his un-
usually thorough knowledge of Chaucer and the
Elizabethan poets. He was also familiar with
modern English literature. Now, however, he
was to begin the study of literature in a systematic and more scholarly way. A distinct advance in his intellectual life must, therefore, be
dated from the winter of 1877–78, when he began
to study English with the aid of the Peabody
Library.

For purposes of research this library was,
during Lanier's lifetime, one of the best in
America. Mr. Peabody indicated its character
when he said, in his announcement of the gift,
that it was to be " well furnished in every de-

---

[1] *Letters,* p. 49.

partment of knowledge, to be for the free use
of all persons who may desire to consult it, to
satisfy the researches of students who may be
engaged in the pursuit of knowledge not ordi-
narily obtainable in the private libraries of the
country." It was modeled on the plan of the
British Museum, and he was anxious to "engraft
in Baltimore the offshoots of the highest culture
obtainable in the great capitals of Europe." In
accordance with his idea, the provost, Dr. Morison, had in the selection of the library consulted
specialists in the leading universities of the country. Besides containing the scientific journals in
the various departments of human learning, it
was especially rich in the publications of the
Early English Text Society, the Chaucer Society,
the Percy Society, and in the reprints of Elizabethan literature made by Alexander B. Grosart
and other English scholars. There had been
some complaint on the part of the citizens of
Baltimore that the library could not be of more
general use. To meet this Dr. Morison said in
1871 : "We cannot create scholars or readers
to use our library, but we can make a collection
of books which all scholars will appreciate, when
they shall appear among us as they surely will
some day." This prophecy was fulfilled when
Johns Hopkins University was established in
1876. In addition to the excellent collection of

books there was a carefully prepared catalogue, which made the investigator's task much easier.

To the Peabody thus furnished and arranged, Lanier came with an eagerness of mind that few men have had. Writing to J. F. Kirk, August 24, 1878, he said, speaking of an edition of Elizabethan sonnets which he was preparing : " I have found the Peabody Library here a rich mine in the collection of material for my book, especially as affording sources for the presentation of the anonymous poems in the early collections which are very interesting." He always expressed himself as grateful that he could find his working material so easily accessible.

Of his habits of study one of the assistant librarians says : " He usually came in the morning, occupying the same seat at the end of the table, where he worked until lunch time, so absorbed with his studies that he scarcely ever raised his eyes to notice anything around him. During the winters that he was a member of the Peabody Orchestra he came back in the afternoons when the rehearsals were held, bringing his flute with him, and continued his studies until it was time to go into the rehearsal. He continued in this way until his increasing weakness prevented him from leaving home, when he would write notes to the desk attendants asking them to verify some reference, or copy some extract for him, and frequently his wife would come to the library to do the copying for him." [1]

This library was Lanier's university. While other Southerners were finding their way to German universities, he was training himself in the methods and ideals of the modern scholar. The dream of his college days was being fulfilled. He lacked the patient and careful training of men who have a lifetime to devote to some special field of work. He could not in the short time at his disposal explore the fields of learning which he entered. Into those two or three years of study and research, however, were crowded results and attainments that many less gifted men, working with less prodigious zest and power, do not reach in a decade.

Writing to Bayard Taylor, October 20, 1878, he said: " Indeed, I have been so buried in study for the past six months that I know not news nor gossip of any kind. Such days and nights of glory as I have had! I have been studying Early English, Middle English, and Elizabethan poetry, from Beowulf to Ben Jonson : and the world seems twice as large." [2] No sooner had he begun this work than he desired to communicate to others his own pleasure in English literature. In March, 1878, he began a series of lectures at the residence of Mrs. Edgworth Bird, who had

[1] Letter of Mr. John Park to the author. [2] *Letters*, p. 214.

welcomed him to her home when he first came
to Baltimore. These lectures on Elizabethan
poetry were attended by many of the most prominent men and women of the city. The following
winter Lanier arranged for a series of lectures
at the Peabody Institute. " In the spring of
1878," says one of his friends, " I was speaking
of the desultory study which women so often do
and of how much better it would be if all this
energy could be directed to some definite end.
He said : ' That is just what I am purposing.
Next winter I am going to have a Shakespearean
revival for women,' and he then proceeded to
tell me of the prospective lectures." He had
become imbued with the idea that much might
be done in the way of establishing " Schools
for Grown People " in all the leading cities of
America. He writes to Gibson Peacock : —

180 St. Paul St., Baltimore, Md.,
November 5, 1878.

I have been " allowing " — as the Southern negroes say — that I would write you, for the last
two weeks ; but I had a good deal to say, and
have n't had time to say it.

During my studies for the last six or eight
months a thought which was at first vague has
slowly crystallized into a purpose, of quite de-
cisive aim. The lectures which I was invited to

deliver last winter before a private class met
with such an enthusiastic reception as to set me
thinking very seriously of the evident delight
with which grown people found themselves receiving systematic instruction in a definite study.
This again put me upon reviewing the whole
business of Lecturing which has risen to such
proportions in our country, but which, every one
must feel, has now reached its climax and must
soon give way — like all things — to something
better. The fault of the lecture system as at
present conducted — a fault which must finally
prove fatal to it — is that it is too fragmentary,
and presents too fragmentary a mass — *indigesta
moles* — of facts before the hearers. Now if,
instead of such a series as that of the popular
Star Course (for instance) in Philadelphia, a
scheme of lectures should be arranged which
would amount to the *systematic presentation* of
a *given subject*, then the audience would receive
a substantial benefit, and would carry away some
genuine possession at the end of the course. The
subject thus systematically presented might be
either scientific (as Botany, for example, or Biology popularized, and the like) or domestic
(as detailed in the accompanying printed extract
under the " Household " School) or artistic or
literary.

This stage of the investigation put me to

thinking of schools for grown people. Men and women leave college nowadays just at the time when they are really prepared to study with effect. There is indeed a vague notion of this abroad, but it remains vague. Any intelligent grown man or woman readily admits that it would be well — indeed, many whom I have met sincerely desire — to pursue some regular course of thought; but there is no guidance, no organized means of any sort, by which people engaged in ordinary avocations can accomplish such an aim.

Here, then, seems to be, first, a universal admission of the usefulness of organized intellectual pursuit for business people; secondly, an underlying desire for it by many of the people themselves; and thirdly, an existing institution (the lecture system) which, if the idea were once started, would quickly adapt itself to the new conditions. In short, the present miscellaneous lecture courses ought to die and be born again as *Schools for Grown People.*

It was with the hope of effecting at least the beginning *of* a beginning of such a movement that I got up the " Shakespeare Course " in Baltimore. I wished to show, to such a class as I could assemble, how much more genuine profit there would be in studying *at first hand*, under the guidance of an enthusiastic interpreter, the writers and conditions of a particular epoch (for instance) than in reading any amount of commentary or in hearing any number of miscellaneous lectures on subjects which range from Palestine to Pottery in the course of a week. With this view I arranged my own part of the Shakespeare course so as to include a quite thorough presentation of the whole *science* of poetry as preparatory to a serious and profitable study of some of the greatest singers in our language.[1]

In accordance with this idea he drew up a scheme for four independent series of class lectures, directed particularly to the systematic guidance of persons — especially ladies — who wished to extend the scope of their culture. There were to be schools of (1) English Literature, (2) the Household, (3) Natural Science, and (4) Art. Thirty lectures were to be given in each school, he to give those on English Literature. He hoped that he would be able to arrange for such series in Washington, Philadelphia, and Southern cities. This scheme is a striking anticipation of popular lectures that have been given in New York city during the past few years, as well as of the University Extension lectures since established at the University of Chicago, the University of Pennsylvania, and other American universities.

[1] *Letters*, p. 53.

The only part of the scheme that took shape was the Shakespeare course planned for the Peabody Institute. In addition to twenty-four lectures by Lanier, two lectures were to be given by Prof. B. L. Gildersleeve, — "one on the Timon of Lucian, compared with Timon of Shakespeare, and one on Macbeth and Agamemnon; two on the State of Natural Science in Shakespeare's Time, by Prof. Ira Remsen; two on Religion in Shakespeare's Time, by Dr. H. B. Adams; two readings from Marlowe's Faust and three lectures on the Mystery Plays as illustrated by the Oberammergau Passion Play, by Prof. E. G. Daves; and three lectures on the Early English Comedy as illustrated by Gammer Gurton's Needle and Ralph Royster Doyster, by Col. Richard M. Johnston."

Of these only Lanier's lectures were given, and they did not prove to be a financial success, although they accomplished much good in Baltimore. Published as they have been recently,[1] they are among the most valuable aids in the study of Lanier's personality and of his attitude to literature. It must be borne in mind that they were not written for publication, nor for an academic audience, and that the only proper way to estimate them is to compare them with

[1] *Shakspere and His Forerunners.* Doubleday, Page & Co., 1903.

lectures of a similar kind, — Lowell's Lowell Institute lectures, for instance. Viewed from this standpoint, one cannot but marvel at the carefulness with which Lanier prepared his lectures, and the vital interest he took in work which has been disagreeable to men of similar temperament. Any one who expects to find in them contributions to present day knowledge of the subjects touched upon will be disappointed; but no one can read them without enjoying the poet's naïve enthusiasm and his clear insight into things that many a plodder never sees, nor can he fail to be impressed with the modernness of his mind. He must have been a successful teacher, — he uses every effort to fix the attention of his hearers, he summarizes frequently, illustrates, vitalizes his subject.

There is evident throughout these lectures the most enthusiastic appreciation of literature and of its place in the life of the world. Few men ever enjoyed reading more than Lanier. He knew something of Stevenson's joy of being "rapt clean out of himself by a book," — the process was "absorbing and voluptuous." And this enthusiasm he shared with all his hearers. After much criticism of the scientific type by followers of Arnold and Brunetière, after many class-room lectures and recitations, in which the spiritual value of literature has been lost sight

of, it is altogether refreshing to read the almost
childlike expressions of Lanier. One feels often
that the worship of what he calls his "sweet
masters" is overdone, and that he praises far
too highly some obscure sonneteer; but there is
in his work the spirit of the romantic critic —
the zest of Charles Lamb and Hazlitt for the old
masters. Lowell, speaking of a period in his
own life when he was delivering his early lectures at Lowell Institute, said: "Then I was at
the period in life when thoughts rose in covies,
. . . a period of life when it does n't seem as if
everything has been said; when a man overesti-
mates the value of what specially interests himself, . . . when he conceives himself a mission-
ary, and is persuaded that he is saving his
fellows from the perdition of their souls if he
convert them from belief in some æsthetic heresy.
That is the mood of mind in which one may read
lectures with some assurance of success. . . .
This is the pleasant peril of enthusiasm." There
could not be a better description of Lanier's lectures. Longfellow, referring to some lectures on
Dante which he had repeated often, said: "It
is become an old story to me. I am tired."
Lanier knew nothing of this *ennui*. He fretted
at times over the fact that he had to give to
work of this kind the time he might have given
to his poetry, but there is not in his lectures a

single note of weariness; there is always the freshness and exuberance of youth, the joy of discovery, of interpretation, of illuminating comment.

He had the power of making even the older English literature vital to a popular audience. An Anglo-Saxon poem was not to him primarily material for the study of philology, although he now and then tried to interest his hearers in the etymology of words — it was a revelation of the life of a race in its childhood. While he lost in technical precision, he gave the listener a real grip on some old poem by which he could always remember it and relate it to other things. A few pages on " Beowulf," for instance, presenting some specially striking scenes therefrom in a translation that in rhythm and substance preserves the spirit of the original, would incite the members of his audience to at least a literary study of the Anglo-Saxon epic. By contrasting " The Address of the Soul to the Dead Body " with " Hamlet," he gave his hearers some clue to its interpretation — he related it to an elementary religious mood.

Is not this passage calculated to make one realize the real meaning of " Beowulf," — especially when accompanied by admirable translations?

" To our old ancestors there were many times

when Nature must have seemed a true Grendel's mother, a veritable hag, mindful of mischief; and these monsters are not silly inventions, — they are true types, ideals, removed very far, if you please, yet born of the old struggle of man against the wild beast for his meat, against the stern earth for his bread, against the cold that cracks his skin and wracks his bones, against the wind that whirls his ship over in the sea, the wave that drowns him, the lightning that consumes him. . . .

"And so, as I said, there is to me an indescribable pathos in these sombre pictures of Nature in our old Beowulf here, — these drear marshes, these monster-haunted meres, that boil with blood and foam with tempests, these fast-rooted, joyless woods that overlean the waters, these enormous, nameless beasts that lie along on promontories all day and wreak vengeance on ships at night — have you not seen them, headlands running out into the sea like great beasts with their forepaws extended? And is it not a huge Gothic picture of the wind rushing down the windy nesse . . . in the evening, and whelming the frail ships of the old Dane, the old Jute and Frisian and Saxon, in the sea? All these, I say, are mere outcroppings of the rude war which was not yet ended against Nature, traces of a time when Nature was still a savage Mother of Grendel, tearing and devouring the sons of men." [1]

Lanier believed strongly that the early English poems ought to be taught in schools and colleges. The following passage does not sound as revolutionary now as it did in 1879 : —

"Surely it is time our popular culture were cited into the presence of the Fathers. That we have forgotten their works is in itself matter of mere impiety which many practical persons would consider themselves entitled to dismiss as a purely sentimental crime; but ignorance of their ways goes to the very root of growth.

"I count it a circumstance so wonderful as to merit some preliminary setting forth here, that with regard to the first seven hundred years of our poetry we English-speaking people appear never to have confirmed ourselves unto ourselves. While we often please our vanity with remarking the outcrop of Anglo-Saxon blood in our modern physical achievements, there is certainly little in our present art of words to show a literary lineage running back to the same ancestry. Of course it is always admitted that there *was* an English poetry as old to Chaucer as Chaucer is to us; but it is admitted with a certain inclusive and amateur vagueness removing it out of the rank of facts which involve grave and im-

[1] *Shakspere and His Forerunners*, vol. i, p. 55.

portant duties. We can neither deny the fact nor the strangeness of it, that the English poetry written between the time of Aldhelm and Cædmon in the seventh century and that of Chaucer in the fourteenth century has never yet taken its place by the hearths and in the hearts of the people whose strongest prayers are couched in its idioms. It is not found in the tatters of use, on the floors of our children's playrooms; there are no illuminated boy's editions of it; it is not on the booksellers' counters at Christmas; it is not studied in our common schools; it is not printed by our publishers; it does not lie even in the dusty corners of our bookcases; nay, the pious English scholar must actually send to Germany for Grein's Bibliothek in order to get a compact reproduction of the body of Old English poetry.

.   .   .   .

"One will go into few moderately appointed houses in this country without finding a Homer in some form or other; but it is probably far within the truth to say that there are not fifty copies of Beowulf in the United States. Or again, every boy, though far less learned than that erudite young person of Macaulay's, can give some account of the death of Hector; but how many boys — or, not to mince matters, how many men — in America could do more than

stare if asked to relate the death of Byrhtnoth?
Yet Byrhtnoth was a hero of our own England
in the tenth century, whose manful fall is recorded in English words that ring on the soul
like arrows on armor. Why do we not draw in
this poem — and its like — with our mother's
milk? Why have we no nursery songs of Beowulf and the Grendel? Why does not the serious education of every English-speaking boy
commence, as a matter of course, with the Anglo-
Saxon grammar? " [1]

There would come from such study a strengthening of English prose and a deepening of culture. He continues :—

" For the absence of this primal Anglicism
from our modern system goes — as was said —
to the very root of culture. The eternal and im-
measurable significance of that individuality in
thought which flows into idiom in speech becomes
notably less recognized among us. We do not
bring with us out of our childhood the fibre of
idiomatic English which our fathers bequeathed
to us. A boy's English is diluted before it has become strong enough for him to make up his mind
clearly as to the true taste of it. Our literature
needs Anglo-Saxon iron, — there is no ruddiness

[1] *Music and Poetry*, p. 136. This quotation is an expansion
of one in the lectures now under consideration. He evidently
overstates his point, but the passage suggests what the study
of old English meant to Lanier himself.

in its cheeks, and everywhere a clear lack of the red corpuscles."

Lanier was more thoroughly at home in the Elizabethan age, however. He reveled in its myriad-mindedness — its adventures and exploits, its chivalry and romance. The sonnets especially appealed to him, for they abounded in conceits. One of the striking characteristics that he noted in the leading men of that age was the union of strength and tenderness. "All this love-making was manly," he says. "It was then as it is now, that the bravest are the tenderest. . . . Stout and fine Walter Raleigh pushes over to America, quite as ready to sigh a sonnet as to plant a colony. Valorous Philip Sidney, who can write as dainty a sonnet as any lover of them all, can at the same time dazzle the stern eyes of warriors with deeds of manhood before Zütphen and touch their hearts to pity and admiration as he offers the cup of water — himself being grievously wounded and in a rage of thirst — to the dying soldier whose necessity is greater than his. Men's minds in this time were employed with big questions ; the old theory of the universe is just losing its long hold upon the intellect, and people are busy with all space, trying to apprehend the relation of their globe to the solar system. To all this ferment the desperate conflict of the Catholic religion with the new form of faith now coming in adds an element of stern strength ; men are pondering not only the physical relation of the earth to the heavens, but the spiritual relation of the soul to heaven and hell. This is no dandy period." [1]

" And if any one should say there is not time to read these poets," he says in a strain of excessive admiration, " I reply with vehemence that in any wise distribution of your moments, after you have read the Bible and Shakspere, you have no time to read anything until you have read these . . . old artists. They are so noble, so manful, so earnest; they have put into such perfect music that protective tenderness of the rugged man for the delicate woman which throbs all down the muscles of the man's life and turns every deed of strength into a deed of love ; they have set the woman, as woman, upon such adorable heights of worship, and by that act have so immeasurably uplifted the whole plane upon which society moves ; they have given to all earnest men and strong lovers such a dear ritual and litany of chivalric devotion ; they have sung us such a high mass of constancy for our love ; they have enlightened us with such celestial revelation of the possible Eden which the modern Adam and Eve may win back for themselves by faithful and generous affection ; that — I speak it

[1] *Shakspere and His Forerunners*, vol. i, p. 168.

with reverence — they have made another religion of loyal love and have given us a second
Bible of womanhood." [1]

Following his study of the sonnet-writers of
the Elizabethan age, comes a somewhat technical
study of the pronunciation of Shakespeare's time
— a restatement of Ellis's monumental work on
that subject. His discussion of music in Shakespeare's time has already been noticed. He next
tried to reproduce for his class the domestic life
of the age, commenting in full on the sermons,
the plays, the customs of the time. In order to
give unity to this study, he sketches in a somewhat fanciful way the boyhood of Shakespeare in
Stratford and his early manhood in London.
The most important part of the lectures, however, is his discussion of the growth of Shakespeare's mind and art, a study made possible by
recent publications of the New Shakespeare Society. Lanier never wrote any more vigorous or
eloquent prose than these chapters, although it
must be said that he makes too much of the
dramatist's personality as revealed in his plays.
Two passages are quoted to indicate in the first
place the standpoint from which he studied the
plays, and in the second place to show his conception of the moral height attained by Shakespeare
as compared with contemporary dramatists : —

[1] *Shakspere and His Forerunners*, vol. i. p. 7.

" The keenest scholarship, the freest discussion, the widest search for external evidence, the most careful checking of conclusions by the Metrical Tests one after another, have all been applied to establish this general succession in time of these three plays ; [1] and it is not in the least necessary to commit ourselves to the exact years here given in order to feel sure that these three plays represent three perfectly distinct epochs, separated from each other by several years, in Shakspere's spiritual existence. . . .

" In short, the young eye already sees the twist and cross of life, but sees it as in a dream : and those of you who are old enough to look back upon your own young dream of life will recognize instantly that the dream is the only term which represents that unspeakable *seeing* of things, without in the least *realizing* them, which brings about that the youth admits all we tell — we older ones — about life and the future, and, admitting it fully, nevertheless goes on right in the face of it to *act* just as if he knew nothing of it. In short, he sees as in a dream. It is the Dream Period. But here suddenly the dream is done, the real pinches the young dreamer and he awakes. This, too, is typical. Every man remembers the time in his own life, somewhere from near thirty to forty, when the actual oppo-

[1] The *Midsummer Night's Dream, Hamlet,* and *The Tempest.*

sitions of life came out before him and refused
to be danced over and stared him grimly in the
face : God or no God, faith or no faith, death or
no death, honesty or policy, men good or men
evil, the Church holy or the Church a fraud, life
worth living or life not worth living, — this, I
say, is the shock of the real, this is the Hamlet
period in every man's life.

" And finally, — to finish this outline, — just
as the man settles all these questions shocked
upon him by the real, will be his Ideal Period.
If he finds that the proper management of these
grim oppositions of life is by goodness, by humility, by love, by the fatherly care of a Prospero
for his daughter Miranda, by the human tenderness of a Prospero finding all his enemies in his
power and forgiving their bitter injuries and
practicing his art to right the wrongs of men
and to bring all evil beginnings to happy issues,
then his Ideal Period is fitly represented by this
heavenly play, in which, as you recall its plot,
you recognize all these elements. Shakspere has
unquestionably emerged from the cold, paralyz-
ing doubts of Hamlet into the human tenderness
and perfect love and faith of *The Tempest*, a faith
which can look clearly upon all the wretched
crimes and follies of the crew of time, and still
be tender and loving and faithful. In short, he
has learned to manage the Hamlet antagonisms,

to adjust the moral oppositions, with the same artistic sense of proportion with which we saw him managing and adjusting the verse-oppositions and the figure-oppositions." [1]

"Surely the genius which in the heat and struggle of ideal creation has the enormous control and temperance to arrange and adjust in harmonious proportions all these æsthetic antagonisms of verse, surely that is the same genius which in the heat and battle of life will arrange the moral antagonisms with similar self-control and temperance. Surely there is a point of technic to which the merely clever artist may reach, but beyond which he may never go, for lack of moral insight; surely your Robert Greene, your Kit Marlowe, your Tom Nash, clever poets all, may write clever verses and arrange clever dramas; but if we look at their own flippant lives and pitiful deaths and their small ideals in their dramas, and compare them, technic for technic, life for life, morality for morality, with this majestic Shakspere, who starts in a dream, who presently encounters the real, who after a while conquers it to its proper place (for Shakspere, mind you, does not forget the real; he will not be a beggar nor a starveling; we have documents which show how he made money, how he bought land at Stratford; we have Richard

[1] *Shakspere and His Forerunners*, vol. ii, p. 260.

Quincy's letter to 'my lovveinge good frend and contreyman Mr. Wm. Shakspere, deliver thees,' asking the loan of thirty pounds 'uppon Mr. Bushells and my securytee,' showing that Shakspere had money to lend), and finally turns it into the ideal in *The Tempest*; if we compare, I say, Greene, Marlowe, Nash, with Shakspere, surely the latter is a whole heaven above them in the music of his verse, as well as in the temperance and prudence of his life, as well also as in the superb height of his later moral ideals. Surely, in fine, there is a point of mere technic in art beyond which nothing but moral greatness can attain, because it is at this point that the moral range, the religious fervor, the true seership and prophethood of the poet, come in and lift him to higher views of all things." [1]

Lanier frequently indulged in little homilies, — " preachments " Thackeray would call them. They were lectures on life as well as on literature in its more technical sense. Two passages indicate a poet's feeling for nature, especially his love of trees : —

" But besides the phase of Nature-communion which we call physical science, there is the other, artistic phase. Day by day we find that the mystic influence of Nature on our human personality

[1] *Shakspere and His Forerunners*, vol. ii, p. 324.

grows more intense and individual. Who can walk alone in your beautiful Druid Hill Park, among those dear and companionable oaks, without a certain sense of being in the midst of a sweet and noble company of friends ? Who has not shivered, wandering among these trees, with a certain sense that the awful mysteries which the mother earth has brought with her out of the primal times are being sucked up through those tree-roots and poured upon us out of branch and leaf in vague showers of suggestions that have no words in any language ? Who, in some day when life has seemed *too* bitter, when man has seemed too vile, when the world has seemed all old leather and brass, when some new twist of life has seemed to wrench the soul beyond all straightening, — who has not flown, at such a time, to the deep woods, and leaned against a tree, and felt his big arms outspread like the arms of the preacher that teaches and blesses, and slowly absorbed his large influences, and so recovered one's self as to one's fellow-men, and gained repose from the ministrations of the Oak and the Pine ? " [1]

" In the sweet old stories of ascetics who by living pure and simple lives in the woods came to understand the secrets of Nature, the conversation of trees, the talk of birds, do we not

[1] *Shakspere and His Forerunners*, vol. i, p. 72.

find but the shadows of this modern communion with Nature to keep ourselves simple and pure, to cultivate our moral sense up to that point of insight that we see all Nature alive with energy, that we hear the whole earth singing like a flock of birds, yet so that we remember Death with Mr. Darwin, so that nothing is any more commonplace, so that death has its place and life its place, so that even a hasty business walk along the street to pay a bill is a walk in fairyland amidst unutterable wonders as long as the sky is above and the trees in sight, — in other words, to be natural . . . natural in our art, natural in our dress, natural in our behavior, natural in our affections, — is not that a modern consummation of culture? For to him who rightly understands Nature she is even more than Ariel and Ceres to Prospero; she is more than a servant conquered like Caliban, to fetch wood for us: she is a friend and comforter; and to that man the cares of the world are but a fabulous *Midsummer Night's Dream*, to smile at — he is ever in sight of the morning and in hand-reach of God." [1]

The lectures close, as they began, with an estimate of the value of the poet to the world and with a word of greeting to his audience: —

" Just as our little spheres of activity in life

[1] *Shakspere and His Forerunners*, vol. i, p. 73.

surely combine into some greater form or purpose which none of us dream of, and which no
one can see save some unearthly spectator that
stands afar off in space and looks upon the whole
of things, — I was impressed anew with the fact
that it is the poet who must get up to this point
and stand off in thought at the great distance of
the ideal, look upon the complex swarm of purposes as upon these dancing gnats, and find out
for man the final form and purpose of man's life.
In short, — and here I am ending this course
with the idea with which I began it, — in short,
it is the poet who must sit at the centre of things
here, as surely as some great One sits at the
centre of things Yonder, and who must teach us
how to control, with temperance and perfect art
and unforgetfulness of detail, all our oppositions,
so that we may come to say with Aristotle, at
last, that poetry is more philosophical than philosophy and more historical than history.

"Permit me to thank you earnestly for the
patience with which you have listened to many
details that must have been dry to you ; and let
me sincerely hope that, whatever may be your
oppositions in life, whether of the verse kind or
the moral kind, you may pass, like Shakspere,
through these planes of the Dream Period and
the Real Period, until you have reached the ideal
plane from which you clearly see that wherever

Prospero's art and Prospero's love and Prospero's forgiveness of injuries rule in behavior, there a blue sky and a quiet heaven full of sun and stars are shining over every tempest." [1]

One of the things which enabled Lanier to produce the effect that he did in teaching literature was the fact that he was an excellent reader. He had a singularly clear and resonant voice and a power to enter so into the spirit of a work of art that he had no trouble in keeping a large audience thoroughly interested. The following account by one of his hearers, written a short time after his death, gives the effect produced by his readings: —

" Mr. Lanier did not lay claim to any extraordinary power as a reader; indeed, he once, when first requested to instruct a class of ladies in poetic lore, modestly demurred, on the ground of his inability to read aloud. ' I cannot read,' he said simply; ' I have never tried.' All, however, who afterwards heard him read such scenes from Shakespeare as he selected to illustrate his lectures were thrilled by his vivid realization of that great dramatist. His voice, though distinct, was never elevated above a moderate tone; he rarely made use of a gesture; certainly, there

[1] *Shakspere and His Forerunners*, vol. ii, p. 328. I have quoted freely from these lectures because they are in a form not easily accessible to the general reader, and because, more than any other of his prose works, they reveal the inner man.

was no approach to action or to the adaptation of his voice to the varied characters of the play; yet many scenes which I have heard him read, I can hardly believe that I have never seen produced on the stage, so truly and vividly did he succeed in presenting them to my imagination. At the time I used to wonder in what element lay the charm. Partly, of course, in his own profound appreciation of the author's meaning, partly also in his clear and correct emphasis, but most of all in the wonderful word-painting with which, by a few masterly strokes, he placed the whole scene before the mental vision. In theatrical representation, a man with a bush of thorn and lantern must 'present moonshine' and another, with a bit of plaster, the wall which divides Pyramus from his Thisbe; but in Mr. Lanier's readings, a poet's quick imagination brought forth in full perfection all the accessories of the play. When he read, in the Johns Hopkins lecture hall, that scene from 'Pericles' in which Cerimon restores Thaisa's apparently lifeless body to animation, a large audience listened with breathless attention. His graphic comments caused the whole rapidly moving scene to engrave itself on the memory." [1]

Such readings and lectures are treasured in the minds of those who heard them. In addition

[1] Letter of Mrs. Arthur W. Machen to the author.

to his work at the Peabody Institute Lanier
taught in various schools, and so extended his
influence. It is easy to overstate the good he
accomplished, but it is within bounds to say
that his efforts to develop the culture life of the
city bore fruit, and that he has his place among
those who have contributed to the new Baltimore. He shared in all the advantages made possible by the philanthropy of George Peabody
and Johns Hopkins, and in such æsthetic influences as the Allston Art Association and the
Walters collection of French and Spanish pictures. In turn he promoted a love of music and
poetry. The successive invasions of Baltimore
by people from New England, Virginia, and
Georgia had added a cosmopolitan and cultured
society. By a wide circle Lanier was much beloved. His admiration for the city and his ideals
for its future are well expressed in his " Ode to
the Johns Hopkins University : " —

And here, O finer Pallas, long remain, —
Sit on these Maryland hills, and fix thy reign,
And frame a fairer Athens than of yore
    In these blest bounds of Baltimore. . . .

Yea, make all ages native to our time,
    Till thou the freedom of the city grant
    To each most antique habitant
        Of Fame, — . . .

And many peoples call from shore to shore,
The world has bloomed again at Baltimore!

CHAPTER IX

THE Peabody lectures led to the appointment of
Lanier as lecturer in English literature at Johns
Hopkins University. As early as the fall of 1876,
he had written to President Gilman, asking for
a catalogue of the institution. In answer to his
first letter of inquiry, President Gilman, who
had followed with interest his Centennial poem,
and had been from the first an admirer of his
poetry, requested an interview for the purpose
of discussing with him the possibility of identify-
ing him with the University. Lanier had then
talked with him about the advisability of establishing a chair of music and poetry, a plan which
appealed to Dr. Gilman. In a letter to his brother
he writes of this interview: " He invited me to
tea and gave up his whole evening to discussing
ways and means for connecting me officially with
the University." He had been delayed in suggesting the matter to him before by his " ignorance as to whether I had pursued any special
course of study in life." Dr. Gilman recom-
mended to the trustees that Lanier be appointed

to such a chair, and the latter looked forward to
a " speedy termination of his wandering and a
pleasant settlement for a long time." For some
reason, however, the plan did not materialize,
and we find Lanier a year later writing a letter
applying for a fellowship : —

WASHINGTON, D. C., Sept. 26, 1877.

DEAR MR. GILMAN, — From a published report of your very interesting address I learn that
there is now a vacant Fellowship. Would I be
able to discharge the duties of such a position ?

My course of study would be : first, constant
research in the physics of musical tone ; second,
several years' devotion to the acquirement of a
thoroughly scientific *general* view of Mineral-
ogy, Botany, and Comparative Anatomy ; third,
French and German Literature. I fear this may
seem a nondescript and even flighty process ; but
it makes straight towards the final result of all
my present thought, and I am tempted, by your
great kindness, to believe that you would have
confidence enough in me to await whatever development should come of it.

Sincerely yours,

SIDNEY LANIER.

Such a plan of study did not fit in with the
scheme of graduate courses, and so he was not

awarded it. President Gilman had, however, heard with much satisfaction Lanier's lectures at Mrs. Bird's, and had coöperated with him in the series of lectures at the Peabody Institute. Finally, the trustees, convinced of Lanier's scholarship, and conscious of his growing influence in Baltimore, agreed to his appointment as lecturer in English literature, and Dr. Gilman had the rare pleasure of announcing the fact on the poet's thirty-seventh birthday — February 3, 1879. Lanier responded in a letter, indicative at once of the spirit in which he received the appointment and of his high personal regard for the president of the University. No story of Lanier's life would be adequate that did not pay tribute to the uniform kindness and thoughtful consideration of the poet's welfare manifested by Dr. Gilman. He has his place in that inner circle of Lanier's friends who meant much to him in opening up new fields of endeavor, and who after his death zealously promoted his fame.

Lanier occupies a place in the history of Johns Hopkins University that has perhaps not been fully appreciated. His appointment was not a merely nominal one, for he threw himself with zeal and energy into the life of the University. He breathed its atmosphere. He was a personal friend of the president, of nearly every member of the faculty, and of the university officers. He

caught its spirit and grew with it into a real sense
of the ideals of University work. While his poem
written on the fourth anniversary of the opening
of the University, is not one of his best, it indicates the great love that he had for the institution : —

> How tall among her sisters, and how fair, —
> How grave beyond her youth, yet debonair
> As dawn! . . .
> Has she, old Learning's latest daughter, won
> This grace, this stature, and this fruitful fame.

What the University meant to Lanier can be
realized only by those who have noted the eager
spirit with which he responded to every great influence brought into his life, and who realize
what " those early days of unbounded enthusiasm
and unfettered ideality," characteristic of the
newly founded University, meant to the American educational system. Her sister institutions
have in later days gone far beyond Johns Hopkins in equipment and in opportunities for research, but students of American education can
never forget the pioneer work of the University
in the line of graduate study. Fortunately its
benefactor had left a board of trustees absolutely
untrammeled by any condition or reservation,
political, religious, or literary. A body of un-
usually strong men, they were fortunate in securing the services of Daniel Coit Gilman, whose

experience in educational matters had commended itself to the judgment of the four leading university presidents of the country to such an extent that each of them without consulting with the others advised his election. The newly elected president and the trustees were accessible to ideas, and finally decided that the wisest thing that could be done was to make possible what had been previously wanting in American universities, a graduate school with high standards. American professors had studied in German universities and distinguished European scholars had been called to chairs in American universities, but neither had succeeded in essentially modifying the type of higher education. Dr. Gilman himself had tried in vain to secure the opportunity for graduate work in this country. Now, without any traditions to bind them, the organizers of the University had the opportunity "which marked the entrance of the higher education in America upon a new phase in its development." " The great work of Hopkins," said President Eliot at the twenty-fifth anniversary of its foundation, " is the creation of a school of graduate studies, which not only has been in itself a strong and potent school, but which has lifted every other university in the country in its departments of arts and sciences."

The trustees were very wise in choosing as

the first faculty men who had the training and
the aspiration to make this work possible: the
" soaring-genius'd Sylvester," —

> That, earlier, loosed the knot great Newton tied,
> And flung the door of Fame's locked temple wide;

Gildersleeve, who combined the best classical
traditions of the old South with recent methods
of German scholarship; Morris, who came from
Oxford, "devout, learned, enthusiastic;" accomplished Martin, who "brought to this country
new methods of physiological inquiry;" Rowland, "honored in every land, peer of the greatest
physicists of our day;" and Adams, "suggestive,
industrious, inspiring, ductile, beneficent," who,
though at first holding a subordinate position,
built up a department of history and economics
which has had a potent influence throughout the
South, and indeed throughout the country.[1] These
men did much original work themselves, and put
before the public in popular articles and scientific journals the ideals of their several departments. It is noteworthy that for every department
a special scientific journal was established. The
library, though small, was composed of special
working collections and of foreign periodicals,
which, when supplemented by the Peabody Li-

[1] The account of the first faculty is based largely on ex-
President Gilman's article, "The Launching of a University,"
in *Scribner's Magazine*, March, 1902.

brary, gave an opportunity for the most diligent research. The students, who came from all parts of the country, were shown " how to discover the limits of the known ; how to extend, even by minute accretions, the realm of knowledge ; how to coöperate with other men in the prosecution of inquiry." Reviewing the work done by the faculty and students of the University, the leading scientific journal of England said, July 12, 1883: " We should like to see such an account of original work done and to be done issuing each year from the laboratories of Oxford and Cambridge."

In addition to the regular courses offered by members of the faculty, the University provided for series of lectures to be given by distinguished scholars from both American and European universities. These lectures, suggested by those given at the Collége de France, appealed at once to the University community and to the citizens of Baltimore. In the course of the first five years they had the chance to hear Lord Kelvin, Freeman, Bryce, Von Holst, Edmund Gosse, William James, Hiram Corson, and shorter series of lectures by Phillips Brooks, Dean Stanley, and others. The most notable of all were delivered in 1877 by Lowell and Child, while at the same time Charles Eliot Norton was lecturing at the Peabody Institute, — " the three wise men of the East."

From far the sages saw, from far they came
And ministered to her.

Lowell lectured on Romance poetry, with Dante
as the central theme, while Child had "a four
weeks' triumph" in Chaucer, producing a corner on that poet's works in all the bookstores
of the city. Readers of Lowell's letters will
remember the joy that he had in renewing his
association with Child and in forming new ac-
quaintances in the circles of Johns Hopkins and
Baltimore. Unfortunately, Lanier was at that
time in Florida, seeking the restoration of his
health, and so missed the opportunity which he
would have coveted, of hearing, and of being
closely associated with, these eminent scholars.

To what degree was Lanier a scholar, worthy
to be named in connection with such men?
There are some who would deny him such a
rank; and indeed, when one finds in his books
inaccuracies, conceits, and hasty generalizations,
one is apt to grow impatient with him. But there
are points which connect him with the modern
English scholar. In the first place, he was a
very hard and systematic student. He had none
of the slipshod methods of many men of his type.
He had respect for the most recent investigations in his special line of work, — he knew the
value of scholarship. The Peabody Library enabled him to have at hand the most recent

publications of the learned societies, and there is no question that he steadfastly endeavored to keep in touch with the authorities in any special field of investigation in which he happened to be interested. The footnotes in the " Science of English Verse " and in the Shakespeare lectures indicate that he had a knowledge of the bibliography of any subject he touched. Furthermore, he consulted with men who were living in Baltimore and had the special information that he desired. While writing the " Science of English Verse," he often talked with Professor Gildersleeve as to Greek metrics. " We never became intimate," says the latter, " and yet we were good friends and there was much common ground. Our talks usually turned on matters of literary form. He was eager, receptive, reaching out to all the knowable, transmuting all that he learned. He would have me read Greek poetry aloud to him for the sake of the rhythm and the musical effect." [1] When the book was finished, he wrote to Mr. Scribner : " I have had no opportunity whatever to submit this book to any expert friend and have often wished that I might do so before it goes finally forth, in order that I might avail myself of any suggestions which would be likely to occur to another mind, approaching the book from another direction.

[1] Letter to the author.

This being impossible, it has occurred to me that perhaps you have sent the manuscript to be read by some specialist in these matters, and that possibly some such suggestions might be offered by him. Pray let me know if you think this worth while." On questions of Anglo-Saxon he conferred with Professor A. S. Cook, at that time instructor in the University, and on matters of scientific interest, such as he pursued in his investigation into the physics of sound, he sought advice from the scientists of the University, even taking courses with them.

For Child, Furnivall, Hales, Grosart, and other workers in the field of English literature he had the greatest reverence. In his preface to the "Boy's Percy," in commenting on the accuracy of modern scholarship, he speaks of the " clear advance in men's conscience as to literary relations of this sort . . . the perfect delicacy which is now the rule among men of letters, the scrupulous fidelity of the editor to his text. . . . I think there can be no doubt that we owe this inestimable uplifting of exact statement and pure truth in men's esteem to the same vigorous growth in the general spirit of man which has flowed forth, among other directions, into the wondrous modern development of physical science. Here the minutest accuracy in observing and the utmost faithfulness in reporting have been found in the outset to be absolutely essential, have created habits and requirements of conscience which extend themselves into all other relations." It may be seen from such quotations that Lanier had respect for the most minute investigations; he had no tirades to make against the peeping and botanizing spirit that many men of his type have found in the modern scholar. Speaking of the monumental work of Ellis on the pronunciation of English in the time of Shakespeare, he pays tribute to his "wonderful skill, patience, industry, keenness, fairness, and learning."

Furthermore, Lanier himself had the spirit of research and original work which we have seen was characteristic of Johns Hopkins University. He not only had the desire to investigate, but he also gave form and shape to his investigations. In this he was in striking contrast with many Southern scholars. Joseph Le Conte, in his recent autobiography, tells of a friend of his who had the making of a great scientist. He met him at Flat Rock in 1858, and heard him talk most intelligently on the origin of species. At that early date this South Carolina planter had Darwin's idea. "Why did n't he publish it?" asks Le Conte, the answer to which question leads him to comment on the lack of productive scholars in the South. "Nothing could be more

remarkable than the wide reading, the deep reflection, the refined culture, and the originality
of thought and observation characteristic of them,
and yet the idea of publication never even enters
their minds. What right has any one to publish
unless it is something of the greatest importance,
something that would revolutionize thought?"
Now Lanier was filled with the spirit of making
contributions, however insignificant, to the development of scholarship in some one direction.
He restates, for instance, with remarkable insight
and conciseness, the investigations of Fleay, Edward Dowden, and other members of the New
Shakespeare Society, as to the metrical development seen in Shakespeare's plays. But he adds to
their investigations a suggestion as to the greater
freedom with which Shakespeare shifted the accent in his later plays: "Several reasons may be
urged for the belief that this might prove one of
the most valuable of all metrical tests. In fact,
when we consider that the matter of rhythmic
accent is one which affects every bar of each line,
while the four tests just now applied affect only
the *last* bar of each line; and when we consider
further that the real result of this freedom in
using the rhythmic accent is to vary the mono-
tonous regularity of the regular system with
the charm of those subtle rhythms which we
employ in familiar discourse, so that the habit

of such freedom might grow with the greatest
uniformity upon a poet, and might thus present us with a test of such uniform development
as to be reliable for nicer discrimination than
any of the more regular tests can be pushed
to, — it would seem fair to expect confirmation
of great importance from a properly constructed
Table of Abnormal Rhythmic Accents in Shakspere."

Lanier not only made these investigations himself, but incited his students to do so, especially
those in the smaller classes of the University. A
good illustration is in the suggestion he made to
a class that they might together work out some
interesting etymological and dialectical points.
" Why should not some of the intelligent ladies
of this class," he asks, " go to work and arrange
the facts — as I have called them — so that
scholars might have before them a comprehen-
sive view of all the word-changes which have
occurred since the earliest Anglo-Saxon works
were written ? The other day a young lady — one
of the very brightest young women I have ever
met — asked me to give her a vocation. She
said she had studied a good many things, of one
sort or another ; that she was merely going over
ground which thousands of others had trodden ;
that she wanted some original work, some method
by which she could contribute substantially to

the world's stock of knowledge : having this kind of outlet she felt sure she had a genuine desire, a working desire, to go forward. Well, of the numerous plans which I can imagine for women to pursue, I have suggested to you one which would combine pleasure with profitable work in a most charming manner. Suppose that some lady — or better a club of ladies — should set out to note down the changes in spelling — and if possible in pronunciation — which have occurred in every word now remaining to us from the Anglo-Saxon tongue. The task would not be a difficult one. All that would be required would be to portion out to each member of the club a specific set of books to be read, each set consisting of some books in Anglo-Saxon, some in Middle English, and some in Modern English. Each member would take her books and fall to reading. As she would come to each word she would write it down; and whenever she would happen on the same word in a book of a later century she would write it down under the first one ; if she came upon the same word in a book of a still later century she would write it down under the other two, and so on. As each member of the club would rapidly accumulate material, the whole body might meet once a month to collate and arrange the results. In this way a pursuit which would soon become perfectly fascinating would in no long time collect material for a thorough and systematic view of the growth of English words for the last thousand years. The most interesting questions concerning the wonderful and subtle laws of word-change might then be solved." [1]

In his zeal for publishing and editing books he conceived of a rather quixotic plan for starting a publishing house. In a letter written June 8, 1879, to his brother, Lanier urges him to come to Baltimore and go into the publishing business with him. They can then both become writers, and thus resume the plan of working together that they had formed just after the war. Lanier himself expects to send forth at least two books a year for the next ten years. "These are to be works, not of one season, but — if popular at all — increasing in value with each year. Besides these works on language and literature and the science of verse, — which I hope will be standard ones, — my poems are to be printed. . . . If you would only be my publisher! Indeed, if we could be a firm together! I have many times thought that ' Lanier Brothers, Publishers,' might be a strong house, particularly as to the Southern States." He then outlines his scheme in detail : they would need only an office, a clerk and a porter, as they could have their

[1] *Shakspere and His Forerunners*, vol. i, p. 134.

printing done elsewhere. He closes with a strong appeal to him to leave the South, inasmuch as political conditions at that time seemed to render the future of that section extremely doubtful.

A still more noteworthy characteristic of Lanier's scholarship is the modernness of his work. It is a striking fact that every subject he wrote about has more and more engaged the attention of scholars since his time. One may not agree with any of his ideas, and may be convinced of the superficiality of his treatment of literature, but there is no question of the insight manifested by him in seizing upon those subjects that have been of notable interest to recent scholars. When he lectured about Shakespeare, for instance, he did not indulge in any of the moralizing that had been characteristic of German commentators. On the other hand, he put himself in thorough accord with the work outlined by Dr. Furnivall and his fellow workers in their efforts to study and interpret Shakespeare as a whole. "The first necessity," said Dr. Furnivall in the introduction to the Leopold Shakespeare (1877), "is to regard Shakespeare as a whole, his works as a living organism, each a member of one created unity, the whole a tree of healing and of comfort to the nations, a growth from small beginnings to mighty ends." And again: "As the growth is more and more closely watched and discerned, we shall more and more clearly see that his metre, his words, his grammar and syntax, move but with the deeper changes of mind and soul of which they are outward signs, and that all the faculties of the man went onward together. . . . This subject of the growth, the oneness of Shakespeare . . . is the special business of the present, the second school of Victorian students . . . as antiquarian illustration, emendation, and verbal criticism were of the first school. The work of the first school we have to carry on, not to leave undone; the work of our own second school we have to do." Into this study, thus outlined by the founder of the New Shakespeare Society, Lanier threw himself with unabated zeal.

The fact is all the more remarkable when we compare his writing on Shakespeare with Swinburne's book published during the same year. Swinburne has only words of contempt for the investigations of the New Shakespeare Society, whom he characterizes as "learned and laborious men who could hear only with their fingers. They will pluck out the heart, not of Hamlet's, but of Shakespeare's mystery by the means of a metrical test; and this test is to be applied by a purely arithmetical process. . . . Every man, woman, and child born with five fingers on each hand was henceforward better qualified as a critic

than any poet or scholar of time past." He calls
them " metre-mongers " and the " bastard brood
of scribblers." Lanier, however, while carefully
avoiding the methods and principles of a mere
dry-as-dust, spiritualizes all their facts, and works
out in passages of remarkable beauty and eloquence the growth of Shakespeare's mind and art.
To Lanier a metrical test or a date is no insignificant thing. " Many a man," he says, " may
feel inclined to say, Why potter about your dates
and chronologies ? . . . But it so happens that
here a whole view of the greatest mind the human race has yet evolved hangs essentially upon
dates." Lanier's reverence for exact scholarship
and his application of seemingly technical standards do not interfere at all with his deeper
appreciation of Shakespeare's plays. While he
overstated the autobiographical value of a chro-
nological study of the plays, — reading into this
study meanings that are not warranted by the
facts, — it must be said that it is difficult to find
in the writings of Americans on Shakespeare more
significant passages than chapters xx–xxiv of
" Shakspere and His Forerunners."

Other illustrations of the modernness of Lanier's scholarly work are easy to cite. His plan
for the publication of a book of Elizabethan sonnets, while not realized by him, has been carried
out during the past year in a far more extensive

and scholarly way than he could have done it by Mr. Sidney Lee. In the light of the recent scholar's investigation, many of Lanier's ideas with regard to the autobiographical value of the sonnets vanish, but his insight into the need of the study of the Elizabethan sonnets is none the less notable. He was the first American to indicate the necessity for the study of the novel as a form of literature that was worthy of serious thought. Lecture courses and books on the novel have multiplied at a rapid rate during the past decade. Whatever may be one's idea of the permanent value of the "Science of English Verse," it is evident that it was a pioneer book in a field which has been much cultivated within recent years. The thesis of the book will be discussed in a later chapter; here it needs to be said that it is one of the best pieces of original work yet produced by an English scholar in America, — in it are seen at their best the qualities that have been noted as distinctive in the author's work.

All these very essential characteristics of a scholar Lanier had. He had not the time to secure results from the plans that he clearly saw. He was moving in the right direction. No scholar should ever speak of him but with reverent lips. Without the training, or the equipment, or the time, of more fortunate scholars of our own day, he should be an inspiration to all men who have scholarly ideals. If not a great scholar himself, he wanted to be one, and he had the finest appreciation of all who were. And besides, did he not have something which is often lacking in scholars? There is more science, more criticism now in American universities, but it would be well to keep in view the ideals of men who saw the spiritual significance of scholarship. President Gilman realized this when he wrote to Lanier: "I think your scheme (of winter lectures) may be admirably worked in, not only with our major and minor courses in English, but with all our literary courses, French and German, Latin and Greek. The teachers of these subjects pursue chiefly *language* courses. We need among us some one like you, loving literature and poetry, and treating it in such a way as to enlist and inspire many students. . . . I think your aims and your preparation admirable."

Dr. Gilman refers here to a scheme for a course in English literature outlined by the poet in the summer of 1879. Lanier indicated three distinct courses of study which would tend to give to students (1) a vocabulary of idiomatic English words and phrases, (2) a stock of illustrative ideas, (3) acquaintance with modern literary forms. To secure the first point, he suggests that students should read with a view to gathering strong and homely English words and phrases from a study of authors ranging from the Scotch poets of the fifteenth and sixteenth centuries to Swift and Emerson. To secure ideas, the student should study systems of thought, ancient and modern. "The expansion of mental range, as well as special facilities in expression, attainable by such a course, cannot be too highly estimated." Under the third head he suggests the study of various forms of writing,—an idea which has been carried out in recent years. The ultimate end of all this study, however, is "the spiritual consolation and refreshment of literature when the day's work is over, the delight of sitting with a favorite poet or essayist at evening, the enlargement of sympathy, derivable from powerful individual presentations such as Shakespeare's or George Eliot's; the gentle influences of Sir Thomas Browne or Burton or Lamb or Hood, the repose of Wordsworth, the beauty of Keats, the charm of Tennyson should be brought out so as to initiate friendships between special students and particular authors, which may be carried on through life." [1]

In another letter he wrote still further of his plans, clearly distinguishing between the popular lectures and the more technical work of the University class-room. It is a long letter, but gives so well Lanier's idea of his work in the Univer-

[1] *The Independent*, March 18, 1886.

sity and his plans for the future that it serves better than much comment : —

180 St. Paul Street, Baltimore, Md.,
July 13, 1879.

My dear Mr. Gilman, — I see, from your letter, that I did not clearly explain my scheme of lectures.

The course marked "Class Lectures" is meant for advanced students, and involves the hardest kind of University work on their part. Perhaps you will best understand the scope of the tasks which this course will set before the student by reading the inclosed *theses* which I should distribute among the members of the class as soon as I should have discovered their mental leanings and capacities sufficiently, and which I should require to be worked out by the end of the scholastic year. I beg you to read these with some care : I send only seven of them, but they will be sufficient to show you the nature of the work which I propose to do with the *University student*. I should like my main efforts to take that direction ; I wish to get some Americans at hard work in pure literature ; and will be glad if the public lectures in Hopkins Hall shall be merely accessory to my main course. With this view, as you look over the accompanying theses, please observe : —

1. That each of these involves original research

and will — if properly carried out — constitute a genuine contribution to modern literary scholarship ;

2. That they are so arranged as to fall in with various other studies and extend their range, — for example, the first one being suitable to a student of philosophy who is pursuing Anglo-Saxon, the second to one who is studying the Transition Period of English, the sixth to one who is studying Elizabethan English, and so on ;

3. That each one necessitates diligent study of some great English work, not as a philological collection of words, but as pure literature ; and

4. That they keep steadily in view, as their ultimate object, that strengthening of manhood, that enlarging of sympathy, that glorifying of moral purpose, which the student unconsciously gains, not from any direct didacticism, but from this constant association with our finest ideals and loftiest souls.

Thus you see that while the course of " Class Lectures " submitted to you nominally centres about the three plays of Shakspere [1] therein named, it really takes these for texts, and involves, in the way of commentary and of thesis, the whole range of English poetry. In fact I have designed it as a thorough preparation for the serious study of the poetic art in its whole

[1] *Midsummer Night's Dream, Hamlet*, and *The Tempest.*

outcome, hoping that, if I should carry it out successfully, the Trustees might find it wise next year to create either a Chair of Poetry or a permanent lectureship covering the field above indicated. It is my fervent belief that to take classes of young men and to preach them the gospel according-to-Poetry is to fill the most serious gap in our system of higher education; I think one can already perceive a certain narrowing of sympathy and — what is even worse — an unsymmetric development of faculty, both intellectual and moral, from a too exclusive devotion to Science which Science itself would be the first to condemn.

As to the first six class lectures on " The Physics and Metaphysics of Poetry :" they unfold my system of English Prosody, in which I should thoroughly drill every student until he should be able to note down, in musical signs, the rhythm of any English poem. This drilling would continue through the whole course, inasmuch as I regard a mastery of the principles set forth in those lectures as vitally important to all systematic progress in the understanding and enjoyment of poetry.

I should have added, apropos of this class course, that there ought to be one examination each week, to every two lectures.

In the first interview we had, after my appointment, it was your intention to place this study among those required by the University for a degree. I hope sincerely you have not abandoned this idea ; and the course outlined in " Class lectures " forwarded to you the other day, and in the theses of which I send the first seven herewith, seems to me the best to begin with. If it should be made a part of the " Major Course in English " (where it seems properly to belong), I could easily arrange a simpler and less arduous modification of it for the corresponding " Minor Course."

I am so deeply interested in this matter — of making a finer fibre for all our young American manhood by leading our youth in proper relations with English poetry — that at the risk of consuming your whole vacation with reading this long and unconscionable letter I will mention that I have nearly completed three works which are addressed to the practical accomplishment of the object named, by supplying a wholly different method of study from that mischievous one which has generally arisen from a wholly mistaken use of the numerous " Manuals " of English literature. These works are my three textbooks : (1) " The Science of English Verse," in which the student's path is cleared of a thousand errors and confusions which have obstructed this study for a long time, by a very simple system

founded upon the physical relations of sound;
(2) " From Cædmon to Chaucer," in which I present all the most interesting Anglo-Saxon poems
remaining to us, in a form which renders their
literary quality appreciable by all students,
whether specially pursuing Old English or not,
thus placing these poems where they ought always
to have stood, as a sort of grand and simple
vestibule through which the later mass of English poetry is to be approached; and (3) my
" Chaucer," which I render immediately enjoyable, without preliminary preparation, by an inter-
lined glossarial explanation of the original text,
and an indication (with hyphens) of those terminal
syllables affecting the rhythm which have decayed
out of the modern tongue. I am going to print
these books and sell them myself, on the cheap
plan which has been so successfully adopted by
Edward Arber, lecturer on English literature in
University College, London. I have been working on them for two months; in two more they
will be finished; and by the middle of November I hope to have them ready for use as text-
books. If they succeed, I shall complete the
series next year with (4) a " Spenser " on the same
plan with the " Chaucer," (5) " The Minor Elizabethan Song-Writers," and (6) " The Minor
Elizabethan Dramatists;" the steady aim of the
whole being to furnish a working set of books

which will familiarize the student with the actual works of English poets, rather than with their names and biographers.

Pray forgive this merciless letter. I could not resist the temptation to unfold to you all my hopes and plans connected with my University work among your young men which I so eagerly anticipate.

I will trouble you to return these notes of theses when you have examined them at leisure.

Faithfully yours,
SIDNEY LANIER.[1]

He endeavored to make his courses fit in with other courses of the curriculum in Greek, Latin, and modern literatures : —

MY DEAR SIR, — I had been meditating, as a second course of public lectures during next term, if you should want them, — twelve studies on " The English Satirists ; " and on my visit to the University to-day I observed from the bulletin that Mr. Rabillon is now lecturing on " The French Satirists." It occurs to me, therefore, that perhaps some additional interest in the subject might be excited if my course on the English satirists should follow the completion of Mr. Rabillon's — which I suppose will not be be-

[1] Published in *South Atlantic Quarterly*, April, 1905.

fore the holidays — and should be given in January and February, instead of the course mentioned in my note to you this morning. I may add that if some other gentleman would offer courses on the Greek and Latin satirists, we might make a cyclus of it.   Faithfully yours,

SIDNEY LANIER.

435 NORTH CALVERT STREET,
        Saturday evening.

Lanier's public lectures were largely attended. What has been said of the Peabody lectures applies to the University lectures. Of the effect produced by him in his smaller University classes, one of his students writes: —

"I think that it was in the winter of 1879–80 that I heard that Mr. Lanier was to conduct a class in English Literature at the Johns Hopkins University, where I was then a Fellow. My field of work was Æsthetics and the History of Art, and as I was eagerly searching for chances to broaden and deepen my ideas, I enrolled myself in the class. We were not many, and I have no recollection of individuals in the group. Neither can I distinctly recall either the topics taken up or the method followed, except that most of the hours consisted of extended readings by Mr. Lanier with all sorts of interjected remarks, often setting aside the reading altogether.

That the course was a real source of intellectual profit to me I cannot doubt, but not in the form of definite information or systemized opinion. The benefit lay in a subtle expansion of the power of appreciation and an undefinable exaltation of the instincts of taste that I have since learned were more precious than any precise increments of cold knowledge.

" What I do remember vividly is the fact that often, almost regularly, I used to wait for Mr. Lanier after the class (which was held in the evening) and walk home with him a mile or so, sometimes walking up and down for a long time. On these occasions we doubtless talked of all manner of things. I was only a student trying to ' find himself ' in reference to the vast areas of thought. I was eager for sympathy and for inspiration. My life-work was still unchosen, but I was conscious of an intense drawing toward artistic topics — not much with the creative impulse of the artist, but rather with the analytic and rational desire of the student. I was beginning to have a profound sense of the interrelations of the fine arts with each other and of all of them with the movement of history. I wanted a chance to talk out what I was thinking and to get new lights and promptings. So in our slow strolls homeward I presume that I often babbled freely of my studies in architecture and music,

and my inconsequent remarks often led Mr.
Lanier to speak somewhat freely, too, of his
speculations and fancies. I now recall with wonder how he put me on such a footing of equality
that I often quite forgot the difference in age and
experience between us and almost felt him to be
a companion student. I now see that this was
the sign of two notable traits, — the extreme native Southern courtesy that clothed him always
in all his dealings with every one, and the essential youthfulness of his mind when moving among
his favorite subjects. His was surely one of the
finest of sympathies, delicate, sensitive, elastic,
vital to the highest degree, the like of which is
all too rare among men, though hardly described
by the term ' feminine.' In it breathed a genuine capacity for love in the most noble sense, for
he was ready to identify himself with the interests
of another, to etherealize and dignify what he
thought he saw in them, and thus absolutely to
transform them by the alchemy of his touch. And,
the more I think of it, the more I recognize that
his soul was incapable of aging. . . . This absolute freshness of heart and spirit seems to me
to have been one of the highest notes of Mr. Lanier's genius. Here he was clearly allied to many
a more famous poet or painter or musician." [1]

[1] Letter to the author from Professor Waldo S. Pratt, now
of Hartford Theological Seminary.

Among American poets Lanier has the same place with regard to the teaching of English that Lowell and Longfellow have in the study of modern languages. There were, to be sure, some greater English scholars in this country during the seventies than Lanier was, just as there were more scientific students of modern languages in the time of Longfellow and Lowell. Professors Child of Harvard, Lounsbury of Yale, March of Lafayette, Corson of Cornell, and Price of Randolph-Macon College — afterwards of Columbia University — have a commanding place in the development of English teaching which has become such a marked feature of educational progress since, say, 1870. Throughout schools and colleges and universities English is now firmly established as perhaps the most important branch of study. It is to the credit of Lanier that before much had been done in this direction he saw the great need of such work. Indeed, as early as 1868, while examining the catalogue of a Southern university, he jotted down in his note-book a suggestion that the most serious defect in the curriculum was the lack of any English training. It is true that there had been from time immemorial chairs of belles lettres in institutions of learning, but the department had rather to do with things in general. Even where English was studied there was a tendency to use manuals of literature rather than the works of authors themselves; and there is now a tendency to use literature as the basis for philological work. Lanier's ideas strike one as singularly balanced and sane, suggesting a compromise between the warring camps of recent years.

By reason of Lanier's sympathy with the ideals of the University, and his influence over some few students, he has a permanent place in the history of Johns Hopkins. Mr. Edmund Clarence Stedman wrote to President Gilman: " It is a fine thing that such an institution as your University should have its shrines — and among them that of its own poet, in a certain sense canonized, and with his most ideal memory a lasting part of its associations." The University has, indeed, kept the fame and the personality of Lanier fresh in its memory. As one enters McCoy Hall and notices the life-size portraits of the first president and the first members of the faculty, he misses the face of Lanier; but on entering Donavan Hall, just at the end of the main hallway, he finds himself in a room dedicated to the highest uses of poetry. There are pictures of men who have delivered lectures on the Percy Turnbull and Donavan foundations, manuscript letters of distinguished American poets and critics, and the bust of Lanier, whose spirit seems to dominate the sur-

BRONZE BUST OF SIDNEY LANIER

By Ephraim Keyser, at Johns Hopkins University

roundings. It is the best of the likenesses of the poet, and is the source of admiration to all visitors, as well as an inspiration to all who labor at Johns Hopkins. Those who were never thrilled by the lustre of his dark eyes or never heard the tones of his voice as he interpreted passages of great poetry, may find some satisfaction in such an image.

CHAPTER X

THE NEW SOUTH

WHILE Lanier was finding his place in the larger spheres of scholarship, of music, and of poetry, he constantly returned in thought and imagination to the South. Even after 1877, when he and his family became residents of Baltimore, his correspondence with his father and brother kept him in touch with that section. He continued to read Southern newspapers and to follow with interest Southern development. In his desk he kept a regular drawer for matters pertaining to the South. Both from his experience, which enabled him to enter with unusual sympathy into the life of the South, and from the larger point of view gained from his life in other sections, his observations on Southern life and literature are of special value. They show that he was not such a detached figure as has been frequently thought. He was of the South, and took delight in every evidence of her progress. He sometimes despaired of her future — so much so that he urged his brother to come to Baltimore in 1879. He had little patience with the prevailing type of political leader at the time when the Silver Bill was passed, so he wrote, June 8, 1879, to Clifford Lanier: —

" I cannot contemplate with any patience your stay in the South. In my soberest moments I can perceive no outlook for that land. Our representatives in Congress have acted with such consummate unwisdom that one may say we have no future there. Mr. —— and Mr. —— (as precious a pair of rascals as ever wrought upon the ignorance of a country) have disgusted all thoughtful men of whatever party; while the shuffling of our better men on the question of public honesty, their folly in allowing such people as Blaine and Conkling to taunt them into cheap hurlings back of defiance (as the silly Southern newspapers term it), their inconceivable mistake in permitting the stalwart Republicans to arrange all the issues of the campaign and to bring on the battle, not only whenever they want it, but on whatever ground they choose, instead of manfully holding before the people the real issues of the time, — the tariff, the prodigious abuses clustered about the capitol at Washington, the restriction of granting powers in Congress, the non-interference theory of government, — all these things have completely obscured the admitted good intentions of Morgan and Lamar and their fellows, and have entirely alienated the feelings of men who at first were quite won over to them. The present extra session has been from the beginning a piece of absurdity such as the world probably never saw before. Our men are such mere politicians, that they have never yet discovered — what the least thoughtful statesmanship ought to have perceived at the close of our war — that the belief in the sacredness and greatness of the American Union among the millions of the North and of the great Northwest is really the principle which conquered us. As soon as we invaded the North and arrayed this sentiment in ar̄̄̄̄ ̄̄̄̄̄t us, our swift destruction followed. But how soon they have forgotten Gettysburg! That the presence of United States troops at the polls is an abuse no sober man will deny; but to attempt to remedy it at this time, when the war is so lately over, when the North is naturally sensitive as to securing the hard-won results of it, when, consequently, every squeak of a penny whistle is easily interpreted into a rebel yell by the artful devices of Mr. Blaine and his crew, — this was simply to invade the North again as we did in '64. And we have met precisely another Gettysburg. The whole community is uneasy as to the silver bill and the illimitable folly of the greenbackers; business men anxiously await the adjournment of Congress, that they may be able to lay their plans with some sense of security against a complete reversal of monetary conditions by some silly legislation; and I do not believe that there is a quiet man in the Republic to whom the whole political caucus at Washington is not a shame and a sorrow.

" And thus, as I said, it really seems as if any prosperity at the South must come long after your time and mine. Our people have failed to perceive the deeper movements under-running the times; they lie wholly off, out of the stream of thought, and whirl their poor old dead leaves of recollection round and round, in a piteous eddy that has all the wear and tear of motion without any of the rewards of progress. By the best information I can get, the country is substantially poorer now than when the war closed, and Southern securities have become simply a catchword. The looseness of thought among our people, the unspeakable rascality of corporations like M——— how long is it going to take us to remedy these things? Whatever is to be done, you and I can do our part of it far better here than there. Come away."

The very next year, however, he wrote his essay on the New South, showing a far more hopeful view. After reading for two years the newspapers of Georgia, with a view to understanding the changed conditions in his native State, Lanier published in October, 1880, an

article on that subject in "Scribner's Magazine." [1] To one who reads it with the expectation of getting an idea of the forces that have
made the New South, it is sadly disappointing ;
for he is told at once that the New South means
small farming, and the article deals largely with
the increase in the number of small farms and a
consequent diversity of products. Insignificant
as such a study may seem, it is noteworthy as
showing Lanier's interest in practical affairs. It
has been seen that ever since the war he had
been interested in the redemption of the agricultural life of the South, that this was the
subject of his first important poem. Since the
writing of "Corn" and of the earlier dialect
poems, he had frequently commented on the
future of the South as to be determined largely
by an improved agricultural system. To him the
best evidence of the enduring character of the
new civilization was a democracy, growing out
of a vital revolution in the farming economy of
the South. "The great rise of the small farmer
in the Southern States during the last twenty
years," he says, "becomes the notable circumstance of the period, in comparison with which
noisier events signify nothing." The hero of the
sketch is a small farmer "who commenced work
after the war with his own hands, not a dollar

[1] *Retrospects and Prospects,* pp. 104–135.

in his pocket, and now owns his plantation, has it well stocked, no mortgage or debt of any kind on it, and a little money to lend." Lanier clips from his newspaper files passages indicating the constantly increasing diversity of crops. The reader is carried into the country fairs and along the roads and through plantations by a man who had a realistic sense of what was going on in the whole State of Georgia. "The last few years," he says, "have witnessed a very decided improvement in Georgia farming: moon-planting and other vulgar superstitions are exploding, the intelligent farmer is deriving more assistance from the philosopher, the naturalist, and the chemist, and he who is succeeding best is he who has thirty or forty cattle, sheep, hogs, and poultry of his own raising, together with good-sized barns and meat-houses, filled from his own fields, instead of from the West."

Lanier saw that out of this growth in small farming — this agricultural prosperity — would come changes of profound significance. He saw an intimate relation between politics, social life, morality, art, on the one hand, and the bread-giver earth on the other. "One has only to remember, particularly here in America, whatever crop we hope to reap in the future, — whether it be a crop of poems, of paintings, of symphonies, of constitutional safeguards, of virtuous behaviors, of religious exaltation, — we have got to bring it out of the ground with palpable plows and with plain farmer's forethought, in order to see that a vital revolution in the farming economy of the South, if it is actually occurring, is necessarily carrying with it all future Southern politics and Southern relations and Southern art, and that, therefore, such an agricultural change is the one substantial fact upon which any really new South can be predicated." It has been seen that Lanier underrated the development of the manufacturing interests in the South ; and yet who does not see that with all the industrial prosperity of this section during the last twenty years, the most crying need now is the rehabilitation of the South's agricultural life ? The present aggressive movement in the direction of the improvement of the rural schools is a confirmation of Lanier's vision of " the village library, the neighborhood farmers'-club, the amateur Thespian Society, the improvement of the public schools, the village orchestra, all manner of betterments and gentilities and openings out into the universe." He saw, too, the effect on the negro of his becoming a landowner, and the consequent obliteration of the color line in politics. He cites from his newspaper clippings evidences of the increasing prosperity of the negro race, — for instance, how " at the Atlanta University for colored people, which is endowed by the State, the progress of the pupils, the clearness of their recitation, their excellent behavior, and the remarkable neatness of their schoolrooms, altogether convince ' your committee that the colored race are capable of receiving the education usually given at such institutions.' " He sees in the appearance of the negro as a small farmer a transition to the point in which " his interests, his hopes, and consequently his politics become identical with those of all other small farmers, whether white or black."

Much as has been accomplished, however, he looks forward with expectancy to a still greater future : " Everywhere the huge and gentle slopes kneel and pray for vineyards, for cornfields, for cottages, for spires to rise up from beyond the oak-groves. It is a land where there is never a day of summer or of winter when a man cannot do a full day's work in the open field ; all the products meet there, as at nature's own agricultural fair. . . . It is because these blissful ranges are still clamorous for human friendship ; it is because many of them are actually virgin to plow, pillar, axe, or mill-wheel, while others have known only the insulting and mean cultivation of the early immigrants who scratched the surface for cotton a year or two, then carelessly abandoned all to sedge and sassafras, and sauntered on toward Texas: it is thus that these lands are with sadder significance than that of small farming, also a New South."

In order to understand the development of the New South, here briefly indicated, and in order to appreciate what Lanier really accomplished, two types of Southerners must be clearly distinguished. After the war the conservative Southerner — ranging all the way from the fiery Bourbon to the strong and worthy protagonist of the old order — failed to understand the meaning of defeat. He interpreted the conflict as the triumph of brute force, — sheer material prosperity, — and comforted himself with the thought that many of the noblest causes had gone down in defeat. He threshed over the arguments of Calhoun with regard to the Constitution of 1787. He quoted Scripture in defense of slavery, or tried to continue slavery — in spirit, if not in name. He saw no hope for the negro, and looked for his speedy deterioration under freedom. Compelled by force of circumstances to acknowledge the supremacy of the Federal government, he was still dominated by the ideas of separation. He saw no future for the nation. "This once fair temple of liberty," one of them said, — "rent from the bottom, desecrated by the orgies of a half-mad crew of fanatics and fools, knaves, negroes, and Jacobins, abandoned wholly by its original worshipers — stands as Babel did of old, a melancholy monument of the frustrate hopes and heaven-aspiring ambition of its builders."

With him the passing away of the age of chivalry was as serious a matter as it was to Burke. He magnified the life before the war as the most glorious in the history of the world. He saw none of its defects ; he resented criticism, either by Northerners or by his own people. He opposed the public school system, as " Yankeeish and infidel," stoutly championing the system of education which had prevailed under the old order. He recognized no standards. " We fearlessly assert," said one of them, speaking of the most distinguished of Southern universities, " that in this university, the standard is higher, the education more thorough, and the work done by both teachers and students is far greater, than in Princeton, or Yale, or Harvard, or in any other Northern college or university." If he ventured into the field of literary criticism, he maintained that the Old South had a literature equal to that of New England ; if he had doubts upon that subject, he looked forward to a time not far off when the Southern cause would find monumental expression in a commanding literature. If he thought on theological or philosophical subjects, he thought in terms of the seventeenth and eighteenth centuries. The watch-words of modern life were so many red flags to him, — science the enemy of religion, German philosophy a denial of the depravity of man, democracy the product of French infidelity and of false humanitarianism, industrial prosperity the inveterate foe of the graces of life. To use Lanier's words, he "failed to perceive the deeper movements underrunning the times." Defeated in a long war and inheriting the provincialism and sensitiveness of a feudal order, he remained proud in his isolation. He went to work with a stubborn and unconquered spirit, with the idea that sometime in the future all the principles for which he had stood would triumph.

Into the hands of such men the reconstruction governments played. Worse even than the effect of excessive taxation, misgovernment, and despair produced in the minds of the people, was the permanent effect produced on the Southern mind. The prophecies that had been made with regard to the triumph of despotism seemed to be fulfilled; every contention that had been made in 1861 with regard to the dangers of Federal usurpation seemed justified in the acts of the government. The political equality of the negro, guaranteed by the Fifteenth Amendment, and the attempt to give him social equality, were stubborn facts which seemed to overthrow the more liberal ideas of Lincoln and of those Southern leaders who after the war hoped that the magnanimity of the North would be equal to the great task ahead of the nation. The conservative leaders were invested with a dignity that recalls the popularity of Burke when his predictions with regard to the French Revolution were realized. During all the years that have intervened since reconstruction days, the conservative has had as a resource for leadership his harking back to those days. The demagogue and the reactionary — enemies of the children of light — have always been able to inflame the populace with appeals to the memories and issues of the past. Such men have forgot nothing and learned nothing.[1]

In striking contrast with the conservative Southerner has been the progressive Southerner, a type ranging all the way from the unwise and unreasonable reformer to the well-balanced and sympathetic worker, who has endeavored to make the transition from the old order to the new a normal and healthy one. If the qualities which have made Lanier's progress possible are recalled, — his lack of prejudice, his inexhaustible energy, the alertness and modernness of his mind, his ability to find joy in constructive work,

[1] I have here sketched a composite picture; it is like no one man, but the type is recognizable. It is the result of a study of the magazines, newspapers, and biographies of the period from 1865 to 1880. The type is not extinct.

his adoption of the national point of view, —
then the reader may see the elements that have
made possible a New South. The same spirit applied to industry, to education, to religion, is now
seen everywhere. The term "New South," used
by Lanier and others, is meant in no way as a
reproach to the Old South, — it is simply the
recognition of a changed social life due to one of
the greatest catastrophes in history. In the early
eighties it was employed by four Georgians, who
had a right to use it, — Benjamin H. Hill, Atticus
G. Haygood, Henry Grady, and Sidney Lanier.

Georgia was the Southern State that led in this
progressive work. Here the readjustment came
sooner, by reason of the fact that a more democratic people lived there, and also that the bur-
dens of reconstruction were less severe. Virginia
gave to the nation at the time of the foundation
of the republic a group of statesmen rarely ex-
celled in the history of the world. South Carolina
statesmen led in the movement towards secession,
and her people were the first to make an aggressive movement in that direction. The leadership
of the New South must be found in a group of
far-seeing, liberal-minded, aggressive Georgians.
The action of the State legislature in repealing
the ordinance of secession and accepting the emancipation of slaves within one minute, was characteristic of her later work. In 1866, Alexander

H. Stephens and Benjamin H. Hill — one before
the legislature of Georgia and the other before
Tammany Hall — sounded the note of patience,
of nationalism, and of hope. "There was a South
of slavery and secession," said the latter ; "that
South is dead. There is a South of Union and
freedom ; that South, thank God! is living,
breathing, growing every hour." These words
became the text of the now celebrated address of
another Georgian who twenty years later, before
the New England Club of New York, gave notable expression to his own ideals and those who
had wrought with him in the genuine reconstruction of the South. Henry Grady, as editor of
the Atlanta "Constitution," was, after 1876, an
exponent of the idea that the future of the South
lay not primarily in politics, but in an industrial
order which should be the basis of a more enduring civilization. At his advice, as Joel Chandler
Harris says, everybody began to take a day off
from politics occasionally and devote themselves
to the upbuilding of the resources of the State.
Another Georgian, the late John B. Gordon,
united with Grady and others in saying " a bold
and manly word in behalf of the American Union
in the ear of the South, and a bold and manly
word in behalf of the South in the ear of the
North." While recounting the last days of the
Confederacy, he awoke in Northern hearts an

admiration for Lee and in Southern hearts an
admiration for Grant, and in all an aspiration
towards nationalism.

Another Georgian, Atticus G. Haygood,— president of Emory College and afterwards bishop
of the Methodist Episcopal Church, South, —
voiced the sentiment of the liberal South with regard to the negro, in a book whose title, "Our Brother in Black," sufficiently indicates the spirit in
which it was written. In a Thanksgiving sermon
on the New South, delivered in 1881, he criticised severely the croakers and the demagogues
who were endeavoring to mislead the people, and
reviewed with sympathy the great progress that
had been made since the war. He pleads guilty
to the charge of having new light and is glad
of it. He points out with keen insight the illit-
eracy of the masses of the Southern people and
the lack of educational facilities. A movement
for the development of a public school system in
the South was led by J. L. M. Curry, a Confederate soldier of Georgia stock. He became an
evangelist in the crusade for public education,
announcing before State legislatures the principle upon which a true democratic order might be
established. "I am not afraid of the educated
masses," he said, in an address before the Georgia
legislature; " I would rather trust the masses than
king, priest, aristocracy, or established church.

No nation can realize its full possibility unless it builds upon the education of the whole people."

By 1885 the forces that have here been briefly sketched were well under way throughout the South. Factories were prospering, farm products were becoming more diversified, more farmers owned their own places, a public school system was firmly established in all the leading cities and towns, colleges and universities — some of the strongest dating from the period just after the war — were enabled to increase their endowments and to modernize their work, the national spirit was growing, and a more liberal view of religion was being maintained. A day of hope, of freedom, of progress, had dawned.

It was natural that along with all these changes, and indeed anticipating some of them, there should arise a group of Southern writers. Indeed, immediately after the war there was a marked tendency in the direction of literary work — "an avalanche of literature in a devastated country." Magazines were started and books were published in abundance. The literary activity was due, no doubt, in the first place, to the poverty of men and women : some who would have looked down upon literature as a profession before the war were now eager to do anything to keep starvation from the door. Furthermore, there was a great desire among some people to

have the Southern side of the war well represented before the civilized world. Hence arose
innumerable biographies, histories, and historical
novels, and hence the demand for Southern text-
books.

It is clearly impossible to give any adequate
sketch of this literary awakening, — if so it may
be called, when contrasted with a later one. Of the
magazines which were started, the most important
were "Debow's Review," "devoted to the restoration of the Southern States and the development
of the wealth and resources of the country," whose
motto was, " Light up the torches of industry ;"
the " Southern Review," edited by Dr. A. T.
Bledsoe and William Hand Browne and dedicated " to the despised, the disfranchised, and the
down-trodden people of the South ; " " The Land
We Love," started in Charlotte, N. C., by Gen.
D. H. Hill, and devoted to literature, military
history, and agriculture ; " Scott's Monthly,"
published in Atlanta, " Southern Field and Fireside," in Raleigh, and " The Crescent Monthly,"
in New Orleans ; the " New Eclectic Magazine "
and its successor, the " Southern Magazine,"
published by the Turnbull Brothers of Baltimore ; and, as if Charleston had not had enough
magazines to die before the war, the " Nineteenth
Century," in that city. Most of these had but a
short career, and none of them survived longer

than 1878. There was in them a continual crying out for Southern literature which might
worthily represent the Southern people. The response came, too — so far as quantity was concerned. One of the editors remarked that he
had enough poetry on hand to last seven years
and five months.

Of these magazines the most important was the
" Southern Magazine," published at Baltimore
from 1871 to 1875, — a magazine which came
nearest filling the place occupied by the " Southern Literary Messenger " before the war. While
it was somewhat eclectic in its character, — re-
printing articles from the English magazines, —
it had as contributors a group of promising young
scholars and writers. The editor was William
Hand Browne, now professor of English literature
in Johns Hopkins University. Professor Gildersleeve, then of the University of Virginia, Professor Thomas R. Price, then professor of English at Randolph-Macon, James Albert Harrison,
later the biographer and editor of Poe, and Margaret J. Preston were regular contributors. Richard Malcolm Johnston contributed his " Dukesborough Tales " to it. One of the publishers of
the magazine, Mr. Lawrence Turnbull, visited
Lanier at Macon in 1871 and became much interested in him. To the magazine Lanier contributed " Prospects and Retrospects " (March

and April, 1871), " A Song " and " A Seashore
Grave " (July, 1871), " Nature-Metaphors "
(February, 1872), " San Antonio de Bexar "
(July and August, 1873), and " Peace " (Oc-
tober, 1874).

Of the books published during this period,
few have survived. John Esten Cooke's novels
and his lives of Stonewall Jackson and Lee,
two or three collections of the war poetry of the
South, Gayarré's histories, the " War between
the States," by Alexander H. Stephens, Craven's
" Prison Life of Jefferson Davis," and Dabney's
"Defense of Virginia" are perhaps the most significant. J. Wood Davidson's " Living Writers
of the South," published in 1869, gives the best
general idea of the extent and quality of the post-
bellum writing. Noteworthy, also, is a series of
text-books projected with the idea that the moral
and mental training of the sons and daughters
of the South should no longer be intrusted to
teachers and books imported from abroad. As
planned originally, the scheme called for Bledsoe's
Mathematics, Maury's Geographies, Holmes's
Readers, Gildersleeve's Latin Grammar, histories
of Louisiana and South Carolina by Gayarré
and Simms respectively, scientific books by the
Le Conte brothers, and English Classics by
Richard Malcolm Johnston.

So much needs to be said of the character of

the literature immediately succeeding the war, if
for no other reason, that it may be contrasted
with the literature of, say, the period from 1875
to 1885. With the death of Timrod in 1867,
and of Simms, Longstreet, and Prentice in 1870,
the old order of Southern writers had passed
away. By 1875 a new group of writers had begun their work, Paul Hamilton Hayne best representing the transition from one to the other. The
younger writers either had been Confederate soldiers, or had been intimately identified with those
who were. They began to write, not out of response to a demand for distinctively Southern
literature, but because they had the artistic spirit,
the desire to create. They were interested in
describing Southern scenery, and in portraying
types of character in the social life of their re-
spective States. Unlike most of the literature of
the Old South, the new literature was related
directly to the life of the people. Men began
to describe Southern scenery, not some fantastic
world of dreamland; sentimentalism was super-
seded by a healthy realism. The writers fell in
with contemporary tendencies and followed the
lead of Bret Harte and Mark Twain, who had
begun to write humorous local sketches and incidents. With them literature was not a diversion,
but a business. They were willing to be known
as men of letters who made their living by litera-

ture. They stood, too, for the national, rather than the sectional, spirit. " What does it matter," said Joel Chandler Harris, " whether I am Northerner or Southerner if I am true to truth, and true to that larger truth, my own true self? My idea is that truth is more important than sectionalism, and that literature that can be labeled Northern, Southern, Western, or Eastern, is not worth labeling at all." Again, he said, speaking of the ideal Southern writer : "He must be Southern and yet cosmopolitan ; he must be intensely local in feeling, but utterly unprejudiced and unpartisan as to opinions, tradition, and sentiment. Whenever we have a genuine Southern literature, it will be American and cosmopolitan as well. Only let it be the work of genius, and it will take all sections by storm."

And it did take all sections by storm. Contrary to the idea which had prevailed after the war that Northern people would be slow to recognize Southern genius, it must be said that Northern magazines, Northern publishers, and Northern readers made possible the success of Southern writers. In 1873, " Scribner's Magazine " sent a special train through the South with the purpose of securing a series of articles on "the great South." While in New Orleans, Mr. Edward King, who had charge of the expedition, discovered George W. Cable, whose story,

" 'Sieur George," appeared in " Scribner's Magazine " in October of that year. Between that time and 1881 the magazine published, in addition to Cable's stories, — afterwards collected into the volume " Old Creole Days," — stories and poems by John Esten Cooke, Margaret J. Preston, Maurice Thompson, Mrs. Burnett, Mrs. Harrison, Irwin Russell, Richard Malcolm Johnston, Thomas Nelson Page, and Sidney Lanier. In an editorial of September, 1881, the editor, referring to the fact that no less than seven articles by Southerners had appeared in a recent number of " Scribner's," said : " We are glad to recognize the fact of a permanent productive force in literature in the Southern States. . . . We welcome the new writers to the great republic of letters with all heartiness." " The Century Magazine," the successor of " Scribner's," continued to be the patron of the new Southern writers. The number for April, 1884, contained Lanier's portrait as a frontispiece, a sketch of Lanier by William Hayes Ward, Thomas Nelson Page's " Marse Chan," an installment of Cable's " Dr. Sevier," Walter B. Hill's article on " Uncle Tom Without a Cabin," and William Preston Johnston's poem, " The Master."

" Harper's Magazine," in January, 1874, began a series of articles on the New South, by Edwin De Leon, and in the following year published a series of articles by Constance F. Woolson, giving sketches of Florida and western North Carolina. In May, 1887, appeared an article giving the first complete survey of Southern literature, which, according to the author, had introduced into our national literature "a stream of rich, warm blood." The "Independent," a paper which had seemed to Southerners extremely severe in its criticism of the life of the South, is especially connected with the rising fame of Lanier. The editor recognized his genius while he was still alive, after his death continued to publish his poems, and in 1884 wrote the Memorial for the first complete edition of his poems. Maurice Thompson, another Southern writer, became its literary editor in 1888.

Nor was the "Atlantic Monthly," which had been identified with the New England Renaissance, slow to recognize the value of the new Southern story-writers and poets. In 1873, while Mr. Howells was editor, Maurice Thompson's poem, "At the Window," was hailed by the editor and by Longfellow as "the work of a new and original singer, fresh, joyous, and true." The author received encouraging letters from Lowell and Emerson. In the same year and in the following appeared a series of articles entitled "A Rebel's Recollections," by George Cary Eggleston. In May, 1878, appeared Charles Egbert

Craddock's first story of the Tennessee Mountains, " A Dancing Party at Harrison's Cove." The value of her work was at once recognized by Mr. Howells and his successor, Mr. Aldrich. In a review of 1880, Cable's stories in " Old Creole Days " are characterized " as fresh in matter, as vivacious in treatment, and as full of wit as were the ' Luck of Roaring Camp ' and its audacious fellows, when they came, while they are much more human and delicate in feeling." In January, 1885, in an article on recent American fiction, appears the following tribute to the work of recent Southern writers : " It is not the subjects offered by Southern writers which interest us so much as the manifestation which seemed to be dying out of our literature. We welcome the work of Mr. Cable and Mr. [*sic*] Craddock, because it is large, imaginative, and constantly responsive to the elemental movements of human nature ; and we should not be greatly surprised if the historian of our literature a few generations hence, should take note of an enlargement of American letters at this time through the agency of a new South. . . . The North refines to a keen analysis, the South enriches through a generous imagination. . . . The breadth which characterizes the best Southern writing, the large free handling, the confident imagination, are legitimate results of the careless yet masterful and hospitable life which has pervaded that section. We have had our laugh at the florid, coarse-flavored literature which has not yet disappeared at the South, but we are witnessing now the rise of a school that shows us the worth of generous nature when it has been schooled and ordered." [1]

The effect of this literature on Northern readers was altogether wholesome, and ministered no doubt to the better understanding both of the Old South and of the New. The stories of Harris, Page, Cable, and Craddock reached the Northern mind to a degree never approached by the logic of Calhoun or the eloquence of impetuous orators, while the poems of Hayne and Lanier, breathing as they did the atmosphere of the larger modern world, and at the same time characterized by the warmth and richness of Southern scenery and Southern life, ministered in the same direction. On Southerners the effect was stimulating; one of the younger scholars of that time, the late Professor Baskervill, recalled "the rapture of glad surprise with which each new Southern writer was hailed as he or she revealed negro, mountaineer, cracker, or creole life and character to the world. There was joy in beholding the roses of romance and poetry blossoming above the ashes of defeat and humiliation, and

[1] In 1896 Mr. Walter H. Page, a native North Carolinian, became editor of the "Atlantic."

that, too, among a people hitherto more remarkable for the masterful deeds of warrior and statesman than for the finer, rarer, and more artistic creations of literary genius." [1]

One of the most significant characteristics of the Southern writers was that they all showed a certain discipline in their artistic work. They had little patience with much of the criticism that had prevailed in the South. As early as 1871 the editor of the " Southern Magazine," in a review of " Southland Writers," said : " We shall not have a literature until we have a criticism which can justify its claims to be deferred to; intelligent enough to explain why a work is good or bad, . . . courageous enough to condemn bad art and bad workmanship, no matter whose it be; to say, for instance, to more than half the writers in these volumes : ' Ladies, you may be all that is good, noble, and fair ; you may be the pride of society and the lights of your homes ; so far as you are Southern women our hearts are at your feet — but you have neither the genius, the learning, nor the judgment to qualify you for literature.' " In the same magazine for June, 1874, Paul Hamilton Hayne condemned severely the provincial literary criticism which had prevailed,

---

[1] Baskervill's *Southern Writers* is the best study that has been made of the Southern literature of this period. A second volume was prepared by his pupils and friends after his death.

— " indiscriminate adulations, effervescing commonplace, shallowness and poverty of thought."
" No foreign ridicule," he said, " however richly deserved, nothing truly either of logic or of laughter, can stop this growing evil, until our own scholars and thinkers have the manliness and honesty to discourage instead of applauding such manifestations of artistic weakness and artistic platitudes as have hitherto been foisted upon us by persons uncalled and unchosen of any of the muses. . . . Can a people's mental dignity and æsthetical culture be vindicated by patting incompetency and ignorance and self-sufficiency on the back ? "

Lanier himself wrote to Hayne, May 26, 1873, commending a criticism that Hayne had passed upon a popular Southern novel : " I have not read that production ; but from all I can hear 't is a most villainous, poor, pitiful piece of work ; and so far from endeavoring to serve the South by blindly plastering it with absurd praises, I think all true patriots ought to unite in redeeming the land from the imputation that such books are regarded as casting honor upon the section. God forbid we should really be brought so low as that we must perforce brag of such works ; and God be merciful to that man (he is an Atlanta editor) who boasted that sixteen thousand of these books had been sold in the South !

This last damning fact ought to have been concealed at the risk of life, limb, and fortune." Lanier himself saw the futility of such praise of his own work by the Southern people. Referring to the defense made of his Centennial poem by Southern newspapers, he wrote from Macon: " People here are so enthusiastic in my favor at present that they are quite prepared to accept blindly anything that comes from me. Of course I understand all this, and any success seems cheap which depends so thoroughly upon local pride as does my present position with the South." And again: " Much of this praise has come from the section in which he was born, and there is reason to suspect that it was based often on sectional pride rather than on any genuine recognition of those artistic theories of which his poem is — so far as he now knows — the first embodiment. Any triumph of this sort is cheap, because wrongly based, and to an earnest artist is intolerably painful."

Lanier's own standards of criticism did not prevent his recognition of the value of the real artists who lived in the South, nor his encouragement of every young man contemplating an artistic career. He wrote to Judge Bleckley about his son: " I am charmed at finding a Georgia young man who deliberately leaves the worn highways of the law and politics for the

rocky road of Art, and I wish to do everything
in my power to help and encourage him." Writing to George Cary Eggleston, December 27,
1876, he said: "I know you very well through
your 'Rebel's Recollections,' which I read in
book form some months ago with great entertainment. Our poor South has so few of the
guild, that I feel a personal interest in the works
of each one." His letters and published writings bear out the truth of this statement. It
has already been seen that he was intimate with
Paul Hamilton Hayne, who had encouraged him
to undertake the literary life at a time when all
other forces were tending in another direction.
Lanier criticised in detail many of Hayne's
poems. In a review of his poems published in
the "Southern Magazine," 1874, he paid a notable tribute to his fellow worker in the realm of
letters. He does not fail to call attention to trite
similes, worn collocations of sound, and commonplace sentiments; and also his diffuseness, prin-
cipally originating in a lavishness and looseness
of adjectives. At the same time he praises the
melody of Hayne's poetry, especially of his poem
"Fire Pictures," which he compares with Poe's
"Bells." In his book on Florida, while giving
an account of Southern cities which travelers are
apt to pass through in going to and from that
State, he has discriminating and sympathetic

passages on Timrod, Randall, Jackson, Hayne, and others. Of Timrod he says: " Few more spontaneous or delicate songs have been sung in these later days than one or two of the briefer lyrics. It is thoroughly evident that he never had time to learn the mere craft of the poet, the technique of verse, and that broader associ- ation with other poets, and a little of the wine of success, without which no man ever does the very best he might do." In his lectures at the Peabody Institute he quoted one of Timrod's sonnets, prefacing it with the words: " And as I have just read you a sonnet from one of the earliest of the sonnet-writers, let me now clinch and confirm this last position with a sonnet from one of the latest, — one who has but recently gone to that Land where, as he wished here, indeed life and love are the same; one who, I devoutly believe, if he had lived in Sir Philip's time, might have been Sir Philip's worthy bro- ther, both in poetic sweetness and in honorable knighthood." [1]

He was one of the first to recognize the genius of Joel Chandler Harris, whose Uncle Remus stories he first read in the " Atlanta Constitu- tion." He refers in his article on the New South to Uncle Remus as a " famous colored philoso- pher of Atlanta, who is a fiction so founded upon

[1] *Shakspere and His Forerunners*, vol. i, p. 170.

fact and so like it as to have passed into true
citizenship and authority, along with Bottom and
Autolycus. This is all the more worth giving,
since it is really negro-talk, and not that suppo-
sititious negro-minstrel talk which so often goes
for the original. It is as nearly perfect as any
dialect can well be; and if one had only some
system of notation by which to convey the *tones*
of the speaking voice, in which Brer Remus and
Brer Ab would say these things, nothing could
be at once more fine in humor and pointed in
philosophy. Negroes on the corner can be heard
any day engaged in talk that at least makes
one think of Shakespeare's clowns; but half the
point and flavor is in the subtle tone of voice,
the gesture, the glance, and these, unfortunately,
cannot be read between the lines by any one who
has not studied them in the living original."

In a letter to his brother, September 24, 1880,
Lanier said : " Have you read Cable's book, ' The
Grandissimes ' ? It is a work of art, and he has
a fervent and rare soul. Do you know him?"
In his announcement of the course on the English Novel at Johns Hopkins University, he included this novel in a list of recent American
novels which he intended to discuss.

Nor was he contented with recognizing the
genius of men who wrote of their own accord.
His letters to "Father" Tabb were especially

stimulating. He was the prime cause in inducing Richard Malcolm Johnston to offer first to the magazines, and then to the publishers, his stories of Middle Georgia. Johnston had published the " Dukesborough Tales " in the " Southern Magazine " as early as 1871, but they had made little or no impression on account of the limited circulation of that periodical. In 1877 " Mr. Neelus Peeler's Condition " was sent by Lanier to Mr. Richard Watson Gilder, then editor of " Scribner's Monthly." He had the rare pleasure of sending Mr. Gilder's letter of acceptance with enclosed check to his friend. The following letter shows how he advised Colonel Johnston as to one of the stories.

55 LEXINGTON STREET, BALTIMORE, MD.,
November 6, 1877.

MY DEAR COL. JOHNSTON, — Mrs. Lanier's illness on Saturday devolved a great many domestic duties upon me, and rendered it quite impossible for me to make the preparations necessary for my visit to you on Sunday. This caused me a great deal of regret; a malign fate seems to have pursued all my recent efforts in your direction.

I have attentively examined your " Dukesborough Tale." I wish very much that I could read it over aloud in your presence, so that I might call your attention to many verbal lapses which I find and which, I am sure, will hinder its way with the magazine editors. I will try to see you in a day or two, and do this. Again, ascending from merely verbal criticism to considerations of general treatment, I find that the action of the story does not move quite fast enough during the *first* twenty-five pages, and the *last* ten, to suit the impatience of the modern magazine man.

Aside from these two points, — and they can both be easily remedied, — the story strikes me as exquisitely funny, and your reproduction of the modes of thought and of speech among the rural Georgians is really wonderful. The peculiar turns and odd angles, described by the minds of these people in the course of ratiocination (Good Heavens, what would Sammy Wiggins think of such a sentence as this !), are presented here with a delicacy of art that gives me a great deal of enjoyment. The whole picture of old-time Georgia is admirable, and I find myself regretting that its *full* merit can be appreciated only by that limited number who, from personal experience, can compare it with the original.

Purely with a view to conciliating the editor of the magazine, I strongly advise you to hasten the movement of the beginning and of the catastrophe : that is, from about p. 1 to p. 34, and from p. 57 to p. 67. The middle, i. e., from p. 34

to p. 57, should not be touched : it is good enough
for me.

I would not dare to make these suggestions
if I thought that you would regard them otherwise than as pure evidences of my interest in the
success of the story.

Your friend,
SIDNEY L.

But Lanier's service to the South and to
Southern literature is greater than the recognition of any one writer or the encouragement
given to any one of them. All of them were
cheered in their work by his heroic life ; not
one but looked to him as a leader. His life,
which in a large sense belongs to the nation, belongs in a peculiar sense to the South. He was
Southern by birth, temperament, and experience.
He knew the South, — he had traveled from San
Antonio to Jacksonville, and from Baltimore to
Mobile Bay. Its scenery was the background of
his poetry, — the marsh, the mountain, the seashore, the forest, the birds and flowers of the
South stirred his imagination. He knew personally many of the leaders of the Confederacy, as
well as the men who made possible the New
South. He was heir to all the life of the past.
His chivalry, his fine grace of manners, his gen-
erosity and his enthusiasm were all Southern

traits; and the work that he has left is in a peculiar sense the product of a genius influenced by that civilization. All these things render him singularly precious to Southerners of the present generation.

He had qualities of mind and ideals of life, however, which have been too rare in his native section. He was a severe critic of some phases of its life. From this standpoint his career and his personality should never lose their influence in the South. There had been men and women who had loved music; but Lanier was the first Southerner to appreciate adequately its significance in the modern world, and to feel the inspiration of the most recent composers. There had been some fine things done in literature; but he was the first to realize the transcendent dignity and worth of the poet and his work. Literature had been a pastime, a source of recreation for men; to him the study of it was a passion, and the creation of it the highest vocation of man. Compared with other writers of the New South, Lanier was a man of broader culture and of finer scholarship. He did not have the power to create character as some of the writers of fiction, but he was a far better representative of the man of letters. The key to his intellectual life may be found in the fact that he read Wordsworth and Keats rather than Scott, George Eliot

rather than Thackeray, German literature as
well as French. He was national rather than
provincial, open-minded not prejudiced, modern
and not mediæval. His characteristics — to be
still further noted in the succeeding chapter —
are all in direct contrast with those of the conservative Southerner. There have been other
Southerners — far more than some men have
thought — who have had his spirit, and have
worked with heroism towards the accomplishment of enduring results. There have been none,
however, who have wrought out in their lives
and expressed in their writings higher ideals.
He therefore makes his appeal to every man who
is to-day working for the betterment of industrial,
educational, and literary conditions in the South.
There will never be a time when such men will
not look to him as the man of letters who, after
the war, struck out along lines which meant most
in the intellectual awakening of this section. He
was a pioneer worker in building up what he
liked to speak of as the New South : —

> The South whose gaze is cast
> No more upon the past,
> But whose bright eyes the skies of promise sweep,
> Whose feet in paths of progress swiftly leap ;
> And whose fresh thoughts, like cheerful rivers, run
> Through odorous ways to meet the morning sun !

CHAPTER XI

CHARACTERISTICS AND IDEAS

PERHAPS the best single description of Lanier is that by his friend H. Clay Wysham : " His eye, of bluish gray, was more spiritual than dreamy — except when he was suddenly aroused, and then it assumed a hawk-like fierceness. The transparent delicacy of his skin and complexion pleased the eye, and his fine-textured hair, which was soft and almost straight and of a light-brown color, was combed behind the ear in Southern style. His long beard, which was wavy and pointed, had even at an early age begun to show signs of turning gray. His nose was aquiline, his bearing was distinguished, and his manners were stamped with a high breeding that befitted the ' Cavalier ' lineage. His hands were delicate and white, by no means thin, and the fingers tapering. His gestures were not many, but swift, graceful, and expressive ; the tone of his voice was low; his figure was willowy and lithe ; and in stature he seemed tall, but in reality he was a little below six feet — withal there was a native knightly grace which marked his every movement." [1] If to this

[1] *Independent,* November 18, 1897.

be added the words of Dr. Gilman as to the impression he produced on people, the picture may be complete: " The appearance of Lanier was striking. There was nothing eccentric or odd about him, but his words, manners, ways of speech, were distinguished. I have heard a lady say that if he took his place in a crowded horse-car, an exhilarating atmosphere seemed to be introduced by his breezy ways." [1]

He was mindful of the conventionalities of life. He had nothing of the Bohemian in his looks, his manners, or his temperament. Poor though he was, he was scrupulous with regard to dress. He was a hard worker, but when his health permitted, he was thoroughly mindful of duties that devolved upon him as a member of society. He wrote to Charlotte Cushman: " For I am surely going to find you, at one place or t' other, — provided heaven shall send me so much fortune in the selling of a poem or two as will make the price of a new dress coat. Alas, with what unspeakable tender care I would have brushed this present garment of mine in days gone by, if I had dreamed that the time would come when so great a thing as a visit to *you* might hang upon the little length of its nap! Behold, it is not only in man's breast that pathos lies, and the very coat lapel that covers it may be a tragedy." Professor Gildersleeve

[1] *South Atlantic Quarterly*, April, 1905.

gives a characteristic incident: " I remember he came to a dinner given in his honor, fresh from a lecture at the Peabody, in a morning suit and with chalk on his fingers. Came thus, not because he was unmindful of conventionalities. He was as mindful of them as Browning, — came thus because he had to come thus. There was no time to dress. The poor chalk-fingered poet was miserable the whole evening, hardly roused himself when the talk fell on Blake, and when we took a walk together the next day he made his moan to me about it. A seraph with chalk on his fingers. Somehow, that little incident seems to me an epitome of his life, though I have mentioned it only to show how busy he was." [1]

He was a welcome guest in many homes. " He had the most gentle, refined, sweet, lovely manners, I think I may say, of any man I ever met," says Charles Heber Clarke. A letter from the daughter of the late John Foster Kirk, former editor of " Lippincott's Magazine," gives an impression of Lanier in the homes of his friends : —

" My first sight of Lanier was when he came into the room with my father at dusk one evening (they had been walking through the Wissahickon woods and came back to tea), and his presence seemed something beautiful in the room, even more from his manner than from his appear-

---

[1] Letter to the author.

ance, gracious and fine as that was. He always seemed to me to stand for chivalry as well as poetry, and his goodness was something you felt at once and never forgot. He was at our house one day with his flute. He and my father were going to Mr. Robert P. Morton's, in Germantown, to play together. We happened to speak of the fact that my sister, then a little girl, though absolutely without ear for music, had a curious delight in listening to it. Mr. Lanier said he would like to play to her; we called her in from the yard where she was playing, and he played some of his own music, explaining to her first what he thought of when he wrote it, describing to her the brook in its course, and other things in nature. He could easily have found a more appreciative listener, but not a happier one.

" I remember his eagerness about all forms of knowledge and expression. We went with him to the Centennial, where we were full of excitement about pictures, though none of us knew much about them. I remember the pleasure Mr. Lanier had in the sense of color and splendor given him by the big Hans Makart ('Caterina Cornaro') and discussions of that and the English and Spanish pictures. Intellectually he seemed to me not so much to have arrived as to be on the way, — with a beautiful fervor and eagerness about things, as if he had never had all that he longed for in books and study and thought." [1]

Lanier had remarkable power for making and keeping friends. This has already been seen in his relations to the Peacocks, Charlotte Cushman, and Bayard Taylor. In the large circle of friends among whom he moved in Baltimore may be seen further attestation of this point. People did not pity him, nor did they dole out charity to him. They did not reverence him merely because he was a poet, a teacher, or a musician of note; they were drawn to him by strong personal ties — he had magnetism. The little informal notes that he wrote to them, or the longer letters he wrote in absence, or the conversations that he had with them, sometimes till far into the night, are cherished as among the most sacred memories of their lives. He knew how to endure human weakness and to inspire human efforts. One of the friends who knew him best has recorded in a tender poem what Lanier meant to those who were intimate with him: —

> That love of man for man,
> That joyed in all sweet possibilities : that faith
> Which hallowed love and life. . . .
> So he, Heaven-taught in his large-heartedness,
> Smiled with his spirit's eyes athwart the veil
> That human loves too oft keep closely drawn. . . .
> So hearts leaped up to breathe his freer atmosphere,

[1] Letter to the author.

And eyes smiled truer for his radiance clear,
And souls grew loftier where his teachings fell,
And all gave love. . . .
                    Aye, the patience and the smile
Which glossed his pain; the courtesy;
The sweet quaint thoughts which gave his poems birth."[1]

She speaks, too, of " his winning tenderness with souls perplexed ; " " his eagerness for lofty converse ; " " his oneness with all master-minds ; " " his thirst for lore ; " " his gratitude for that the Lord had made the earth so good ! " "

In the house of this same friend, Mme. Blanc (Th. Bentzon) first realized the dead poet's personality ; she there caught something of the after-glow of his presence : —

" The morning that I spent with Mrs. Turnbull was almost as interesting as an interview with Sidney Lanier himself would have been, so fully does his memory live in that most æsthetic interior, where poetry and music are held in perpetual honor, and where domestic life has all the beauty of a work of art. The hero of Mrs. Turnbull's novel, 'A Catholic Man,' is none other than Sidney Lanier, and that scrupulously faithful presentment of a 'universal man' was of the greatest assistance to me.

" The beautiful mansion on Park Avenue has almost the character of a temple, where

---

[1] Poem by Mrs. Lawrence Turnbull, read at the presentation of the Lanier bust to Johns Hopkins University.

nothing profane or vulgar is allowed admission.
Passing through the reception rooms, I was introduced into a private parlor out of which
opened a music-room, from whose threshold I
recognized the man whom I had come to seek, —
the poet himself, as he was represented in his
latest years, by the German sculptor, Ephraim
Keyser. . . . By way of contrast, Mrs. Turnbull
exhibits a glorified Lanier, crowned with his
ultimate immortality. He appears in a symbolic
picture, ordered by this American art patroness,
from the Italian painter Gatti, where are grouped
all the great geniuses of the past, present, and
future, — the latter emerging vaguely from the
mists of the distance, and including a large
number of women. This innumerable multitude
of the *élite* of all ages encircles a mountain which
is dominated by Jesus Christ; and from this
figure of the Christ emanates the light which
Mrs. Turnbull has caused to be shed upon the
figures of the picture, with more or less brilliancy
according to her own preferences. Designating
a tall, draped figure who walks in the front rank
of the poets, the lady said to me : ' This is
Sidney Lanier ; ' and when I, despite my admiration for the poet of the marshes, ventured to offer
a few modest suggestions, she went on to develop
the thesis, that what exalts a man is less what
he has done than what he has aspired to do."

". . . . .

" Mrs. Turnbull had too much tact to multiply her personal anecdotes of Sidney Lanier, but she pictured him to me as he loved to sit by the fireside, where he had always his own special place ; coming, of an evening, unannounced, into the room where we then were, rising like a phantom beside her husband and herself, in the hour between daylight and dark, and pouring forth those profound, unexpected, and delightful things which seem to belong to him alone, which characterize his correspondence also, and all his literary remains." [1]

The quality of affection in Lanier reached its climax in his home life. There he was seen and known at his best. An early aspiration of his was " to show that the artist-life is not necessarily a Bohemian life, but that it may coincide with and *be* the home-life." Such poems as " Baby Charley " and " Hard Times in Elfland," and the story of " Bob " reveal the playful and affectionate father, while " My Springs," " In Absence," " Laus Mariae " and many published and unpublished letters are but variations of the oft-recurring theme : —

When life 's all love, 't is life : aught else, 't is naught.

[1] *Revue des Deux Mondes*, 1898. Translated for *Littell's Living Age*, May 14 and May 21, 1898.

A letter written to his wife will serve to give the spirit which prevailed in the home : —

January 1, 1875.

A thousand-fold Happy New Year to thee, and I would that thy whole year may be as full of sweetness as my heart is full of thee.

All day I dwell with my dear ones there with thee. I do so long for one hearty romp with my boys again! Kiss them most fervently for me, and say over their heads my New Year's prayer, that whether God may color their lives bright or black, they may continually grow in a large and hearty manhood, compounded of strength and love.

Let us try and teach them, dear wife, that it is only the small soul that ever cherishes bitterness ; for the climate of a large and loving heart is too warm for that frigid plant. Let us lead them to love everything in the world, above the world, and under the world adequately ; that is the sum and substance of a perfect life. And so God's divine rest be upon every head under the roof that covers thine this night, prayeth thy

HUSBAND.

Sweetness of disposition, depth of emotion, and absolute purity of life are frequently regarded as feminine traits. These Lanier had, but they were fused with the qualities of a virile and healthy manhood. He attracted strong and intellectual men as well as refined and cultivated women. The bravery manifested during the Civil War and the fortitude that he displayed after the war became elemental qualities in his character. His admiration of the heroic deeds of the age of chivalry arose from a certain inherent knightliness in his own character. He had the combination of tenderness and strength to which he called attention in Sir Philip Sidney. His admiration for old English poetry was due to the "ruddiness in its cheek and the red corpuscles in its veins." There is in his later prose the " send and drive " of a vigorous soul. It was this elemental manhood that attracted him to Whitman, despite all his protests against the latter's carelessness of form and lack of grace. " Reading him," he says, " is like getting the salt sea spray into one's face."

He had some of the Southerner's resistance to anything like insult. A story is frequently told in Baltimore of the way in which Lanier resented the conductor's words to a young lady at a rehearsal of the Peabody Orchestra. " ———, irritated in his undisciplined musician's nerves, vented that irritation in a rude outburst towards a timid young woman who was playing the piano, either with orchestra or voice or in solo. In an instant Lanier's tall, straight figure shot up from his seat and, taking the chair he occupied in his hand, he said : 'Mr. ——, you must retract every word you have uttered and apologize to that young lady before you beat another bar.' There was no mistake of his resoluteness and determination, and Mr. —— retracted and apologized ; the orchestra went on only after the same had been done."

Another element that contributed to the admirable symmetry of Lanier's character was that of humor. One would misjudge him entirely if he took into account only the highly wrought letters on music or the great majority of his poems. From one standpoint he seems a burning flame. As a matter of fact, however, his enthusiasm for anything that was fine and the ecstatic rapture into which he passed under the spell of great music or nature or poetry, were balanced by humor that was playful and delicate and at times irresistible. His pranks as a college boy and as a soldier have already been noted. His enjoyment of the negro and of the Georgia " Cracker " may be seen in his dialect poems, " A Florida Ghost," " Uncle Jim's Baptist Revival Hymn," " Jones's Private Argument," and others. With his children his spirit of fun-making knew no bounds. The point may still further be seen by any one who reads his lectures, and especially those letters to his friends in which he constantly indulged in playful conceits and fine humor. He even laughed at his poverty, and got off many a jest in the very face of death. In this respect, as in others, he was strikingly like Robert Louis Stevenson.

Lanier's modernness of mind has already been illustrated in his attitude to music and to scholarship. Asked one time what age he preferred, he said, " the Present," and the answer was typical of his whole attitude to things. He did not rail at his age. He was a close student of current events. He spoke strongly sometimes, as did Wordsworth and Ruskin, against the materialism of the nineteenth century; he delivered his protest against it in many of his poems; and yet he never lost his faith that all material progress would eventually contribute to the moral and artistic needs of man. " It is often asserted," he said, " that ours is a materialistic age, and that romance is dead; but this is marvelously untrue, and it may be counter-asserted with perfect confidence that there was never an age of the world when art was enthroned by so many hearthstones and intimate in so many common houses as now." He accepted the facts of his time, and sought to make them subservient to the healthy idealism that reigned in his soul.

Furthermore, he was an absolutely open-minded man, eager for any new world which he might enter. He had nothing of the provincialism

of the parish or of the period. One of the most
striking illustrations of this quality of mind is
seen in comparing him with Poe, who was irri-
table and prejudiced. Poe shared the ante-bellum
Southerner's prejudice against New England and
all her writers. There is nowhere in Lanier any
indication that such a spirit found lodgment in
his mind. Emerson — the transcendentalist —
was one of his " wise masters."

Another striking illustration of his breadth of
view was his profound reverence for science. That
he had this so early was due, as has been already
seen, to the influence of Professor Woodrow at
college. In " Tiger Lilies " he said, in commenting on Macaulay's idea of poetry declining as
science grows : " How long a time intervened
between Humboldt and Goethe ; how long between Agassiz and Tennyson ? One can scarcely
tell whether Humboldt and Agassiz were not as
good poets as Goethe and Tennyson were certainly good philosophers." " The astonishing
effect of the stimulus which has been given to
investigation into material nature by the rise of
geology and the prosperity of chemistry " is seen
in the literary development of the day. " To-
day's science bears not only fruit, but flowers also !
Poems, as well as steam engines, crown its growth
in these times." The passage closes with these
significant words : " Poetry will never fail, nor

science, nor the poetry of science." This view remained with him till the end of his life. He hailed the scientific progress of the nineteenth century as one of its greatest achievements, and constantly related it to the rise of landscape painting, modern nature poetry, modern music, and the English novel. His attitude thereto is made all the more notable by the fact that throughout the country, and especially in the South, there prevailed the utmost distrust of scientific investigations and hypotheses. During the seventies the criticism of the invitation extended to Huxley to deliver the principal address at the opening of Johns Hopkins University, and the controversy arising out of President White's enunciation of the principles that would dominate the newly created Cornell University, all tended to make the controversy between science and religion especially acute. American poets, notably Poe and Lowell, had expressed their distrust of modern scientific methods and conclusions. But Lanier saw no danger either to religion or to poetry in science. He constantly referred to Tyndall, Huxley, and Darwin, in a way which suggested his familiarity with their writings. I have seen a copy of the " Origin of Species " owned by Lanier, — the marks and annotations indicating the most careful and thoughtful reading thereof. In his lectures on the English Novel, in contrasting ancient science with modern science, he says : "In short, I find that early thought everywhere, whether dealing with physical fact or metaphysical problems, is lacking in what I may call the intellectual conscience, — the conscience which makes Mr. Darwin spend long and patient years in investigating small facts before daring to reason upon them, and which makes him state the facts adverse to his theory with as much care as the facts which make for it." Again he refers to him as " our own grave and patient Charles Darwin."

He did not write about science at second-hand, either, — he studied it. Mrs. Sophie Bledsoe Herrick, Lowell's Baltimore friend, tells of Lanier's interest in microscopic work : " Mrs. Lanier and family were not with him then, and he was busy writing some articles on the science of composition. Evening after evening he would bring the manuscript of these articles and read them, and talk them over.

" I was at that time intensely interested in microscopic work. It was curious and interesting to see how Mr. Lanier kindled to the subject, so foreign to his ordinary literary interests. I was too busy with editorial work to go on with my microscopic work then, and it was a great pleasure to leave my instrument and books on the subject with him for some months. He plunged in with all the ardor of a naturalist, not using the microscope as a mere toy, but doing good hard work with it. I think I can detect in his work after this time, — as well as in his letters, — many little touches which show the influence this study of nature had upon his mind." [1]

So he had little patience with " those timorous souls who believe that science, in explaining everything, — as they singularly fancy, — will destroy the possibility of poetry, of the novel, in short of all works of the imagination: the idea seeming to be that the imagination always requires the hall of life to be darkened before it displays its magic, like the modern spiritualistic séance-givers who can do nothing with the rope-tying and the guitars unless the lights are put out." [2] And again: " Here are thousands upon thousands of acute and patient men to-day who are devoutly gazing into the great mysteries of Nature and faithfully reporting what they see. These men have not destroyed the fairies: they have preserved them in more truthful and solid shape."

But while he estimated at its proper value the development of modern physical science, he saw it in its proper relation to music, poetry, and religion. " The scientific man," he says in his "Legend of St. Leonor," " is merely the minister

---

[1] Letter to the author.   [2] *The English Novel*, p. 28.

of poetry. He is cutting down the Western
Woods of Time ; presently poetry will come there
and make a city and gardens. This is always so.
The man of affairs works for the behoof and the
use of poetry. Scientific facts have never reached
their proper function until they emerge into new
poetic relations established between man and
man, between man and God, or between man
and nature."

Lanier's view of the theory of evolution is
interesting. "I have been studying science, biology, chemistry, evolution, and all," he writes to
J. F. Kirk, June 15, 1880. "It pieces on, perfectly, to those dreams which one has when one
is a boy and wanders alone by a strong running
river, on a day when the wind is high but the
sky clear. These enormous modern generalizations fill me with such dreams again.

"But it is precisely at the beginning of that
phenomenon which is the underlying subject
of this poem, 'Individuality,' that the largest of
such generalizations must begin, and the doctrine of evolution when pushed beyond this point
appears to me, after the most careful examination
of the evidence, to fail. It is pushed beyond this
point in its current application to the genesis of
species, and I think Mr. Huxley's last sweeping
declaration is clearly parallel to that of an enthusiastic dissecter who, forgetting that his obser-

vations are upon dead bodies, should build a physiological conclusion upon purely anatomical facts.

" For whatever can be proved to have been evolved, evolution seems to me a noble and beautiful and true theory. But a careful search has not shown me a single instance in which such proof as would stand the first shot of a boy lawyer in a moot court, has been brought forward in support of an actual case of species differentiation.

" A cloud (see the poem) *may* be evolved ; but not an artist ; and I find, in looking over my poem, that it has made itself into a passionate reaffirmation of the artist's autonomy, threatened alike from the direction of the scientific fanatic and the pantheistic devotee."

With all of Lanier's development — whether in science and scholarship, or in music and literature — he retained a vital faith in the Christian religion. He reacted against the Calvinism of his youth to almost as great a degree as did some of the New England poets. He at times felt keenly the narrowness and bigotry of the church — the warring of the sects over the unessential points.[1] In his thinking he found no place for the rigid and severe creed which dominated his youth. He gave up the forms, not the spirit, of

[1] See especially the poem " Remonstrance."

worship. He lived the abundant life, and all
of the roads which he traveled led to God. His
faith was as broad as "the liberal marshes of
Glynn." In the spirit of St. Francis he said : —

> I am one with all the kinsmen things
> That e'er my Father fathered.

Notwithstanding his vivid realization of the
evil of dogma and of sect, he maintained throughout his life a reverent faith; he could distin-
guish, as Browning said Shelley could not, between churchdom and Christianity. Not only in
the "Crystal" and "A Ballad of Trees and the
Master," and in the spirit of nearly all of his
poems, is this evident; but throughout his lectures, essays, and letters he never missed an opportunity to relate knowledge to faith. "He was
the most Christlike man I ever knew," said one
of his intimate friends, and those who have
looked upon his bust at Johns Hopkins have
involuntarily found the resemblance of physical
form. Certainly there has been no tenderer poem
written about the Master than the lines written
during Lanier's last year : —

> Into the woods my Master went,
> Clean forspent, forspent.
> Into the woods my Master came,
> Forspent with love and shame.
> But the olives they were not blind to Him,
> The little gray leaves were kind to Him :

The thorn-tree had a mind to Him
When into the woods He came.

Out of the woods my Master went,
And He was well content.
Out of the woods my Master came,
Content with death and shame.
When Death and Shame would woo Him last,
From under the trees they drew Him last :
'T was on a tree they slew Him — last
When out of the woods He came.

CHAPTER XII

THE LAST YEAR

ONE of the pieces of advice that Lanier gave to consumptives who went to Florida for their health was, " Set out to get well, with the thorough assurance that consumption is curable." He had literally followed his own advice, and had fought death off for seven years. By the spring of 1880 he had won his fight over every obstacle that had been in his way. He had a position which, supplemented by literary work, could sustain him and his family. By prodigious work he had overcome, to a large extent, his lack of training in both music and scholarship. The years 1878 and 1879 were his most productive. By the " Science of English Verse " and the " Marshes of Glynn " he had won the admiration of many who had at first been doubtful about his ability. From an obscure man of the provinces out of touch with artists or musicians, he had become the idol of a large circle of friends and admirers.

During all these years he had had to fight the disease which he inherited from both sides of his family and which was accentuated by hardships

during the war and the habits of a bent student.
His flute-playing had helped to mitigate the disease. Finally, however, in the summer of 1880,
he entered upon the last fight with his old enemy.
Lanier had laughed in the face of death, and
each new acquisition in the realms of music and
poetry had been a challenge to the enemy. In
1876 he almost succumbed, but in the mean time
three years of hard work had intervened. What
he had suffered from disease, even when he was
at his best, may be divined by one of imagination. He once referred to consumptives as " beyond all measure the keenest sufferers of all the
stricken of this world," and he knew what he was
talking about. He wrote to Hayne, November 19,
1880 : " For six months past a ghastly fever has
been taking possession of me each day at about
twelve M., and holding my head under the surface of indescribable distress for the next twenty
hours, subsiding only enough each morning to let
me get on my working-harness, but never inter-
mitting. A number of tests show it not to be the
' hectic ' so well known in consumption ; and to
this day it has baffled all the skill I could find
in New York, in Philadelphia, and here. I have
myself been disposed to think it arose purely
from the bitterness of having to spend my time
in making academic lectures and boy's books —
pot-boilers all — when a thousand songs are sing-

ing in my heart that will certainly kill me if I do not utter them soon. But I don't think this diagnosis has found favor with any practical physician ; and meantime I work day after day in such suffering as is piteous to see." [1] With his fever at 104 degrees he wrote "Sunrise," which, though considered by many his best poem, shows an unmistakable weakness when compared with the "Marshes of Glynn." There is a letting down of the robust imagination. He delivered his lectures on the English Novel under circumstances too harrowing to describe. His audience did not know whether he could finish any one of them.

And yet the story of his life shall not close with a pathetic account of those last sad months. Even during the last year he maintained his cheerfulness, his playfulness, his good humor, and also his buoyancy. In August, a fourth son, Robert Sampson Lanier, was born at West Chester, and the father writes letters to his friends, announcing his joy thereat. One is to his old friend, Richard Malcolm Johnston.

WEST CHESTER, PA., August 28, 1880.

MY DEAR AND SWEET RICHARD, — It has just occurred to me that you were *obliged* to be as sweet as you are, in order to redeem your name ; for the other three Richards in history were very

[1] *Letters*, p. 244.

far from being satisfactory persons, and something had to be done. Richard I, though a man of muscle, was but a loose sort of a swashbuckler after all; and Richard II, though handsome in person, was "redeless," and ministered much occasion to Wat Tyler and his gross following; while Richard III, though a wise man, allowed his wisdom to ferment into cunning and applied the same unto villainy.

But now comes Richard IV, to wit, you, — and, by means of gentle loveliness and a story or two, subdues a realm which I foresee will be far more intelligent than that of Richard I, far less turbulent than that of Richard II, and far more legitimate than that of Richard III, while it will own more, and more true loving subjects than all of those three put together.

I suppose my thoughts have been carried into these details of nomenclature by your reference to my own young Samson, who, I devoutly trust with you, shall yet give many a shrewd buffet and upsetting to the Philistines. Is it not wonderful how quickly these young fledgelings impress us with a sense of their individuality? This fellow is two weeks old to-day, and every one of us, from mother to nurse, appears to have a perfectly clear conception of his character. This conception is simply enchanting. In fact, the young man has already made himself absolutely indispensable to us, and my comrade and I wonder how we ever got along with *only* three boys.

I rejoice that the editor of " Harper's " has discrimination enough to see the quality of your stories, and I long to see these two appear, so that you may quickly follow them with a volume. When that appears, it shall have a review that will draw three souls out of one weaver — if this pen have not lost her cunning.

I'm sorry I can't send a very satisfactory answer to your health inquiries, as far as regards myself. The mean, pusillanimous fever which took under-hold of me two months ago is still *there*, as impregnably fixed as a cockle-burr in a sheep's tail. I have tried idleness, but (naturally) it won't *work*. I do no labor except works of necessity — such as kissing Mary, who is a more ravishing angel than ever — and works of mercy — such as letting off the world from any more of my poetry for a while. But it's all one to my master the fever. I get up every day and drag around in a pitiful kind of shambling existence. I fancy it has come to be purely a go-as-you-please match between me and the disease, to see which will wear out first, and I think I will manage to take the belt, yet.

Give my love to the chestnut trees [1] and all the rest of your family.

---

[1] It is said that he wrote the *Marshes of Glynn* under one of these.

Your letter gave us great delight. God bless you for it, my best and only Richard, as well as for all your other benefactions to

Your faithful friend,

S. L.

A few days before, he had written a more serious letter to his friend, Mrs. Isabelle Dobbin, of Baltimore. The concluding words show his realization of the deeper meaning of childhood.

WEST CHESTER, August 18, 1880.

Here is come a young man so lovely in his person, and so gentle and high-born in his manners, that in the course of some three days he has managed to make himself as necessary to *our* world as the sun, moon, and stars; at any rate, these would seem quite obscured without him. It just so happens that he is very vividly associated with *you;* for among the few treasures we allowed ourselves to bring away from home is the photograph you gave us, and this stands in the most honorable coign of vantage in Mary's room.

.   .   .   .

You'll be glad to know that my dear Comrade is doing well. . . . We have reason to expect a speedy sight of our dear invalid moving about her accustomed ways again. If you could see the Boy asleep by her side! The tranquillity of his slumber, and the shine of his mother's eyes thereover, seem to melt up and mysteriously absorb the great debates of the agnostics, and of science and politics, and to dissolve them into the pellucid Faith long ago reaffirmed by the Son of Man. Looking upon the child, this term seems to acquire a new meaning, as if Christ were in some sort reproduced in every infant.

In the fall he was busy again with his books for boys, — books, it may be said, that had their origin in the stories he told his own boys.[1] The spirit in which he worked on these "pot-boilers" is seen in a letter to his publisher, Mr. Charles Scribner : —

> 435 N. CALVERT ST., BALTIMORE, MD.,
> November 12, 1880.

MY DEAR MR. SCRIBNER, — You have certainly made a beautiful book of the "King Arthur," and I heartily congratulate you on achieving what seems to me a real marvel of bookmaking art. The binding seems even richer than that of the "Froissart;" and the type and printing leave a new impression of graciousness upon the eye with each reading.

I suspect there are few books in our language

---

[1] Of these *The Boy's Froissart* was published in 1878, *The Boy's King Arthur* in 1880, *The Boy's Mabinogion* in 1881, and *The Boy's Percy* in 1882.

which lead a reader — whether young or old —
on from one paragraph to another with such
strong and yet quiet seduction as this. Familiar
as I am with it after having digested the whole
work before editing it and again reading it in
proof — some parts twice over — I yet cannot
open at any page of your volume without reading on for a while; and I have observed the same
effect with other grown persons who have opened
the book in my library since your package came
a couple of days ago. It seems difficult to believe otherwise than that you have only to make
the book well known in order to secure it a great
sale, not only for the present year but for several
years to come. Perhaps I may be of service in
reminding you — of what the rush of winter business might cause you to overlook — that it would
seem wise to make a much more extensive outlay
in the way of special advertisement, here, than was
necessary with the "Froissart." It is probably
quite safe to say that a thousand persons are familiar with at least the name of Froissart to one
who ever heard of Malory; and the facts (1)
that this book is an English classic written in the
fifteenth century; (2) that it is the very first piece
of melodious English prose ever written, though
melodious English *poetry* had been common for
seven hundred years before, — a fact which seems
astonishing to those who are not familiar with

the circumstance that all nations appear to have produced good poetry a long time before good prose, usually a long time before *any* prose; (3) that it arrays a number of the most splendid ideals of energetic manhood in all literature; and (4) that the stories which it brings together and arranges, for the first time, have furnished themes for the thought, the talk, the poems, the operas of the most civilized peoples of the earth during more than seven hundred years, — ought to be diligently circulated. I regretted exceedingly that I could not, with appropriateness to youthful readers, bring out in the introduction the strange melody of Malory's sentences, by reducing their movement to musical notation. No one who has not heard it would believe the effect of some of his passages upon the ear when read by any one who has through sympathetic study learned the rhythm in which he *thought* his phrases. . . .

Sincerely yours,

SIDNEY LANIER.

In January, he began his lectures at Johns Hopkins. Who would have thought that a dying man could give expression to such vigorous ideas in such rhythmic and virile prose as are some of the passages in the " English Novel " ? There is not the intellectual strength in this book that there is in the " Science of English Verse."

There is more of a tendency to go off in digressions, "to talk away across country," and the whole lacks in unity and in scientific precision. But there are passages in it that men will not willingly let die. His discussion of the growth of personality, of the relations of Science, Art, Religion, and Life, of Walt Whitman and Zola, and above all, of George Eliot, are worthy of Lanier at his best. These passages and the still more important one on the relation of art to morals are too well known to be quoted; they will be considered in another chapter dealing with Lanier's work as critic. They are mentioned here only to show the range of Lanier's interest and the alertness of his mind when his body was fast failing.

Frances E. Willard heard these lectures, and her words descriptive of them indicate that even in those days of intense suffering Lanier impressed her favorably. "It was refreshing," she says, "to listen to a professor of literature who was something more than a *raconteur* and something different from a bibliophile, who had, indeed, risen to the level of generalization and employed the method of a philosopher. . . . [His] face [was] very pale and delicate, with finely chiseled features, dark, clustering hair, parted in the middle, and beard after the manner of the Italian school of art. . . . He sits not very reposefully in his professorial armchair, and reads from dainty slips of MS. in a clear, penetrating voice full of subtlest comprehension, but painfully and often interrupted by a cough. . . . As we met for a moment, when the lecture was over, he spoke kindly of my work, evincing that sympathy of the scholar with the work of progressive philanthropy. 'We are all striving for one end,' said Lanier, with genial, hopeful smile, 'and that is to develop and ennoble the humanity of which we form a part.' " [1]

Just after finishing his lectures, which were reduced from twenty to twelve out of consideration for his health, Lanier went to New York to consult his publishers about future work. The impression made by him on one of his old students is seen in this passage: "One day I had a startling letter from Mrs. Lanier, saying that he was coming to New York on business, though he was in no condition for such an effort, and begging me, as one whom he loved, to meet him and to watch over him as best I could. I found him at the St. Denis, and we had dinner together. I now know how completely he deceived me as to his condition. With the intensity and exaltation often characteristic of the consumptive, he led me to think that he was only slightly ailing, was gay and versatile as ever, insisted on going some-

[1] *Independent*, Sept. 1, 1881.

where for the evening 'to hear some music,' and absolutely demanded to exercise through the evening the rights of host in a way that baffled my inexperience completely. Only just as I left him did he let fall a single remark that I later saw showed how severe and unfortunate, probably, was the strain of it all."

Brave as he was, however, and eager to keep at his work, he finally submitted to the inevitable, and in May started with his brother to the mountains of western North Carolina. His final interview with Dr. Gilman is thus related by the latter : —

"The last time that I saw Lanier was in the spring of 1881, when after a winter of severe illness he came to make arrangements for his lectures in the next winter and to say good-bye for the summer. His emaciated form could scarcely walk across the yard from the carriage to the door. 'I am going to Asheville, N. C.,' he said, ' and I am going to write an account of that region as a railroad guide. It seems as if the good Lord always took care of me. Just as the doctors had said that I must go to that mountain region, the publishers gave me a commission to prepare a book.' 'Good-bye,' he added, and I supported his tottering steps to the carriage door, never to see his face again."[1]

[1] *South Atlantic Quarterly*, April, 1905.

The last months of Lanier's career seem to bring
together all the threads of his life. He was in
the mountains which had first stimulated his love
of nature and were the background of his early
romance. He was lovingly attended by father,
brother, and wife, and took constant delight in
the little boy who had come to cheer his last days
of weariness and sickness. He named the tent
Camp Robin, after his youngest son, and from
that camp sent his last message to the boys of
America. They are the words of the preface
to " The Boy's Mabinogion," or " Knightly Le-
gends of Wales : " " In now leaving this beautiful book with my young countrymen, I find myself so sure of its charm as to feel no hesitation
in taking authority to unite the earnest expression of their gratitude with that of my own to
Lady Charlotte Guest, whose talents and scholarship have made these delights possible ; and I
can wish my young readers few pleasures of finer
quality than that surprised sense of a whole new
world of possession which came with my first
reading of these Mabinogion, and made me remember Keats's

> watcher of the skies
> When a new planet swims into his ken."

A letter to President Gilman indicates his continued interest in scientific investigation : —

ASHEVILLE, N. C., June 5, 1881.

DEAR MR. GILMAN, — Can you help me — or tell me how I can help myself — in the following matter? A few weeks from now I wish to study the so-called no-frost belt on the side of Tryon Mountain; and in order to test the popular account I propose to carry on two simultaneous series of meteorological observations during a fortnight or longer, — the one conducted by myself in the middle of the belt, the other by a friend stationed well outside its limits. For this purpose I need two small self-registering thermometers, two aneroid thermometers, and two hygrometers of any make. It has occurred to me that since these observations will be conducted during the University recess I might — always provided, of course, that there is any authority or precedent for such action — procure this apparatus from the University collection, especially as no instrument is included which could not easily be replaced. Of course I would cheerfully deposit a sum sufficient to cover the value of the whole outfit.

Should this arrangement be possible, I merely ask that you turn this letter over to Dr. Hastings, with the request that he will have this apparatus packed at my expense and shipped by express to me at this point immediately.

Yours very sincerely, SIDNEY LANIER.

The impulse to poetry was with him, too. He jotted down or dictated to his wife outlines and suggestions of poems which he hoped to write. Of these one has been printed : —

I was the earliest bird awake,
It was a while before dawn, I believe,
But somehow I saw round the world,
And the eastern mountain top did not hinder me.
And I knew of the dawn by my heart, not by mine eyes.

One agrees with " Father " Tabb that no utterance of the poet ever betrayed more of his nature, — " feeble and dying, but still a ' bird,' awake to every emotion of love, of beauty, of faith, of star-like hope, keeping the dawn in his heart to sing, when the mountain-tops hindered it from his eyes."

On August 4 the party started across the mountains to Lynn, Polk County, North Carolina. On the way they stopped with a friend in whose house Lanier gave one more exhibition of his love of music. " It was in this house," says Miss Spann, " the meeting-place of all sweet nobility with nature and with the human spirit, that he uttered his last music on earth. At the close of the day Lanier came in and passed down the long drawing-room until he reached a western window. In the distance were the far-reaching Alleghany hills, with Mt. Pisgah supreme among them, and the intervening valley bathed in sunset beauty. Absorbed away from those around him, he watched the sunset glow deepen into twilight, then sat down to the piano, facing the window. Sorrow and joy and pain and hope and triumph his soul poured forth. They felt that in that twilight hour he had risen to an angel's song." [1]

Lynn is in a sheltered valley among the mountains of Polk County, whose "climate is tempered by a curious current of warm air along the slope of Tryon Mountain, its northern boundary, a sort of ethereal Gulf Stream." Here death came sooner than was anticipated by the brother, who had gone back to Montgomery, preceded already by his father. Mrs. Lanier's own words tell the story of the end in simplicity and love: "We are left alone (August 29) with one another. On the last night of the summer comes a change. His love and immortal will hold off the destroyer of our summer yet one more week, until the forenoon of September 7, and then falls the frost, and that unfaltering will renders its supreme submission to the adored will of God." His death before the open window was a realization of Matthew Arnold's wish with regard to dying : —

> Let me be,
> While all around in silence lies,

[1] *Independent*, June 28, 1894.

> Moved to the window near, and see
> Once more, before my dying eyes, —
>
> Bathed in the sacred dews of morn
> The wide aerial landscape spread,
> The world which was ere I was born,
> The world which lasts when I am dead."

The closing lines of "Sunrise" express better than anything else Lanier's own confident faith as he passed behind the veil : —

> And ever my heart through the night shall with know-
>   ledge abide thee,
> And ever by day shall my spirit, as one that hath tried
>   thee,
> Labor, at leisure, in art — till yonder beside thee
> My soul shall float, friend Sun,
> The day being done.

His body was taken to Baltimore, where it rests in Greenmount Cemetery in the lot of his friends, the Turnbulls, close by the son whose memory they have perpetuated by the endowment of a permanent lectureship on poetry in Johns Hopkins University. The grave is unmarked — even by a slab. It divides the interest of visitors to Baltimore with the grave of Poe, which, however, is in another part of the city. So these two poets, whose lives and whose characters were so strikingly unlike, sleep in their adopted city.

Shortly after Lanier's death memorial services

were held at Johns Hopkins University, at which
time beautiful tributes were paid to him by his
colleagues and friends. A committee of the citizens of Baltimore was appointed to raise a fund
for the sustenance and education of the poet's
family. They were aided in this by admirers of
Lanier and public-spirited citizens throughout
the country. Meantime his fame was growing,
the publication of his poems in 1884 giving
fresh impetus thereto.

Seven years after his death a bust of the poet
was presented to the University by Mr. Charles
Lanier of New York.[1] "The hall was filled,"
says ex-President Gilman, "with a company of
those who knew and admired him. On the ped-
estal which supported the bust hung his flute
and a roll of his music; a garland of laurels
crowned his brow, and the sweetest of flowers
were strewn at his feet. Letters came from Lowell, Holmes, Gilder, Stedman; young men who
never saw him, but who had come under his influence, read their tributes in verse; a former
student of the University made a critical estimate of the 'Science of Verse;' a lady read
several of Lanier's own poems; another lady sang
one of his musical compositions adapted to words
of Tennyson, and another song, one of his to

[1] For a full record of the exercises see *A Memorial of Sidney Lanier*, Baltimore, 1888.

which some one else wrote the music; a college
president of New Jersey held up Lanier as a
teacher of ethics; but the most striking figure
was the trim, gaunt form of a Catholic priest,
who referred to the day when they, two Confederate soldiers (the Huguenot and the Catholic),
were confined in the Union prison, and with tears
in his eyes said, his love for Lanier was like that
of David for Jonathan. The sweetest of all the
testimonials came at the very last moment, un-
solicited and unexpected, from that charming
poetess, Edith Thomas. She heard of the memorial assembly, and on the spur of the moment
wrote the well-known lines, suggested by one of
Lanier's own verses : —

On the Paradise side of the river of death."

The aftermath of Lanier's home life is all
pleasant to contemplate. His wife, although still
an invalid, has, by her readings from her husband's letters and poems, and by her sympathetic help for all those who have cared to know
more about him, done more than any other person to extend his fame. With tremendous obstacles in her way, she has reared to manhood
the four sons, three of whom are now actively
identified with publishing houses in New York
city, and one of whom, bearing the name of his
father, is now living upon a farm in Georgia.

Charles Day Lanier is president of the Review
of Reviews Company, and is associated with his
youngest brother, Robert Sampson Lanier, in
editing "The Country Calendar." Henry Wysham Lanier is a member of the firm of Double-
day, Page & Company, and editor of "Country
Life in America." They all inherit their father's
love of music and poetry, and through their magazines are doing much to foster among Americans
a taste for country life. By a striking coinci-
dence — entirely unpremeditated on their part —
three of the sons and their mother live at Greenwich, Connecticut. It will be remembered that
the home of the English Laniers was at Greenwich, — and so the story of the Lanier family
begins and ends with this name, — one in the
Old World and one in the New.

CHAPTER XIII

·THE ACHIEVEMENT IN CRITICISM AND IN POETRY

SPECULATIONS as to what Lanier might have done with fewer limitations and with a longer span of years inevitably arise in the mind of any one who studies his life. If, like the late Theodore Thomas, he had at an early age been able to develop his talent for music in the musical circles of New York; if, like Longfellow, he had gone from a small college to a German university, or, like Mr. Howells, from the provinces to Cambridge, where he would have come in contact with a group of men of letters; if, after the Civil War, he had, like Hayne, retired to a cabin and there devoted himself entirely to literary work; if, like Lowell, he could have given attention to literary subjects and lectured in a university without teaching classes of immature students or without resorting to " potboilers," " nothings that do mar the artist's hand; " if, like Poe, he could have struck some one vein and worked it for all it was worth, — if, in a word, the varied activity of his life could have given way to a certain definiteness of purpose and concentration of effort, what might have been the difference! Music and poetry strove for the mastery of his soul. Swinburne, speaking of those who attempt success in two realms of art, says, " On neither course can the runner of a double race attain the goal, but must needs in both races alike be caught up and resign his torch to a runner with a single aim." And yet one feels that if Lanier had had time and health to work out all these diverse interests and all his varied experiences into a unity, if scholarship and music and poetry could have been developed simultaneously over a long stretch of time, there would have resulted, perhaps, a more many-sided man and a finer poetry than we have yet had in America.

So at last the speculation reduces itself to one of time. Lycidas was dead ere his prime. From 1876 till the fatal illness took hold of him he made great strides in poetry. Up to the very last he was making plans for the future. His letters to friends outlining the volumes that he hoped to publish, — work demanding decades instead of years, — the memoranda jotted down on bits of paper or backs of envelopes as the rough drafts of essays or poems, would be pathetic, if one did not believe with Lanier that death is a mere incident in an eternal life, or with Browning, that what a man would do exalts him. The lines of Robert Browning's poems in which he sets forth the glory of the life of aspiration — aspiration independent of any achievement — ring in one's ears, as he reads the story of Lanier's life.

> This low man seeks a little thing to do,
>   Sees it and does it;
> This high man, with a great thing to pursue,
>   Dies ere he knows it.

The imperfect poems, the unfinished poems, the sheaves unharvested, not like Coleridge's for lack of will, but for lack of time, are suggestive of one of the finest aspects of romantic art. " I would rather fail at some things I wot of than succeed at others," said Lanier. There are moods when the imperfection of Lanier pleases more than the perfection of Poe — even from the artistic standpoint. What he aspired to be enters into one's whole thought about his life and his art. The vista of his grave opens up into the unseen world.

On earth the broken arcs; in the heaven a perfect round.

But the time comes when none of these considerations — neither admiration for the man, nor speculations as to what he might have done under different circumstances, nor thoughts as to what he may be doing in larger, other worlds than ours — should interfere with a judicial estimate of what he really achieved. It would have been the miracle of history if with all his obstacles he had not had limitations as a writer ; and yet many who have insisted most on his sufferings, have resented any criticism passed upon his work. One has the authority of Lanier's writings about other men and his letters about his own poems for judging him only by the highest standards. Did he in aiming at a million miss a unit? Was he blinded by the very excess of light? How will he fare in that race with time of which a contemporary essayist has written? " When the admiration of his friends no longer counts, when his friends and admirers are themselves gathered to the same silent throng," will there be enough inherent worth in his work to keep his fame alive ? These are questions that one has a right to ask.

And, first, as to Lanier's prose work. He has suffered from the fact that so many of his unrevised works have been published ; these have their excuse for being in the light they throw on his life ; but otherwise some of them are disappointing. If, instead of ten volumes of prose, there could be selected his best work from all of them, there would still be a residue of writing that would establish Lanier's place among the prose writers of America. There is no better illustration of his development than that seen in comparing his early prose — the war letters and " Tiger Lilies," for instance, or such essays as " Retrospects and Prospects " — with that of his maturer years. I doubt if justice has been done to Lanier's best style, its clearness, fluency, and eloquence. It may be claimed without dispute that he was a rare good letter-writer; perhaps only Lowell's letters are more interesting. The faults of his poetry are not always seen in his best letters. In them there is a playfulness, a richness of humor, an exuberance of spirits, animated talk about himself and his work, and withal a distinct style, that ought to keep them alive. There might be selected, too, a volume of essays, including " From Bacon to Beethoven," " The Orchestra of To-Day," " San Antonio de Bexar," " The Confederate Memorial Address," " The New South," and others.

A volume of American Criticism, edited by Mr. William Morton Payne, includes Lanier among the dozen best American critics, giving a selection from the " English Novel " as a typical passage. Has he a right to be in such a book? His work as a scholar has been discussed in a previous chapter; his rank as a critic is a very different matter. It goes without saying that Lanier was not a great critic. He did not have the learning requisite for one. One might turn the words of his criticism of Poe and say that he needed to know more. He knew but little of the

classics beyond what he studied in college; while
he read French and German literature to some
extent, he did not go into them as Lowell did.
Homer, Dante, and Goethe were but little more
than names to him. Furthermore, his criticism
is often marked by a tendency to indulge in
hasty generalizations, due to the fact that he had
not sufficient facts to draw upon. An illustration
is his preference of the Elizabethan sonnets to
the English sonnets written on the Italian model,
or his discussion of personality as found in the
Greek drama. His generalizations are often
either patently obvious or far-fetched. He was
too eager to "bring together people and books
that never dreamed of being side by side." His
tendency to fancy, so marked in his poetry, is
seen also in his criticism, as for instance, his comparison of a sonnet to a little drama, or his statement that every poem has a plot, a crisis, and a
hero. He had De Quincey's habit of digressing
from the main theme, — what he himself called
in speaking of an Elizabethan poet, the "constant temptation, to the vigorous and springy
mind of the poet, to bound off wherever his
momentary fancy may lead him." This is especially seen in his lectures on the English
Novel, where he is often carried far afield from
the general theme. In his lectures on "Shakspere and His Forerunners," he was so often

troubled with an embarrassment of riches that he did not endeavor to follow a rigidly formed plan.

A more serious defect, however, was his lack of catholicity of judgment. He had all of Carlyle's distaste for the eighteenth century; his dislike of Pope was often expressed, and he went so far as to wish that the novels of Fielding and Richardson might be " blotted from the face of the earth." His characterization of Thackeray as a " low-pitched artist " is wide of the mark. As Lanier had his dislikes in literature and expressed them vigorously, so he over-praised many men. When he says, for instance, that Bartholomew Griffin " will yet obtain a high and immortal place in English literature," or that William Drummond of Hawthornden is one of " the chief glories of the English tongue," or that Gavin Douglas is " one of the greatest poets of our language," one wonders to what extent the " pleasant peril of enthusiasm " will carry a man. One may be an admirer of George Eliot and yet feel that Lanier has overstated her merits as compared with other English novelists, and that his praise of " Daniel Deronda " is excessive.

Such defects as are here suggested should not, however, blind the reader to some of Lanier's better work. The history of criticism, especially of romantic criticism, is full of just such unbalanced judgments. It is often true in criticism

that a man " should like what he does like ; and
his likings are facts in criticism for him." Without very great learning and with strong preju-
dices in some directions, Lanier yet had remarkable insight into literature. Lowell's saying that he was " a man of genius with a rare
gift for the happy word " is especially true of
some of his critical writing. Examples are his
well-known characterizations of great men in
" The Crystal : " —

> Buddha, beautiful! I pardon thee
> That all the All thou hadst for needy man
> Was Nothing, and thy Best of being was
> But not to be.
>
> .   .   .   .   .   .
>
>   Langley, that with but a touch
> Of art had sung Piers Plowman to the top
> Of English song, whereof 't is dearest, now
> And most adorable.
>
> .   .   .   .   .   .
>
>   Emerson,
> Most wise, that yet, in finding Wisdom, lost
> Thy Self, sometimes.
>
> .   .   .   .   .   .
>
>   Tennyson, largest voice
> Since Milton, yet some register of wit
> Wanting.

There are scattered throughout his prose works
criticisms of writers that are at once penetrating
and subtle. The one on Browning has already
been quoted. The best known of these criticisms
is that on Walt Whitman, but it is too long for

insertion here. There is a sentence in one of his
letters to Bayard Taylor, however, that hits the
mark better than the longer criticism, perhaps:
" Upon a sober comparison, I think Walt Whitman's ' Leaves of Grass ' worth at least a million
of ' Among my Books ' and ' Atalanta in Caly-
don.' In the two latter I could not find anything
which has not been much better said before ;
but ' Leaves of Grass ' was real refreshing to me
— like rude salt spray in your face — in spite
of its enormous fundamental error that a thing
is good because it is natural, and in spite of the
world-wide difference between my own conceptions of art and the author's." Another good
one is that on Shelley : " In truth, Shelley appears always to have labored under an essential
immaturity : it is very possible that if he had
lived a hundred years he would never have become a man ; he was penetrated with modern
ideas, but penetrated as a boy would be, crudely,
overmuch, and with a constant tendency to the
extravagant and illogical ; so that I call him
the modern boy."

Lanier writes of the songs of the twelfth and
thirteenth centuries as " short and unstudied little songs, as many of them are, songs which come
upon us out of that obscure period like brief
little bird-calls from a thick-leaved wood." He
speaks of Chaucer's works as " full of cunning

hints and twinkle-eyed suggestions which peep between the lines like the comely faces of country children between the fence bars as one rides by." He draws a fine comparison between William Morris and Chaucer: " How does the spire of hope spring and upbound into the infinite in Chaucer; while, on the other hand, how blank, world-bound, and wearying is the stone *façade* of hopelessness which rears itself uncompromisingly behind the gayest pictures of William Morris ! . . . Again, how openly joyful is Chaucer, how secretly melancholy is Morris ! Both, it is true, are full of sunshine ; but Chaucer's is spring sunshine, Morris's is autumn. . . . Chaucer rejoices as only those can who know the bound of good red blood through unobstructed veins, and the thrilling tingle of nerve and sinew at amity ; and who can transport this healthy animalism into their unburdened minds, and spiritualize it so that the mere drawing of breath is at once a keen delight and an inwardly felt practical act of praise to the God of a strong and beautiful world. Morris too has his sensuous element, but it is utterly unlike Chaucer's ; it is *dilettante*, it is amateur sensualism; it is not strong, though sometimes excessive, and it is nervously afraid of that satiety which is at once its chief temptation and its most awful doom.

" Again, Chaucer lives, Morris dreams. . . .

'The Canterbury Tales' is simply a drama with somewhat more of stage direction than is common ; but the 'Earthly Paradise' is a reverie, which would hate nothing so much as to be broken by any collision with that rude actual life which Chaucer portrays.

" And, finally, note the faith that shines in Chaucer and the doubt that darkens in Morris. Has there been any man since St. John so lovable as the 'Persoune'? or any sermon since that on the Mount so keenly analytical, . . . as 'The Persoune's Tale'? . . . A true Hindu life-weariness (to use one of Novalis' marvelous phrases) is really the atmosphere which produces the exquisite haze of Morris's pictures. . . . Can any poet shoot his soul's arrow to its best height, when at once bow and string and muscle and nerve are slackened in this vaporous and relaxing air, that comes up out of the old dreams of fate that were false and of passions that were not pure? " [1]

Lanier's enthusiasm for Chaucer is typical of much of his critical writing. He was a generous praiser of the best literature, and generally his praise was right. " Lyrics of criticism " would be a good title for many of his passages. There was nothing of indifferentism in him. In a letter to Gibson Peacock he wrote of a certain type of

[1] *Music and Poetry*, p. 198.

criticism which, it may be said, has been widely prevalent in recent years : " In the very short time that I have been in the hands of the critics, nothing has amazed me more than the timid solicitudes with which they rarefy in one line any enthusiasm they may have condensed in another — a process curiously analogous to those irregular condensations and rarefactions of air which physicists have shown to be the conditions of producing an indeterminate sound. Many of my critics have seemed — if I may change the figure — to be forever conciliating the yet-unrisen ghosts of possible mistakes." Enough quotations have already been given from his lectures in Baltimore to show his enthusiasm for many of the periods and many of the authors of English literature. It is a distinction for him as a critic that he has set forth in so many passages his conception of the mission of poetry, — passages that are in the line of succession of defenses of poetry by Sidney, Hazlitt, and Shelley.

There is enough good criticism in the Shakespeare lectures and in the " English Novel," in the prefaces of the boy's books and in his letters, to make a volume of interest and importance. Suppose we cease to think of the first two as formal treatises on the subjects they discuss, and rather select from them such passages as the discussion of personality, the relation of music,

science, and the novel, the criticism of Whitman's
theory of art, the discussion of the relation of
morals to art, the best passages on Anglo-Saxon
poetry and the Elizabethan sonneteers, and the
finer passages on Shakespeare's growth as a man
and as a dramatist.   Such a volume would, I
believe, confirm one in the opinion that Lanier
belongs by right among the best American critics.
Certainly, the " Science of English Verse " en-
titles him to that distinction.

About 1875 Lanier became interested in the
formal side of poetry and projected a work on a
scientific basis.   It was natural that one who
had so much reverence for science and who had
studied the " physics of music," should apply the
scientific method to the study of poetry.   He
knew that the science of versification was not
the most important phase of poetry : in the preface, as in the epilogue, to the " Science of English Verse," he makes clear that " for the artist
in verse there is no law : the perception and love
of beauty constitute the whole outfit."   In many
other passages in his writings may be seen his
view of the moral significance of poetry.   He
desired, however, to formulate for himself and
for students certain metrical laws.   What differentiates poetry from prose ? How does a writer
produce certain effects with certain rhythms
and vowel and consonant arrangements ?   The

student wishes to know why the forms are fair and hear how the tale is told. By the study of rhythm, tune, and color, Lanier believed that one might receive " a whole new world of possible delight." He believed with Sylvester that " versification has a technical side quite as well capable of being reduced to rules as that of painting or any other fine art." His book was intended to furnish students with such an outfit of facts and principles as would serve for pursuing further researches.

The time was ripe for such a study. Lanier wrote to Mr. Stedman that " in all directions the poetic art was suffering from the shameful circumstance that criticism was without a scientific basis." The book at once received commendation from competent critics. Edward Rowland Sill wrote Dr. Gilman that it was " the only thing extant on that subject that is of any earthly value. I wonder that so few seem to have discovered its great merit," — an opinion afterwards repeated by him in the " Atlantic Monthly." The late Richard Hovey, in a series of articles in the " Independent " on the technic of poetry, said that Lanier had begun such a scientific study with " great soundness and common sense ; " the book is " accurate, scientific, suggestive." The editor of the " Dial " referred to it as " the most striking and thoughtful exposition yet published on the technics of English poetry." Within the past ten years books on English verse have multiplied fast. In Germany, in England, and in America, the discussion of metrics has gone on. While dissenting from some of Lanier's conclusions, few of the writers have failed to recognize his work as of great importance.[1] One man rarely sees all round any great subject like this, — each man sees some one special point and states it in an individual way, and finally, in the course of time, the truth is evolved.

There is little objection to Parts II and III of the " Science of English Verse." They are generally recognized as strikingly suggestive and helpful. It is with the main thesis of the first part that many disagree — the author's insistence that the laws of music and of verse are identical. According to Lanier, verse is in all respects a phenomenon of sound. From time immemorial the relation of music and of poetry has been spoken of in figurative terms, as in Carlyle's discussion of the subject in the essay on the " Hero as Poet." Lanier, however, was the first to work the idea out in a thorough-going fashion. He was especially qualified to do so

[1] See, for instance, Winchester's *Principles of Literary Criticism*, Alden's *English Verse*, Paul Elmer More's *Shelburne Essays*, and Omond's *English Metrists*.

because of his knowledge of the two arts. His
general conclusion was the same as that reached
by Professor Gummere in his searching discussion
of " Rhythm as the Essential Fact of Poetry." [1]
Both of them saw that the origin of poetry was
in the dance and the march, and later the song.
In modern times the two arts had become distinct. Lanier believed that, in accordance with
its origin and the practice of the best poets, the
basis of rhythm is time and not accent. Every
line is made up of bars of equal time value.
" If this equality of time were taken away, no
possibility of rhythm would remain." " The
accent serves only to mark for the ear these
equal intervals of time, which are the units of
poetic measurement." Lanier's theory of quantity, however, is different from the rigid laws of
classic quantity, for he allows for variations from
the regular type of verse that may prevail in a
certain poem or line, thus providing for " an es-
cape out of the rigidities of the type into the infinite field of those subtle rhythms which pervade
familiar utterance." He separates himself therefore from such writers as Abbott and Guest, who
applied the rule of thumb to English verse. To
such men " Shakspere's verse has often seemed
a mass of 'license,' of 'irregularity,' and of
lawless anomaly to commentators; while, ap-

[1] *The Beginnings of Poetry*, chapter 2.

proached from the direction of that great rhythmic sense of humanity displayed in music, in all manner of folk-songs, and in common talk, it is perfect music."

Lanier's theory is a good one in so far as it applies to the ideal rhythm, for the melody of verse does approximate that of music. If one considers actual rhythm, however, he is forced to come to the conclusion that no such mathematical relation exists between the syllables of a foot of verse as that existing between the notes of a musical bar. In poetry another element enters in to interfere with the ideal rhythm of music, and that is what Mr. More has called "the normal unrhythmical enunciation of the language." The result is a compromise shifting toward one extreme or another. Lanier's theory would apply to the earliest folk-songs. He illustrated his point by referring to the negro melodies, which, says Joel Chandler Harris, "depend for their melody and rhythm upon the musical quality of the time, and not upon long or short, accented or unaccented syllables." His citation of Japanese poetry was also a case in point. Unquestionably, the lyrics and choruses of the Greek drama were thoroughly musical; Sophocles and Æschylus were both teachers of the chorus. Many of the lyrics of the Elizabethan age were written especially for music, and more

than one collector of these lyrics has bemoaned
the fact that in later times there has been such
a divorce between the two arts. Who will say
that Coleridge's "Christabel" and "Kubla
Khan" are not disembodied music? Lamb said
that Coleridge repeated the latter poem "so en-
chantingly that it irradiates and brings heaven
and elysian bowers into any parlor when he says
or sings it to me." Mr. Arthur Symons has recently said: "'Christabel' is composed like music;
you might set at the side of each section, especially of the opening, *largo vivacissimo*, and as
the general expressive signature, *tempo rubato*."
Tennyson realized the musical effect of "Paradise
Lost" when he spoke of Milton as "England's
God-gifted organ-voice;" and he himself in such
lyrics as those in the "Princess" and the eighty-
sixth canto of "In Memoriam" wrought musical
effects with verse. Mr. Theodore Watts-Dunton
says of Poe's "Ulalume" that, if properly in-
toned, "it would produce something like the
same effect upon a listener knowing no word of
English that it produces upon us." It needs to be
said, in parenthesis, that in all these cases, while
there is the musical effect from the standpoint
of time and tone-color, there is still the perfection of speech. The theory will not hold, however, in much dramatic verse, or in meditative
blank verse, as used by Wordsworth. Much of

the poetry of Byron, Browning, Keats, and Shakespeare, while supremely great from the standpoint of color, or dramatic power, or picturesqueness, or thought, is not musical. To bring some poems within the limit of musical notation would be impossible.

While then one must modify Lanier's theory, the book emphasizes a point that needs constantly to be emphasized, both by poets and by students of poetry. Followed too closely by minor poets, it will tend to develop artisans rather than artists. Followed by the greater poets,— consciously or unconsciously,— it may prove to be one of the surest signs of poetry. This phase of poetical work needed to be emphasized in America, where poetry, with the exception of Poe's, has been deficient in this very element. Whatever else one may say of Emerson, Bryant, Whittier, or Longfellow, he must find that their poetry as a whole is singularly lacking in melody. Moreover, the poet who was the most dominant figure in American literature at the time when Lanier was writing, prided himself on violating every law of form, using rhythm, if at all, in a certain elementary or oriental sense. " I tried to read a beautifully printed and scholarly volume on the theory of poetry received by mail this morning from England," said Whitman, " but gave it up at last as a bad job." One may be thoroughly just to Whitman and grant the worth of his work in American literature, and yet see the value of Lanier's contention that the study of the formal element in poetry will lead to a much finer poetry than we have yet had in this country. Other books will supplant the "Science of English Verse" as text-books, and few may ever read it understandingly; but the author's name will always be thought of in any discussion of the relations of music and poetry. It is not only a scientific monograph, but a philosophical treatise on a subject that will be discussed with increasing interest.

While Lanier thus stated his conception of the formal element in poetry, he has, in many other places, given his ideas of the poet's character and his work in the world. If on the one hand he criticised Whitman for lack of form, on the other he blamed Swinburne for lack of substance. Seemingly a follower of Poe, he yet would have incurred the displeasure of that poet for adopting the " heresy of the didactic." He had an exalted sense of what poetry means in the redemption of mankind. He had little patience with the cry, " Art for art's sake," or with the justification so often made for the immorality of the artist's life. Milton himself did not believe more ardently that a poet's life ought to be a true poem. In the poems " Individuality," " Clover," " Life and Song," and the " Psalm of the West," Lanier expresses his view of the responsibility of the artist. In the first he says : —

> Awful is Art because 't is free;
> The artist trembles o'er his plan
> Where men his Self must see,

In the " English Novel " he says : " For, indeed, we may say that he who has not yet perceived how artistic beauty and moral beauty are convergent lines which run back into a common ideal origin, and who is therefore not afire with moral beauty just as with artistic beauty ; that he, in short, who has not come to that stage of quiet and eternal frenzy in which the beauty of holiness and the holiness of beauty mean one thing, burn as one fire, shine as one light within him, he is not yet the great artist."

Lanier believed that he was, or would be, a great poet. While for a time he considered music as his special field of work and " poetry as a mere tangent," after 1875 his aspiration took the direction of poetry. Criticism of his work only strengthened his conviction that it was of a high order. Letters to his father and to his wife indicate his positive conviction that he was meeting with the misunderstanding that every great artist has met since the world began : " Let my

name perish, — the poetry is good poetry and the
music is good music, and beauty dieth not, and
the heart that needs it will find it." " I *know*,
through the fiercest tests of life, that I am in soul,
and shall be in life and utterance, a great poet,"
he said again.

Accordingly he hoped that he would accomplish
something different from the popular poetry of
the period. Time and again he spoke of " the
feeble magazine lyrics " of his time. " This is
the kind of poetry that is technically called culture poetry, yet it is in reality the product of a
want of culture. If these gentlemen and ladies
would read the old English poetry . . . they
could never be content to put forth these little
diffuse prettinessess and dandy kickshaws of
verse." And again : " In looking around at the
publications of the younger American poets, I
am struck with the circumstance that none of
them even *attempt* anything great. . . . Hence
the endless multiplications of those little feeble
magazine lyrics which we all know : consisting
of one minute idea each, which is put in the
last line of the fourth verse, the other three
verses and three lines being mere surplusage."
His characterizations of contemporary poetry are
strikingly like those of Walt Whitman. Different as they were in nearly every respect, the
two poets were yet alike in their idea that there

should be a reaction against the conventional and artificial poetry of their time, — the difference being, that Whitman's reaction took the direction of formlessness, while Lanier's was concerned about the extension and revival of poetic forms. In both poets there is a range and sweep, both of conception and of utterance, that sharply differentiates them from all other poets since the Civil War.

The question then is, whether Lanier, with his lofty conception of the poet's work, and with his faith in himself, succeeded in writing poetry that will stand the test of time. He undoubtedly had some of the necessary qualities of a poet. He had, first of all, a sense of melody that found vent primarily in music and then in words which moved with a certain rhythmic cadence. " A holy tune was in my soul when I fell asleep; it was going when I awoke. This melody is always moving along in the background of my spirit. If I wish to compose, I abstract my attention from the things which occupy the front of the stage, the *dramatis personae* of the moment, and fix myself upon the deeper scene in the rear." " All day my soul hath been cutting swiftly into the great space of the subtle, unspeakable deep, driven by wind after wind of heavenly melody," he writes at another time. His best poems move to the cadence of a tune. He probably heard them as did Milton the lines of "Paradise Lost." Sometimes there was a lilt like the singing of a bird, and sometimes the lyric cry, and yet again the music of the orchestra. "He has an ear for the distribution of instruments, and this gives him a desire for the antiphonal, for introducing an answer, or an echo, or a compensating note," says Mr. Higginson. Sometimes, as in the "Marshes of Glynn" and in the best parts of "Sunrise," there is a cosmic rhythm that is like unto the rhythmic beating of the heart of God, of which Poe and Lanier have written eloquently.

Besides this melody that was temperamental, Lanier had ideas. He was alive to the problems of his age and to the beauties of nature. One has only to think of the names of his poems to realize how many themes occupied his attention. He wrote of religion, social questions, science, philosophy, nature, love. "My head and my heart are both [so] full of poems," he says. "So many great ideas for art are born to me each day, I am swept into the land of All-delight by their strenuous sweet whirlwind." "Every leaf that I brush against breeds a poem." "A thousand vital elements rill through my soul." So he is in no sense a "jingle man." There is a note of healthy mysticism in his poetry that makes him akin to Wordsworth and Emerson. A series of poems might be selected that would entitle him to the praise of being " the friend and aider of those who would live in the spirit."

With the spiritual endowment of a poet and an unusual sense of melody, where was he lacking in what makes a great poet? In power of expression. He never attained, except in a few poems, that union of sound and sense which is characteristic of the best poetry. The touch of finality is not in his words; the subtle charm of verse outside of the melody and the meaning is not his — he failed to get the last " touches of vitalizing force." He did not, as Lowell said of Keats, "rediscover the delight and wonder that lay enchanted in the dictionary." He did not attain to " the perfection and the precision of the instantaneous line." Take his poem " Remonstrance," for instance. It is a strong utterance against tyranny and intolerance and bigotry, hot from his soul; but the expression is not worthy of his feeling. A few lines of Lowell's " Fable for Critics " about freedom are better. The same may be said of his attack on agnosticism in "Acknowledgment." " Corn " while representing an extremely poetical situation, leaves one with the feeling of incompleteness: the ideas are not adequately or felicitously expressed. There is melody in the " Marsh Song at Sunset," but the poem is not clear. Or take what many consider his masterpiece, "Sunrise." There is one of the most imaginative situations a poet could have, — the ecstasy of the poet's soul as he rises from his bed to go to the forest, the silence of the night, the mystery of the deep green woods, the coming of "my lord, the Sun." There is nothing in American poetry that goes beyond the sweep and range of this conception. But look at the words; with the exception of the first stanza and those that describe the dawn, there is a nervousness of style, a strain of expression. If one compare even the best parts with the "Evening of Extraordinary Splendor and Beauty" by Wordsworth, he sees the difference in the art of expression. There is in Wordsworth's poem the romantic mood, — the same uplift of soul in the presence of the greater phenomena of nature, — but there is a classic restraint of form; it is "emotion recollected in tranquillity."

What, then, is the explanation of this defect in Lanier? Undoubtedly lack of time to revise his work is one cause. Speaking of one of his poems, he said, "Being cool next day, I find some flaws in my poem." And again, "On seeing the poem in print, I find it faulty; there's too much matter in it." Sickness, poverty, and hard work prevented him from having that repose which is the proper mood of the artist. He

had to write as long a poem as " The Symphony " in four days, the " Psalm of the West "
in a few weeks. " Sunrise " was dictated on his
death-bed. The revision of " Corn " and of all
other poems which I have been able to compare
with the first drafts shows conclusively that he
had the power of improving his work. With
more time he might have achieved with all of his
poems some of the results attained by such careful workmen as Tennyson and Poe.

But lack of time for revision will not explain
all. There were certain temperamental defects
in Lanier as poet. There was a lack of spontaneous utterance. Writing once of Swinburne,
he used words that characterize well one phase
of his own work: " It is always the Fourth of
July with Mr. Swinburne. It is impossible in
reading this strained laborious matter not to remember that the case of poetry is precisely that
where he who conquers, conquers without strain.
There was a certain damsel who once came to
King Arthur's court, ' gért ' (as sweet Sir Thomas
Malory hath it) ' with a sword for to find a man
of such virtue to draw it out of the scabbard.'
King Arthur, to set example to his knights, first
essayed, and pulled at it eagerly, but the sword
would not out. ' Sir,' said the damsel, ' ye need
not to pull half so hard, for he that shall pull it
out shall do it with little might.' " This is not

to say that Lanier simulated poetic expression, but his words are not inevitable enough. He often lacked simplicity.

Furthermore, he suffered from a tendency to indulge in fancies, " sucking sweet similes out of the most diverse objects." He was inoculated with the " conceit virus " of the seventeenth century. In a letter already quoted, he pointed out this defect to his father, and he never overcame it. He did not restrain his luxuriant imagination. The poem " Clover " is almost spoiled by the conceit of the ox representing the " Course-of-things " and trampling upon the souls (the clover-blossoms) of the poets. " Sunrise " is marred by the figure of the bee-hive from which the " star-fed Bee, the build-fire Bee, . . . the great Sun-Bee," emerges in the morning. Such examples might be easily multiplied.

Lanier was undoubtedly hampered, too, by his theory of verse. The very poem " Special Pleading," in which he said that he began to work out his theory, is a failure. Alliteration, assonance, compound words, personifications, are greatly overused. Some of the rhymes are as grotesque as Browning's. Instead of the perfect union of sound and sense, there is often a mere chanting of words.

It is futile to deny these tendencies in Lanier. They vitiate more than half his poems, and are defects even in some of the best. Sometimes, in his very highest flight, he seems to have been winged by one of these arrows. But it is equally futile to deny that he frequently rises above all these limitations and does work that is absolutely unique, and original, and enduring. Distinction must be made, as in the case of every other man who has marked qualities of style, between his good work and his bad work. He has done enough good work to entitle him to a place among the genuine poets of America. No American anthology would be complete that did not contain some dozen or more of his poems, and no study of American poetry would be complete that did not take into consideration twice this number. It is too soon yet to fix upon such poems, but surely they may be found among the following: such lyrics as "An Evening Song," "My Springs," "A Ballad of the Trees and the Master," "Betrayal," "Night and Day," "The Stirrup-Cup," and "Nirvâna;" such sonnets as "The Mocking-Bird" and "The Harlequin of Dreams;" such nature poems as "The Song of the Chattahoochee," "The Waving of the Corn," and "From the Flats;" such poems of high seriousness as "Individuality," "Opposition," "How Love looked for Hell," and "A Florida Sunday;" such a stirring ballad as "The Revenge of Hamish;" the opening lines and the

Columbus sonnets of the " Psalm of the West ; " and the longer poems, " The Symphony," " Sunrise," and " The Marshes of Glynn."

The first may be quoted as an illustration of Lanier's lyric quality. Those who have heard it sung to the music of Mr. Dudley Buck can realize to some extent Lanier's idea of the union of music and poetry : —

Look off, dear Love, across the shallow sands,
    And mark yon meeting of the sun and sea,
How long they kiss in sight of all the lands.
        Ah ! longer, longer, we.

Now in the sea's red vintage melts the sun,
    As Egypt's pearl dissolved in rosy wine,
And Cleopatra night drinks all. 'T is done,
        Love, lay thine hand in mine.

Come forth, sweet stars, and comfort heaven's heart ;
    Glimmer, ye waves, round else unlighted sands.
O night ! divorce our sun and sky apart,
        Never our lips, our hands.

Throughout his poems — some of them imperfect enough as wholes — there are lines that come from the innermost soul of poetry : —

But the air and my heart and the earth are a-thrill.

The little green leaves would not let me alone in my
    sleep.

        Happy-valley hopes
Beyond the bend of roads.

I lie as lies yon placid Brandywine,
Holding the hills and heavens in my heart
For contemplation.

Sweet visages of all the souls of time
Whose loving service to the world has been
In the artist's way expressed.

A perfect life in perfect labor wrought.

The artist's market is the heart of man;
The artist's price, some little good of man.

He summ'd the words in song.

The whole sweet round
Of littles that large life compound !

My brain is beating like the heart of Haste.

Where an artist plays, the sky is low.

Thou 'rt only a gray and sober dove,
But thine eye is faith and thy wing is love.

Oh, sweet, my pretty sum of history,
I leapt the breadth of Time in loving thee !

Music is love in search of a word.

His song was only living aloud,
His work, a singing with his hand !

And Science be known as the sense making love to the
          All,
And Art be known as the soul making love to the All,
And Love be known as the marriage of man with the All.

Indeed, if one had to rely upon one poem to keep alive the fame of Lanier, he could single out " The Marshes of Glynn " with assurance that there is something so individual and original about it, and that, at the same time, there is such a roll and range of verse in it, that it will surely live not only in American poetry but in English. Here the imagination has taken the place of fancy, the effort to do great things ends in victory, and the melody of the poem corresponds to the exalted thought. It has all the strong points of " Sunrise," with but few of its limitations. There is something of Whitman's virile imagination and Emerson's high spirituality combined with the haunting melody of Poe's best work. Written in 1878, when Lanier was in the full exercise of all his powers, it is the best expression of his genius and one of the few great American poems.

The background of the poem — as of " Sunrise " — is the forest, the coast and the marshes near Brunswick, Georgia. Early in life Lanier had been thrilled by this wonderful natural scenery, and later visits had the more powerfully impressed his imagination. He is the poet of the marshes as surely as Bryant is of the forests, or Wordsworth of the mountains.

The poet represents himself as having spent the day in the forest and coming at sunset into

full view of the length and the breadth and the
sweep of the marshes. The glooms of the live-
oaks and the emerald twilights of the "dim
sweet woods, of the dear dark woods," have been
as a refuge from the riotous noon-day sun. More
than that, in the wildwood privacies and closets
of lone desire he has known the passionate pleasure of prayer and the joy of elevated thought.
His spirit is grown to a lordly great compass
within, — he is ready for what Wordsworth calls
a " god-like hour : " —

But now when the noon is no more, and riot is rest,
And the sun is a-wait at the ponderous gate of the West,
And the slant yellow beam down the wood-aisle doth
    seem
Like a lane into heaven that leads from a dream, —
Ay, now, when my soul all day hath drunken the soul of
    the oak
And my heart is at ease from men, and the wearisome
    sound of the stroke
  Of the scythe of time and the trowel of trade is low,
  And belief overmasters doubt, and I know that I know,
  And my spirit is grown to a lordly great compass
    within,
That the length and the breadth and the sweep of the
    marshes of Glynn
Will work me no fear like the fear they have wrought
    me of yore
When length was fatigue, and when breadth was but
    bitterness sore,
And when terror and shrinking and dreary unnamable
    pain
Drew over me out of the merciless miles of the plain, —

Oh, now, unafraid, I am fain to face
  The vast sweet visage of space.
To the edge of the wood I am drawn, I am drawn,
Where the gray beach glimmering runs, as a belt of the
     dawn,
    For a mete and a mark
    To the forest-dark: —
          So:
Affable live-oak, leaning low, —
Thus — with your favor — soft, with a reverent hand
(Not lightly touching your person, Lord of the land !)
Bending your beauty aside, with a step I stand
On the firm-packed sand,
       Free
By a world of marsh that borders a world of sea.

.   .   .   .

And what if behind me to westward the wall of the woods
    stands high ?
The world lies east: how ample, the marsh and the sea
    and the sky !
A league and a league of marsh-grass, waist-high, broad
    in the blade,
Green, and all of a height, and unflecked with a light or
    a shade,
Stretch leisurely off, in a pleasant plain,
To the terminal blue of the main.

Oh, what is abroad in the marsh and the terminal sea ?
  Somehow my soul seems suddenly free
From the weighing of fate and the sad discussion of sin,
By the length and the breadth and the sweep of the
    marshes of Glynn.

.   .   .   .

As the marsh-hen secretly builds on the watery sod,
Behold I will build me a nest on the greatness of God:

I will fly in the greatness of God as the marsh-hen flies
In the freedom that fills all the space 'twixt the marsh
    and the skies:
By so many roots as the marsh-grass sends in the sod
I will heartily lay me a-hold on the greatness of God:
Oh, like to the greatness of God is the greatness within
The range of the marshes, the liberal marshes of Glynn.

And the sea lends large, as the marsh: lo, out of his
    plenty the sea
Pours fast: full soon the time of the flood-tide must be:
Look how the grace of the sea doth go
About and about through the intricate channels that flow
        Here and there,
          Everywhere,
Till his waters have flooded the uttermost creeks and the
    low-lying lanes,
And the marsh is meshed with a million veins,
That like as with rosy and silvery essences flow
  In the rose-and-silver evening glow.
          Farewell, my lord Sun !
The creeks overflow: a thousand rivulets run
'Twixt the roots of the sod; the blades of the marsh-grass
    stir;
Passeth a hurrying sound of wings that westward whirr;
Passeth, and all is still; and the currents cease to run;
And the sea and the marsh are one.

How still the plains of the waters be !
The tide is in his ecstasy.
The tide is at his highest height:
        And it is night.

And now from the Vast of the Lord will the waters of
    sleep
Roll in on the souls of men,
But who will reveal to our waking ken

The forms that swim and the shapes that creep
               Under the waters of sleep?
And I would I could know what swimmeth below when
    the tide comes in
On the length and the breadth of the marvelous marshes
    of Glynn.

In the light of such a poem Lanier's poetry and his life take on a new significance. The struggles through which he passed and the victory he achieved are summed up in a passage which may well be the last word of this biography. For Sidney Lanier was

            The catholic man who hath mightily won
God out of knowledge and good out of infinite pain
And sight out of blindness and purity out of a stain.

INDEX

16-19; life in Macon, 19-23;
early schools, 23; fondness
for music and books, 24, 25;
at Oglethorpe University, 26-
41; influence of Dr. Woodrow,
28-30; of comrades, 32; vacation at Montvale Springs,
Tenn., 35-37; tutor in Greek, 38;
plans to go to Heidelberg, 39;
catches war fever and joins
Macon Volunteers, 42-48; at
Norfolk, 48; in battles around
Richmond, 48, 49; at Petersburg, 49; vacation in Macon,
52, 53; as scout at Fort Boykin reads German poetry and
begins "Tiger Lilies," 54-56,
84; captured on blockade-run-
ner at Wilmington, N. C., 57;
and taken to Point Lookout
Prison, 58-60; rescue from
death, 60; after illness in Macon, goes to Point Clear on
Mobile Bay, 64; hotel clerk at
Exchange Hotel, Montgom-
ery, Alabama, 64-78; resumes
literary work, 74; goes to
New York with "Tiger Lil-
ies," 78; teaches school at
Prattville, Alabama, 91-97;
suffers from reconstruction
governments, 91-95; marriage,
93; practices law at Macon,
99; delivers Confederate
Memorial address, 103; goes
to Alleghany Springs, Virginia, 112, to New York, 114, to
San Antonio, 117; resolves to
give the remainder of his life
to music and poetry, 120-126;
goes to New York to study
music, 129; first flute in Peabody Orchestra in Baltimore,
130; popularity in Baltimore,
135; on a visit to Georgia
writes "Corn," 153; at work
on other poems, and books,

161-165; appointed to write
a cantata for the opening
of Centennial Exposition in
Philadelphia, 166; publishes
first volume of poems, 181;
meets wider circle of literary
men and women, 181; visit to
Boston, 190; attends Century
Club and Goethe celebration,
192; moves family to Chadd's
Ford, Pa., 194; goes to Florida
for health, 195, 196; seeks
in vain for government
position in Washington, 198,
199; settles with family in
Baltimore, 200; at work in
Peabody Library on English
literature, 202; lectures at
the Peabody Institute, 206-
210; appointed lecturer at
Johns Hopkins University,
233; writes article on the
"New South," 264; last illness begins, 321; birth of
fourth son at West Chester,
Pa., 322; lectures at Johns
Hopkins, 328-330; goes to
New York, 330; to Asheville,
N. C., 331; death, 335; burial
in Baltimore, 336; memorial
exercises at Johns Hopkins
University, 337-338.
Characteristics: physical appearance, 190 (Lowell), 193
(Stedman), 300 (Wysham),
301 (Gilman; humor, 21, 32,
33, 79, 80, 100, 200, 204, 310,
311; buoyancy of spirit,
4-7, 96, 322, 323; lack of Bohemianism, 18, 301, 302, 307;
knightliness and chivalry, 54,
158, 309; capacity for hard
work, 129-130, 134, 163, 187, 211,
238; capacity for friendship,
302-307; fondness for children,
79, 80, 303, 307; love of nature,
18, 19, 37, 112-114, 224-226; pu-

rity of life, 59, 60, 162; reverence for science, 28, 29, 138, 232, 312–317, 333, 334 (*see also* Darwin, Gilman, Kirk); enthusiasm for literature, 32–34, 108–110, 205, 211, 212, 350 (*see also* Elizabethan poetry and old English); as a scholar, 7, 34, 238–250; as teacher, 258–260; as critic, 344–366; as poet, 360–375; as musician, 24, 31, 32, 38, 55, 58, 59, 74, 86, 115–117, 120–123, chapter vi; his national spirit, 175–181; his religious faith, 6, 17, 22, 23, 27, 28, 87, 145, 317–319, 326; inheritor of unfulfilled renown, 3, 341, 342.

Works: A Birthday Song, 76; A Florida Ghost, 310; A Florida Sunday, 197, 368; Acknowledgment, 364; An Evening Song, 197, 368, 369 (quoted); Baby Charley, 100, 307; Ballad of Trees and Master (quoted), 318, 368; Barnacles, 76; Betrayal, 368; Bob, 307; Boy's Froissart, The, 326; Boy's King Arthur, The, 109, 326–328; Boy's Mabinogion, The, 326, 332; Boy's Percy, The, 326; Cantata, the Centennial, 166–176, 291; Clover, 360, 367, 369, 370; Confederate Memorial Address, 103–106, 344; Corn, 153–157, 181, 183, 268, 364, 366; Crystal, The, 318, 347, 370; English Novel, The, 294, 314, 315, 322, 328–330, 344, 351, 352, 360; Florida, 36 (note), 164–166, 187; From Bacon to Beethoven, 140, 344; From the Flats, 197, 368, 369; Hard Times in Elfland, 307; Harlequin of Dreams, The, 368; How Love looked for Hell, 368; In Absence, 307; In the Foam, 76 (note); India, Sketches of, 163;

Individuality, 360, 368; Jacquerie, The, 38, 101, 118, 158, 159; Laughter in the Senate, 76 (note), 92, 93 (quoted); Laus Mariae, 307; Legend of St. Leonor, The, 315; Life and Song, 76, 370; Marsh Song at Sunset, 364; Marshes of Glynn, The, 3, 320, 322, 324, 363, 370–375; Mazzini on Music, 145–147; Mocking - Bird, The, 197, 368; Modern Orchestra, The, 140; Music and Poetry, 172, 217; My Springs, 97, 98, 307, 368; Nature - Metaphors, 96; New South, The, 157, 264–272, 344; Night and Day, 368; Nirvâna, 108, 368; Ode to Johns Hopkins University, The, 230, 234, 236, 238; Opposition, 128, 368; Orchestra of To-day, 344; Power of Prayer, The, 185, 186; Psalm of the West, The, 176–178, 181, 360, 366, 369; Raven Days, 93; Remonstrance, 364; Retrospects and Prospects (essay), 19, 70–72, 94, 96, 344; Retrospects and Prospects (book), 103–106, 117–122, 264–272; Revenge of Hamish, The, 368; San Antonio de Bexar, 117–122, 344; Science of English Verse, The, 3, 239, 249, 320, 329, 337, 352–359; Shakspere and His Forerunners, 98, 210–228, 243–245, 351, 352; Song of the Chattahoochee, The, 197, 368; Special Pleading, 367; Steel in Soft Hands, 93; Stirrup-Cup, The, 197, 368; Sunrise, 322, 336, 363, 365–367; Symphony, The, 158–163, 181, 185, 187, 368; Tampa Robins, 197; Tiger Lilies, 35–37, 43, 44, 55, 57, 58, 72, 74, 78, 80–89, 143, 144, 312, 344; Tyranny, 76, 93; Under the Cedarcroft Chestnut,

The Riverside Press

Electrotyped and printed by H. O. Houghton & Co.
Cambridge, Mass., U. S. A.